LNER Workshops

Peter Tuffrey

First published in 2018

© Peter Tuffrey 2018

A CIP record for this book is available from the British Library

Printed in Turkey by Olas Solutions

ISBN 9780860936732

Crécy Publishing Limited
1a Ringway Trading Estate, Shadowmoss Road, Manchester
M22 5LH
www.crecy.co.uk

Front cover, top A4 No 4500 (left), as built named 'Carganey' (later renamed 'Sir Ronald Matthews') complete and ready for service, and another member of the same class No 2515 'Quicksilver', seen in the Doncaster paint shop. The latter has yet to be fitted with coupling rods, chimney and side fairing to partly cover the driving wheels.

Front cover, lower Hoisted high, a brand new Peppercorn Pacific – note the stepped footplate - ready for wheeling.

Rear cover, top Firebox / throatplate rivetting, one of the nosiest tasks in the workshops undertaken here without any form of ear protection.

Rear cover, centre 1930's style and luxury. We should not forget that aside from his premier steam engines, Nigel Gresley also designed the luxury coaches behind the engine. Here we see the interior of a First-Class saloon from the 'Coronation'.

Rear cover, lower Standing in front of No 2001 *Cock o' the North* (left to right) are R. A. Thom, Mechanical Engineer, Doncaster; E. Windle, Chief Locomotive Draughtsman; J. S. Jones, Assistant Works Manager; F. H. Eggleshaw, Works Manager; the Paint Shop Foreman; unidentified; the Erecting Shop Foreman; and two chargehand fitters.

Contents

Introduction

If the average person on the street was asked if he or she had heard of *Mallard* or *Flying Scotsman*, the answer would surely be yes. However, ask the same person where they were built and a quizzical look could betray their inability to voice the correct response. A railway enthusiast would know that both were built in the London & North Eastern Railway's workshops at Doncaster, but how much more information could be given about the establishment or any of the other places that produced the company's locomotives, carriages and wagons between 1923 and 1948?

At the Grouping the LNER inherited twelve main facilities, which employed approximately 25,000 people: Darlington, Doncaster, Stratford, Temple Mills, Shildon, Faverdale, Gateshead, York, Inverurie, Cowlairs, Gorton and Dukinfield. Most of these had been in existence since the dawn of the railways and many had pioneered many advances in technology subsequently. In 1923 the role of several of these changed dramatically, while others continued to be leaders in the fields of locomotive, carriage and wagon construction and maintenance. Only a relatively short time later British Railways was formed and the workshops saw a further change in direction, and in this instance some would not survive longer than the early 1960s.

LNER Workshops traces the history of these places from their birth to the end of steam and beyond to determine how they changed over this period and what influence the changes of ownership had on new designs, pre-Grouping types and stock built for British Railways. Also detailed are the new systems for construction and repairs that were implemented to improve productivity and save money. Items of interest regarding the workforce are given throughout the book, such as working hours, pay, relationships with management, and events organised for pleasure and charitable causes.

One facet of workshop life that became abundantly clear as the research for this book progressed was the numerous activities available for the staff to pursue during their leisure time. There were sports teams competing against other areas and rival railway companies – in addition to ambulance brigades – educational classes were taken, excursions organised to various places, and bands formed.

The evolution of the railway workshop occurred slowly over a number of decades, mirroring that of the locomotive, carriage and wagon stock. In the beginning the facilities mainly catered for repairs and a gap usually existed between establishment and the first items of stock being built from scratch. These places were usually small and were soon found to be inadequate. Expansions were implemented in a piecemeal fashion as there was generally very little planning carried out when many of the works were created, or due regard given to their locations, but subsequently this became a necessity. Darlington's formation illustrates this point, as buildings were erected for the requirements of the time, but space was acquired for expansion to take place as the need arose, although the forecast proved to be slightly cautious.

Equipment and tools played an important part in how successfully the tasks were completed and, more significantly, how reliable the products were in traffic. In the early 1800s the apparatus was quite basic and slowly evolved as understanding of the physics of the railways improved. This is evidenced by the use of wheel balancing machines, which only became prominent towards the end of the 19th century when comfort for all passengers was taken more seriously. Furthermore, as the 20th century began thoughts turned to mass production of certain items, such as nuts and bolts and similar articles, in addition to the practice of machining multiple parts at once to reduce time and save labour.

After the Grouping of 1923 the LNER fully evaluated the organisation of construction and repairs at all the sites and adopted the 'progressive' system, whereby the work started at one point and moved along a set route where various tasks were undertaken, then at the end the job was complete and the vehicle entered traffic. Being not too dissimilar to the assembly line practice popular at the time, the use of this method drastically reduced the amount of time that rolling stock spent in works, increased productivity and saved money.

As mentioned, the locomotives are perhaps the best-known products of the workshops. These comprised the express train classes – from Gresley's 'A4s', 'A3'/'A1' 'Pacifics' to the constituents' 4-6-0, 'Atlantic', 4-4-0 and 'Single' types – to freight designs of Gresley and Robinson in the robust 2-6-0s and 2-8-0s and the many 0-6-0s of the North British, North Eastern and Great Eastern railways. The many locomotive engineers who had occupied the top positions on the railways also liked to experiment with various types, systems and gadgets for locomotives, and several interesting engines were built. Gresley's Class 'W1' with its water tube boiler was one, the 'Decapod' 0-10-0T built by the Great Eastern Railway (GER) to Holden's design was another, while a number attempted to harness the use of compound working, meeting with varying degrees of success. Gresley's primary trials during his tenure concerned poppet valves and feedwater heaters, which culminated in 1934 with the erection of 'P2' 2-8-2 'Mikado' No 2001 *Cock o' the North* at Doncaster. This was the largest and most powerful British passenger engine to be built at the time. The GER held the record for the shortest time taken to construct a fully functioning locomotive in 1891 when Holden 0-6-0 No 930 was sent to work in less than 10 hours.

Both World Wars had a tremendous impact on the railways. During the 1914-18 conflict, construction of new stock and the repairs and maintenance of existing locomotives, carriages and wagons were seriously curtailed and this caused a rolling stock shortage and backlog that lasted into the 1920s. The workshops were engaged on large-scale production of armaments and other war materials, as well as stock for the armed forces. Many of the places shattered targets for production and received high praise from the Government for the standard of the work. As many of the men employed in the workshops either joined the forces or were called up, women had to enter the profession and in the vast majority of instances demonstrated extreme capability with the tasks set, laying the foundations for increased integration of females in the workforce for subsequent generations.

The war had a strong effect on wages, with the cost of living rising as the years passed, leading to a war bonus being paid to workers to compensate for this; the increase reached 110% by 1918 compared to 1914. However, the rise became a burden to the Government and the railway companies – contributing to losses of up to £40 million annually – and subsequently caused conflict when attempts were made to reduce or hold the figures at a certain level.

Upon the LNER's formation, several similar workshops came under the jurisdiction of the company. The capacity of these was generally in excess of the company's projected requirements, which in fact were never realised, leaving certain places vulnerable to cutbacks and even closure.

The main decision made following amalgamation was for locomotive construction to be concentrated at Doncaster and Darlington, while Gorton sporadically contributed small numbers, but Stratford and Cowlairs were stripped of this responsibility. From the 757 locomotives of Gresley design built under the LNER, 687 were the product of either Doncaster or Darlington and the remainder were bought from contractors. However, all the works remained fully accountable for the maintenance of the stock operating in their respective areas. Similar edicts covered carriage and wagon building – which was focused at Doncaster and York, and Shildon and Faverdale respectively – and maintenance. The use of several firms to supplement orders placed in the company's shops also occurred. The vast majority of the stock built by and for the LNER was standardised to certain specifications depending on its use, although there were several instances of detail variations between batches from the different workshops.

The financial crisis of the late 1920s and early 1930s seriously disrupted construction projects and by 1933 the amount of new stock sent into traffic was extremely low. Coupled with falling passenger and freight receipts, the situation forced the closure of Gateshead Works in 1932 and job losses were experienced at several shops. Wage cuts were also part of the economy drive and affected all employees of the company, even the Directors. Further reduction of the wage bill through the Railway Wages Board caused the 'Big Four' companies to leave the negotiations with the former and the unions, as a 10% cut was wanted but only 2% was granted. Future talks were held directly between the two as the railway companies thought the Board was not acting in fairness to both parties. The process was perhaps not helped by the fact that the employees of the works were considered separately from other railway employees and a number of different unions represented the men.

Despite these difficulties the LNER rose to finish the 1930s on a high note, doing this by embracing a modern image. The substance of this was created in the company's workshops, beginning with No 2001 *Cock o' the North* in 1934, 'A4' 'Pacific' No 2509 *Silver Link* in 1935, and 'V2' Class No 4771 *Green Arrow* in 1936. Representing power, speed and reliability, these locomotives served to interest and impress the general public, which would hopefully increase their patronage of the railway. New carriage sets built at Doncaster for the 'Silver Jubilee', 'Coronation' and 'West Riding Limited' expresses and at York for the 'Flying Scotsman' offered modern comforts such as air-conditioning and soundproofing, in addition to a high standard of decoration in new styles that dispensed with the fussy formality of previous years. The wagon stock also moved forward through the introduction of steel underframes – constructed using the relatively new technique of welding – metal bodywork and vacuum brakes.

Before the start of the war Dukinfield Carriage & Wagon Works was hit by the loss of carriage construction and maintenance to Doncaster and York, in addition to the erection of new wagons. This left many hundreds without a job and an area with depressed heavy industry, while the offer of relocation for more than 200 to York was unappealing to some, given the ties of friends and family. With the Second World War breaking out soon afterwards the loss of work was perhaps tempered somewhat as munitions tasks were again undertaken. The role of the LNER's shops was similar to that between 1914 and 1918, and women were again accepted into the workplace to make a valuable contribution. A new feature of the second conflict was the possibility of aerial attack. Although the damage was not too serious or permanent, Stratford suffered the most due to its proximity to London's dockyards. The biggest losses were not inflicted by the enemy, but from accidents. In 1940 the Carriage Shop at Doncaster was completely gutted by a fire and the same fate befell the facility at York in 1944.

Upon nationalisation of the 'Big Four', the LNER workshops became a part of a much larger group of engineering establishments, but ranked second in the number of locomotives, carriages and wagons for which they had responsibility. Generally, the different regions remained focussed on their own networks and rarely intruded on each other. The main task for the management of British Railways was the reorganisation of the systems in use for taking stock into works for repair, which was a process that differed from place to place. The responsibility for carriages and wagons – usually in the same department – was split and the two became sections in their own right at the works. Both of these were successful in improving the amount of stock accepted for maintenance and reducing the amount of time spent under attention.

The drawing office at Doncaster was able to join forces early on with those of the former London Midland & Scottish (LMS), Southern (SR) and Great Western (GWR) railways to produce the new standard designs. The works at Doncaster and Darlington carried out a moderate amount of construction of these, while the remainder of the shops would only receive them for repair if at work in the area; the use of Gorton for construction purposes was officially drawn to a close. As with the LNER designs after the Grouping, the BR locomotives featured many standardised components to make repairs and maintenance as easy and cheap as possible. The same policy extended to new carriages produced by Doncaster and York and wagons built at Shildon and Faverdale. The latter gradually lost orders as the stock switched from timber to metal construction, as other shops were better equipped to meet this requirement, coupled with a large amount of work being placed with private firms.

BR's Modernisation Plan of 1955 signalled the beginning of the end for many of the former works of the LNER. The dismissal of the steam fleet was at first to be a gradual process, but soon became a pressing matter, and from 1955, when there were 18,000 engines in service, scrapping gained momentum, eventually including the BR Standard classes that were only a few years old.

The influx of diesel and electric locomotives, as well as multiple units, never reached this figure, perhaps being just over half, by the end of steam. Therefore there was a wide discrepancy between the available space and that required in the workshops. A similar situation was forecasted for carriages and wagons, especially the latter. Much of the vehicle stock in operation at the time was still devoid of adequate brakes and the hope was that these would be replaced by higher-capacity fully fitted vacuum-braked types to improve the freight services on offer. However, this proved far too optimistic and the traffic never materialised.

Soon after the plan was announced another report was compiled on the future of the various shops, and recommendations were made with the planned actions of BR in mind. These included the closure of a number of facilities and the removal of functions from others, with the establishment of local repair depots in key places. The first round of cuts was scheduled for 1959 and included Gateshead and Dukinfield, followed by a reduction in the responsibilities at Stratford in 1960, then closure for Gorton and Cowlairs within the following three years. Certain tasks were also to be discontinued at Darlington, Doncaster and Faverdale. With the re-evaluation of the Modernisation Plan and the appointment of Dr Richard Beeching in the early 1960s as the 'hatchet man' to bring increased profitability to the railways, further cuts were deemed necessary after the centralisation of responsibility for the workshops as part of the Transport Act 1962. Darlington and Faverdale were now scheduled for closure together with Gorton, Cowlairs and Stratford. Doncaster, York, Shildon, Temple Mills and Inverurie were to carry on maintaining the new stock and later adding fresh vehicles for service. In all, these actions led to the redundancies of 26,000 people.

The main reasons behind the Modernisation Plan were falling freight receipts – traditionally the backbone of many railway companies – and rising costs, particularly wages, which continued to increase throughout the war and into the early 1950s. Each year in the early part of the decade was characterised by disputes between the unions and the British Transport Commission over the issue, and rises of varying percentages under 10% were generally agreed. This increased the amount payable annually to the staff by millions of pounds and in the early 1960s a railwayman's wage was more than 70% greater than that of the early 1950s. The price of raw materials had also gone up, although not as sharply, and steel cost some 40% more, while coal was bought at a price nearly 30% higher. From the mid-1950s BR operated at a loss and this only became greater as the years wore on until 1962, when the railways lost more than £160 million and drastic action had to be taken.

Many of the shops remaining after the cull saw a number of improvements take place in the intervening years. Doncaster became the repair centre for the Eastern Region, also undertaking new construction in subsequent years and York was given the task of building the vast majority of the electric multiple units for BR, while Shildon was at the forefront of wagon matters. Temple Mills was the repair depot for the London area, but Inverurie's role was less secure due to its northerly location, and the shops were abandoned at the end of the decade. At this time further changes were made through the Transport Act 1968, affecting the workshops by placing them in a separate company – British Rail Engineering Limited. The main benefit of this was that the workshops were now allowed to build stock to order from industry or other international railways, breaking the reliance on BR for new orders.

Of the four surviving works only Doncaster remains operational today, although in a reduced capacity. Shildon and Temple Mills fell in the early 1980s as freight traffic had continued to decline throughout the 1970s. York closed first in 1996 from a lack of orders from home and abroad, but was resurrected under a new guise for a time before succumbing again early in the new millennium.

The story of the LNER's works closely mirrors the trajectory of the fortunes of British industry over more than 100 years. Even though the engineering trade is not as strong as in the past, the establishment of Hitachi Rail Europe at Newton Aycliffe, County Durham, and a new maintenance facility for the Hitachi express trains for the East Coast Main Line at Doncaster Carr, gives hope that the traditions of the heyday of railway workshops can be regained and improved upon with modern technology for future prosperity.

Acknowledgements

I am grateful for the help received from the following people: Doug Brown, John Chalcraft, David Clay, David Dippie, David Dunn, Norman Ellis, Brian Longbone, Hugh Parkin, Derek Porter, David Postle, Bill Reed and Howard Turner.

Special thanks are due to my son Tristram for his help and tremendous encouragement throughout the project.

Photographs

Every effort has been made to gain permission to use the photographs in this book. If you feel you have not been contacted please let me know at petertuffrey@ rocketmail.com.

Information

I have taken reasonable steps to verify the accuracy of the information in this book but it may contain errors or omissions. Any information that may be of assistance to rectify any problems will be gratefully received. Please contact me by email at petertuffrey@rocketmail.com or in writing at 8 Wrightson Avenue, Warmsworth, Doncaster, South Yorkshire, DN4 9QL.

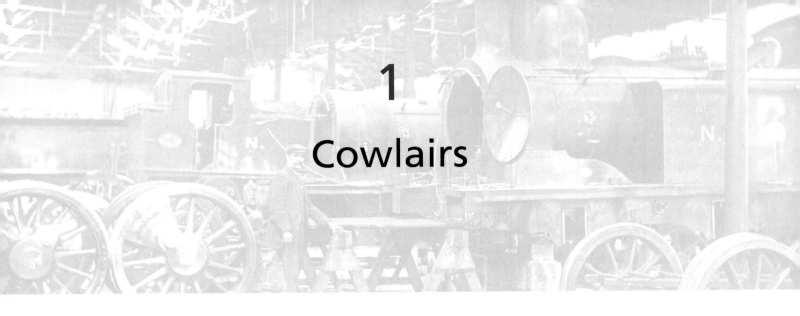

1
Cowlairs

Two canals dominated the movement of mineral traffic to Glasgow in the early 1800s. These were the Monkland and the Forth & Clyde, both having been opened in the latter half of the 18th century, and which charged high fees for their use. One of the first railways to be built in the Glasgow area – the Monkland & Kirkintilloch – served the canals, but the mode of transport was soon used to break the stranglehold. The Glasgow &

Garnkirk was opened in 1831 to bring coal into the city at lower rates and the company was generally successful in this aim.

Around this time there were also plans to connect Glasgow with Edinburgh. Grainger and Miller were engaged to survey a route, but this met with opposition and soon faltered. The scheme was resurrected at the end of the 1830s and the Act for the Edinburgh & Glasgow

This map shows Cowlairs Works at Springburn, Glasgow, during the 1920s; note the close proximity of the North British Locomotive Company's works to the east.

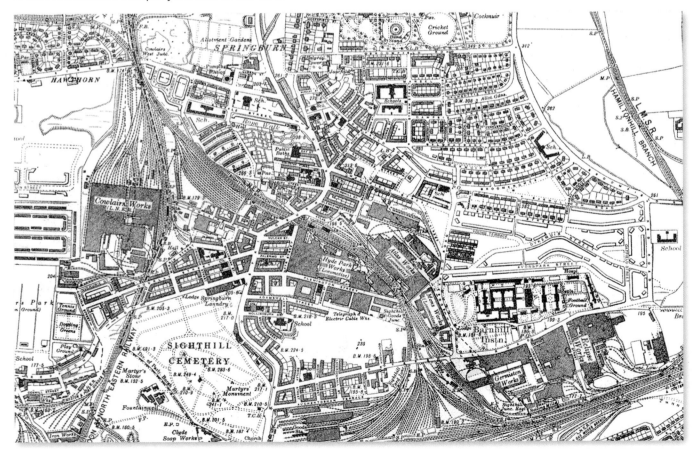

The problem of working the steep Cowlairs incline prompted the construction of the first locomotives at the works. Here, men are seen with the rope used for hauling trains out of the station and at the rear are a number of brake wagons (curiously labelled 'break') used during the process.

Railway (E&GR) was authorised in 1838. Beginning at Edinburgh Haymarket, the line took a northern course – where the land was favourable – and paralleled the Union Canal, which, from 1822, connected Edinburgh with the Forth & Clyde. Unfortunately, the canal companies were directly affronted by this and successfully prevented the E&GR from passing over the Forth & Clyde at Port Dundas, Glasgow. As a result the railway was forced to go beneath the waterway by means of a long, steep tunnel to the station, which faced on to George Street. From the opening on 21 February 1842 until the early 20th century the Cowlairs bank (with gradients around 1 in 41) was operated by a rope haulage system.

A short distance to the north of the Cowlairs incline, the company established Cowlairs Works on the western side of the route through Springburn. The works took their name from the country house a short distance to the south and consisted of facilities for the repair and maintenance of locomotives, carriages and wagons, being one of the first workshops in the country to offer facilities for all three items of rolling stock. William Paton was the Superintendent of Locomotives, and the first engines were bought from Edward Bury & Co and R. & W. Hawthorn, being of 2-2-0, 2-2-2, 0-4-0 and 2-4-0 wheel arrangements for passenger and goods trains.

Soon after the opening of the line the limitations of using ropes to drag the trains up Cowlairs incline became very apparent through the frequent breakages and the high cost of replacing the equipment. Paton decided to use two powerful locomotives to escort the trains out of the station, and instead of passing a design to the trade for construction he took the bold step of having the pair erected in Cowlairs Works. The first was 0-6-0T *Hercules*, which was built in January 1844 with 4ft 3½in-diameter wheels and 15½-inch-diameter cylinders, and the second – named *Sampson* – followed later in the year, being slightly modified with larger cylinders. Both locomotives performed well and reduced the cost of working the trains out to Cowlairs, but were too powerful for the time as the rails were too fragile and kept breaking, leading to the reinstatement of the rope haulage system in 1847.

Towards the end of the 1840s the Caledonian Railway (CR) began a rival service to the E&GR using a southerly route over difficult terrain. To attract passengers, the CR reduced fares and soon a fierce competition broke out between the two companies, forcing down the passenger fares to unsustainable levels. When sense prevailed thoughts turned to speeding up the trains running between the two cities, and Cowlairs was again called into action. Two locomotives were built in 1848 with 15-inch by 20-inch cylinders and 6-foot-diameter driving wheels; they were named *Orion* and *Sirius*. The shops continued to be used sparingly, however, as the majority of the other locomotives were bought from Sharp, Stewart & Co.

In 1861 Paton was replaced by William Steel Brown. At this time the Cowlairs Works Manager was William Stroudley (later of the London, Brighton & South Coast Railway [LB&SCR]) and one of the foremen was Dugald

Gresley 'A4' 'Pacific' No 60004 *William Whitelaw* works hard up Cowlairs incline with the help of a banking engine. This 'A4' was one of the few class members to visit Cowlairs for repairs.

Drummond (who subsequently held the top position with both the North British Railway and the CR). Brown ordered six 2-4-0 tender engines to be used on express trains in 1862, which was the largest number of locomotives yet received from the E&GR shops. Unfortunately, Brown died suddenly in mid-1864 and was succeeded by S. W. Johnson, who spent two years at the helm of the E&GR's locomotive affairs. During this time the company was absorbed by the North British Railway (NBR), and one of the main benefits of the merger was the acquisition of Cowlairs Works (employing just over 800 at the time), which replaced the NBR's shops at St Margaret's, Edinburgh. The latter had more experience with construction, however, as some thirty-three locomotives had been erected since 1856, but the shops were subsequently dedicated to repairs and remained so until just after the Grouping.

For a time after the merger the NBR had an unusual arrangement whereby S. W. Johnson was Locomotive Superintendent with William Hurst, who had been with the NBR since 1854. The latter was the superior in the relationship and this was undoubtedly the reason why Johnson did not carry on for too long after the amalgamation. Another was the rapidly declining liquidity of the company, which was in such dire straits that any scrap metal on the system had to be immediately sold to raise money. At Cowlairs 250 men in the Wagon Department were dismissed when there were in excess of 700 wagons awaiting repairs, while significant numbers of locomotives and carriages stood idle in sidings in Glasgow and Edinburgh desperate for attention that the NBR could

not afford. Hurst was subsequently used as a 'scapegoat' for the trouble with the rolling stock and he was given his notice in 1866.

Thomas Wheatley was recruited from the London & North Western Railway, beginning work in 1867 as the company regrouped from the recent turmoil. The new Locomotive Superintendent embraced the workshops at Cowlairs and during his tenure increased the output significantly to around forty engines per year. The first of his designs for express traffic was the '141' Class 2-4-0, of which two were erected in 1869, with 6ft 6in driving wheels and 16-inch by 24-inch cylinders. Soon afterwards the first inside-frame and inside-cylinder 4-4-0 in Britain was built at Cowlairs – No 224 – and this was followed by another of the same design, then a modified version in 1873. No 224 is infamous for being the locomotive that was at the head of the train that plunged into the Firth of Tay when the bridge collapsed in 1879, and holds the distinction of being the only NBR compound engine when transformed in 1885 – after being rebuilt following the disaster. The most numerous type built by Wheatley at Cowlairs was the 0-6-0 tender engine, and these formed two standard classes; thirty-eight were of the '251' Class and sixty-two of the '151' Class. Smaller groups of 0-6-0STs were built from 1870 to the mid-point of the decade to work in the various yards across the NBR network.

Wheatley left under a cloud in 1874 after J. M. Douglas, an NBR Director, found irregularities in the accounting for repairs and renewals carried out at Cowlairs. Wheatley's brother was in charge of the Carriage Department at

Wheatley '224' Class 4-4-0 No 224 seen after rebuilding by Holmes.

Cowlairs at this time and also departed, together with the head of the Stores Department. In the 1870s the NBR produced very few carriages at the works, and these consisted of composite vehicles, which were adopted as standard, with all earlier stock being converted to this arrangement. The first British sleeping carriage was bought by the NBR from the Ashbury Railway Carriage & Iron Company in 1873; it had two berths with three beds in each, which were convertible for daytime occupation. Washing facilities, a luggage area and a fixed-seat compartment were also provided. Little success or plaudits came to the NBR with the carriage in service, and the vehicle later passed into the East Coast Joint Stock (ECJS). The vast majority of the wagon stock was bought

or rented from contractors and maintained at Cowlairs.

Drummond returned to the NBR as Locomotive Superintendent in 1874 after spells with the Highland Railway and the LB&SCR. His first task was improving the passenger stud at work on the new Edinburgh to Carlisle route, where the gradients were difficult. Those engines already employed were having so much trouble keeping time that several 0-6-0s on order from Neilson & Co were changed before appearing as 4-4-0s in 1877 and 1878. Four also appeared from Cowlairs in 1879, and these had 6ft 6in driving wheels, 18-inch by 26-inch cylinders, and a 4ft 6¼in-diameter boiler with a heating surface of 1,099.3sq ft and a boiler pressure of 150lb per sq in. The locomotives from the NBR's shops were also fitted

Wheatley '141' Class 2-4-0 No 141.

Drummond '476' 'Abbotsford' Class 4-4-0 No 497 was built at Cowlairs in 1879.

with Westinghouse brakes after extensive tests had been conducted by Drummond to illustrate their superiority over the vacuum system.

During this period Cowlairs was re-equipped and modernised, leading to a reduction in capacity for new construction, with orders placed at local firms, and for repairs. As a result the NBR attempted to compel the men to work longer hours without an increase in pay. The employees were forced to defend their position by striking and the company underhandedly recruited recently redundant workers from Dübs & Co. These men were soon sympathetic and dropped their tools, leaving the NBR to take on applicants with only basic mechanical skills. These employees were at work for nearly two months before the original Cowlairs men went back to work, having made concessions for this privilege. Another conflict between the NBR hierarchy and Drummond occurred when the men wanted to form an ambulance brigade. The company refused any use of rooms for the meetings and contributed no money towards the cost of instruction. A similar position was maintained against the creation, in the early 1880s, of a Co-operative Society, which occurred in the works canteen. Members were threatened with dismissal before local community leaders leapt to their defence and the NBR backed down.

John Thomas, in *The North British Railway*, *Volume Two*, records that Drummond resigned his position in 1882 a short time before further investigations were made into the finances at Cowlairs, which were in arrears. This came after a certain amount of friction had developed between the Locomotive Superintendent and the Board over several matters. Drummond subsequently joined fierce rival the Caledonian Railway. Matthew Holmes almost immediately replaced him at Cowlairs, being promoted from within the NBR, having started with the E&GR in the 1840s. Holmes relied more on Cowlairs than

his predecessor and the first design produced there was for an 0-6-0 similar to the Drummond goods engines but with an improved tender and other details. These engines were subsequently developed into the 'C' Class (a later designation), which appeared in 1888 and possessed a larger boiler than their forerunners. A total of 138 were erected at Cowlairs up to 1900, supplemented by fifteen each from Neilson & Co and Sharp, Stewart & Co. The express stock was also updated by the addition of nearly 100 4-4-0s during Holmes's tenure. These were generally similar, but there were variations, such as a reduction in driving wheel diameter from 7 feet to 6ft 6in, the lowering of boiler pressure to 140lb per sq in, later reinstated to 150lb per sq in., and an increase in the boiler heating surface. Two other deviations were a small version for the West Highland line, which had 5ft 7in wheels and 18-inch by 24-inch cylinders, and an enlarged 6ft 6in design for main-line traffic.

Near the turn of the century the Institution of Mechanical Engineers called in to visit Cowlairs and a description of the site was given in the body's *Journal* for 1895. The total area taken up by the shops was 25 acres and from east to west comprised the Locomotive, Wagon and Carriage Departments. At the south end of the latter two shops was a Timber Yard served by a 10-ton overhead crane, and in the area was a timber drying shed; a fire station was situated close by in case of emergency. On the eastern edge of the yard, adjacent to the main line, was the Iron Foundry where smaller components for the locomotives were produced, in addition to certain items for the permanent way; the Brass Foundry was connected to the southern end of the building. To the north were the Forge and Smithy. Serving these were seventy fires and seven furnaces, as well as seventeen steam hammers with capacities of 5cwt to 5 tons, and hydraulic presses. A heat exchange system had been devised so that the waste

Holmes Class 'C' 0-6-0 No 626 was erected at the works in 1890.

heat from the furnaces could be collected and used to power boilers. The Machine Shop was close by to receive the products of the aforementioned and finish them for attachment to a locomotive. Running alongside the eastern flank of the Erecting Shop was the Boiler Shop, which contained all of the associated equipment for the production of the barrels and fireboxes.

The Erecting Shop was organised into three bays, each with three roads, and as many as sixty engines could be received in the building, together with twelve tenders; two 30-ton overhead cranes served each bay. Immediately outside was the Weigh House. The Wagon Shop next door was a much larger building with more than ten lines running the length of the structure, and accommodated in the south-east corner was the Sawmill. The Carriage Shop was split into two sections – one for repair and the other for erection of new stock. On the western edge was

the Paint Shop (erected in the early 1890s and insured for £20,000 after a bad fire in the works' stores in 1895), which was used for all vehicles; a section in the southern half was given over to trimming the carriage seats, etc. Across all the departments there were some 2,112 men and boys engaged in the various tasks.

A relative of the first Superintendent at Cowlairs replaced Holmes after his retirement in 1903 – William Paton Reid. At this time the working hours were 6.00am to 5.30pm, with the men called to the shops at 5.30am by a horn, which sounded again at 5.53. Such organisation did not spread to the Running Department; John Thomas, in *The North British Railway, Volume Two*, notes that in 1905 a 'head count' of all the locomotives and carriages was performed only to find that a number of tenders and carriages had been mislaid! The former discrepancy was discovered to be an administrative error, while five carriages

While No 633 was the first of the class of the same designation, the engine later became part of the larger Class 'M', which encompassed several groups of 4-4-0s.

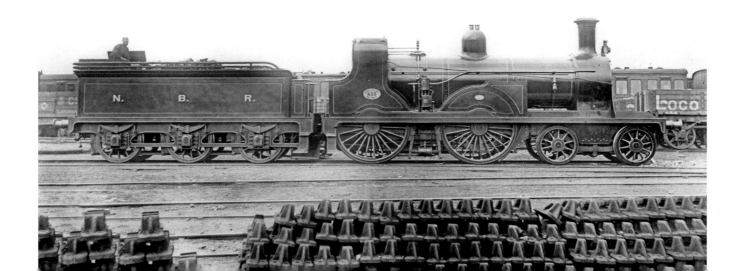

A rare shot inside Cowlairs Works Erecting Shop.

had to be written off as they were nowhere to be found. Reid was employed on a probationary basis for the first year and another twelve months passed before his first design was formulated. This proved to be an 'Atlantic' for express passenger trains on the Waverley and Edinburgh to Aberdeen routes. The North British Locomotive Co (NBLC) was engaged to construct the locomotives as the company could turn them out much faster than Cowlairs, although in the event the manufacturer missed the NBR's spring deadline and there was a shortage of motive power as a result. Even though the engines and subsequent members of the class were 'sired' by a third party, the men at Cowlairs were particularly keen to make sure they were maintained to an exceptionally high standard. Thomas, in *The Springburn Story*, records that there was a separate 'Atlantic Section' at the works where the best craftsmen were employed. Soon after the introduction of the 'Atlantics' in 1906 new stock followed for the Aberdeen service, using a four-wheel bogie; they were 53 feet long and 8ft 6in wide with an elliptical roof.

Appearing after the 'Atlantics' was a mixed traffic 4-4-0 design; twelve were built at Cowlairs between 1906 and 1907, and the same number of a very similar version was constructed in 1909-10. Reid also sent an updated 0-6-0 goods type into service, with 18½-inch by 26-inch

cylinders and a 5ft 4¼in-diameter boiler. Only two were built initially in the NBR's shops, as ten were ordered from the NBLC; of the class total in 1913, when the last was completed, thirty-six had been erected in Cowlairs and forty by the NBLC. A financial crisis hit the NBR during the second half of the century's first decade, and one of the measures implemented to save money was the reduction

The first of twenty-two 'Atlantics', No 868 *Aberdonian*, was erected by the North British Locomotive Co in 1906.

of the working week at Cowlairs to just four days. One of the outcomes of the resulting investigation into the running of the company was that the role of Cowlairs was to be reduced to focus on repairs rather than new construction, which was to be limited to just twelve locomotives per year. In the event this did not occur, as more were built, but outside contractors did take a stronger hand in the NBR's orders, which had been the case for much of Reid's tenure.

Before the First World War commenced the NBR adopted superheating for the principal designs. In 1912 two 'J' Class 4-4-0s, with 6ft 6in-diameter wheels, were fitted with the Schmidt pattern, but the company soon favoured the Robinson version, which commanded a £40 royalty fee. A further twenty-five locomotives – named after Sir Walter Scott characters, earning them the sobriquet 'Scotts' – were completed at Cowlairs to 1920. The 6-foot 4-4-0 was similarly treated and ten were built initially in 1913 before a further twenty-two were ordered before the end of the decade. Finally, the 0-6-0 goods design was modified and these appeared from the works in 1914, but subsequently the NBLC took the upper hand and completed sixty-nine to Cowlairs's thirty-five.

Cowlairs continued to build six-wheel carriages into the early 20th century, even though both 1st and 3rd Class bogie vehicles had been erected in small numbers since the late 1880s. When the latter became standard, 1st, 3rd and Composite variations were constructed, though the 1st Class coaches were bought from the trade. These were 58 feet long and 8ft 6in wide and had eight compartments, while the 3rds had the same dimensions but a further compartment squeezed in; the Brake 3rd had five compartments. The carriage stock was principally non-corridor with few corridor coaches. Six-wheel bogie vehicles were quite rare and after the first four were built in 1879 the next were not seen until the early 20th century. These were Composite dining carriages for the Aberdeen trains, but another long gap ensued before a set of twelve-wheelers was bought from Cravens after the First World War. Built from steel, there were 1st and 3rd Class diners together with Composites, and the dimensions varied.

While the majority of the wagon stock continued to be produced at the works, there were several instances of orders being placed outside. From the turn of the century to the Grouping the standard features were mostly wooden underframes and sides (oak and pine respectively), grease axleboxes and hand-operated brakes. Even though Westinghouse brakes were employed, there was little will to fit these to the wagon stock, although some were so fitted and as a result were given oil-lubricated axleboxes. For the transportation of general goods traffic open

Reid 'J' Class 'Scott' 4-4-0 No 9339 *Ivanhoe* passes over the Forth Bridge with a Stirling to Edinburgh train on 20 August 1937.

Above Class 'J' 4-4-0 No 895 *Rob Roy* was constructed by the NBLC in 1909 and was later the first of the class to be fitted with a Robinson superheater after the Grouping.

Below The second Class 'B' 0-6-0 to be built at Cowlairs was No 330.

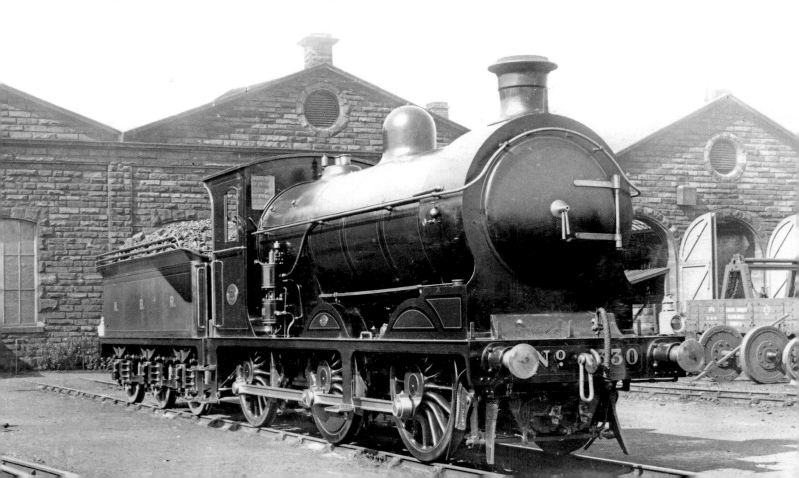

Class 'J' 4-4-0 No 9409 *The Pirate* was built new with a superheater in 1914. The engine is seen at Edinburgh Haymarket shed with the mechanical coaler under construction in the background, c1930.

wagons and goods vans were of 8- and 10-ton capacity, while mineral wagons could carry 16 tons. In the main, the types were those typically required by a railway at the time, but some specialised wagons included some for casks for the distilling and brewing businesses and tanks mounted on a normal underframe for the movement of oils, chemicals and volatile liquids.

As with other railway companies, the NBR and Cowlairs served the country and armed forces admirably during the 1914-18 conflict. However, by the end of the decade the working conditions and restrictions of materials had not eased and this led to a crisis with engines unavailable for work – nearly a quarter of the approximately 1,000 locomotives awaited attention at Cowlairs, which was grossly overstretched. The NBR resorted to sending a number to private firms for overhaul, but this was only in small numbers, while the company's own shops employed men on night shifts in an attempt to clear the backlog, which was only achieved slowly. With the extra workload during the war years came much increased expenditure, and the railway companies were entitled to claim from the Ministry of Transport for work arising to

This 16-ton ore wagon, with a welded steel underframe, was built in 1903.

No 69224, of the 'A' Class (LNER 'N15'), was the last locomotive built at Cowlairs. The engine is seen here late in life at Aberdeen Ferryhill shed. *Bill Reed*

serve the conflict. In 1921 *The Engineer* reported that NBR Chairman William Whitelaw had taken the Ministry to task for only paying £186,914 of the £616,914 that had been claimed. The case was subsequently taken to the Court of Arbitration and the NBR was found to be fully justified in requesting the original sum and the remainder was ordered to be paid.

At the Grouping 1,075 locomotives, 3,576 carriages and 58,970 wagons were taken from the NBR into the stock of the LNER, which also recruited William Whitelaw as Chairman. Reid had retired in 1919 and was replaced by Walter Chalmers, the son of Robert Chalmers, Chief Draughtsman and Assistant Locomotive Superintendent for many years. The younger Chalmers was only in office for a brief period as he chose to take retirement in 1924 and was succeeded by R. A. Thom from Gorton. Design work had been undertaken at Cowlairs for a new eight-coupled freight engine, but this scheme was dropped after the Grouping.

Cowlairs was engaged on completing an order for twenty Reid Class 'A' 0-6-2T locomotives between the end of 1923 and early 1924, which had been placed by the LNER shortly after amalgamation. After the Railways Act 1921 was passed the NBR only placed one order, for ten of the class from Robert Stephenson & Co, which appeared in early 1923. The design originated in 1909 and the preceding class members had been built by the NBLC. The principal dimensions were two 18-inch by 26-inch cylinders fed by slide valves operated by Stephenson motion, a 4ft 8 in-diameter boiler with 1,309sq ft of heating surface working at 175lb per sq in pressure, a tractive effort of 23,205lb, and 4ft 6in-diameter coupled wheels. The Cowlairs series began at number 19, then filled

in various gaps to the last four, which took LNER '9'-prefix numbers 9147, 9174, 9225 and 9227 – the latter being the last locomotive turned out of the workshops, in April 1924. Thereafter the locomotive department was only called upon to conduct repairs to the engines operating in the area and to complete minor rebuilding work, such as fitting new types of boilers and cylinders.

The Carriage Department saw a similar downgrading of responsibility, while the Wagon Shops were busy briefly in 1924 erecting 200 brake-fitted high-sided open wagons, and in 1925 building 250 more, in addition to 500 unfitted. *LNER Wagons Volume 4A: LNER Standard Designs* by Peter Tatlow gives the price of the latter as £150 each, while the former amounted to £202 per wagon for the first batch and £179 for the second. In both instances this was greater than the cost from other workshops that produced the same type: Doncaster's and Dukinfield's prices were £139 and £117 for the unfitted wagons, while with brakes the charges were £150 in 1928. The example of the unfitted wagons is perhaps illustrative of the savings that could be achieved by building elsewhere, and helps to explain why Cowlairs was only rarely asked subsequently to contribute new wagon stock. The next order did not arrive until 1937 when 300 high-sided open wagons to Diagram 92 were requested, together with another 500 in the following year. In 1940 100 Type 'BD' containers to Diagram 94 were also constructed.

The Institution of Mechanical Engineers returned to Cowlairs almost twenty years after the first visit and the *Journal* gave an account illustrating the shops in use and their role. The Brass and Iron Foundries – located in the south-east corner – had an output of 15 and 118 tons per week respectively. The Carriage Wheel and Locomotive

This 12-ton open wagon, which is fitted with automatic vacuum brakes, was erected at Cowlairs in 1928.

Wheel Shops were close by and contained a number of lathes and balancing equipment. In the Spring Shop there was a large double furnace and a double ram hydraulic press; there were water troughs nearby for treating metal. The Machine Shop was supplied with all the necessary tools and lathes, and also housed a hydraulic engine and accumulator for all the hydraulic apparatus used in the building. The Boiler Shop could hold eighteen boilers in the space that was not taken up by the multitude of presses, benders, punchers, rollers and drills. This was relatively new and had been fitted into space between the Sawmill and the metal-working shops to the south of the Erecting Shop. A Tender Shop was also accommodated on the western side in the building, and a total of twelve tenders could be held there. The Wagon Shops had a capacity of 250, either new builds or repairs, and the Carriage Shops had berths for ten under construction and twenty-eight being repaired; sixty could be in the Paint Shop at any one time. The total number of people employed was 2,470.

The men working at Cowlairs underwent a turbulent first decade under the LNER. At first the Drawing Office staff were suspended indefinitely and a number of blacksmiths were released in 1924. During 1926 the men were put on short time for a period (working just four days a week from June to November) due to the financial problems. Further short time was implemented from July 1928 to April 1929, and as a result the Wagon Shops had to be opened three nights a week for overtime to take place and the accumulation of wagon repairs to be overcome. The general reduction in work subsequently forced the men to consider taking action, but this did not

occur as there was a certain amount of reorganisation in the shops to improve the efficiency of the repairs. Cowlairs was responsible for constructing new boilers for the locomotives overseen during the 1920s, although this duty was also rescinded in the early 1930s, the difference in cost being the reason given.

In the *LNER Magazine* for February 1935 the Works Manager of Cowlairs, R. A. Smeddle, gave an account of

Thompson 'B1' No 61349 with an unidentified BR Standard locomotive and a Stanier Class 5 4-6-0 are seen in the Erecting Shop on 27 July 1965. *Brian Robbins, courtesy of Rail Photoprints*

Gresley 'J38' 0-6-0 No 65908, Reid Class 'G' (LNER 'Y9') 0-4-0ST No 68097 and 'B1' No 61402 make up a portion of the engines in the works on 7 April 1957. *Bill Reed*

the changes that had been made in the Erecting Shop to improve the flow of engines through the various stages of repair. Two of the three bays had the number of tracks reduced to one while the other had one turned over to light repairs and the other to tender repairs. The tracks not in use were covered over and utilised to store the material taken off the engine and the refurbished or new parts to be refitted. With the reduction in the space available the number of locomotives given attention fell from fifty-four in 1923 to just twenty. Four 50-ton capacity cranes had recently been installed to cope with the ever-growing size of the locomotives and these were supplemented by two of 40-ton capacity and three of 15 tons.

All of the 'feeder' shops had also undergone a rationalisation of their role and layout. New machinery was bought and arranged with the older tools to provide an assembly line-type environment that moved components in one direction with the utmost efficiency. An example of how this was applied was given in relation to axleboxes. As these weighed around 5cwt, a conveyor system was devised for their movement between the different stages in the Machine Shop, which eased the burden of the men and increased productivity. Electric hoists were also used for the

installation of the axleboxes to the journals. In all, the time in works had been reduced from between thirty and fifty days to just eighteen.

Just before the war the Foundry was fully modernised with the addition of new plant for charging the cupolas and furnaces and also for cleaning the castings. The continuous casting machine for moulds could produce 120 an hour and consumed 20 tons of sand. The three cupolas all had a capacity of 6 tons and these were moved by an electric overhead travelling crane capable of lifting 10 tons. This work, which cost £40,000, caused a great deal of turmoil in the department as up to fifty men were given their dismissal notices in July 1939 due to a lack of work entering the shop. Furthermore, the moulders were in dispute with the management over their rate of pay. At the end of August strike action was threatened over this matter until the LNER agreed to pay the same rate while discussions with the unions were ongoing. These likely did not get very far as the war began soon afterwards and pay rates were drastically altered during the conflict.

K. S. Robertson became Cowlairs Works Manager in 1941 when R. A. Smeddle moved to Darlington under the general reshuffle implemented by new CME Edward

A BR Standard Class 5 is in the midst of a repair. *Brian Robbins, courtesy of Rail Photoprints*

Thompson; the Mechanical Engineer, Scotland, remained T. E. Heywood. To keep morale up during the hostilities the *LNER Magazine* reported that in 1943 a concert had been staged in the works canteen, becoming a regular attraction for the employees. The same publication gave details of an interesting public health initiative taking place at Cowlairs in 1946. A pair of standard vestibule carriages had been converted to accommodate X-ray equipment for the assessment of the men's chests, looking for any signs of disease. Thirty men could be examined in 15 minutes, and of the 3,000 employed 2,000 had undergone the test.

Nationalisation did not change the position of Cowlairs in the new hierarchy of workshops, even with the LMS establishment at St Rollox being a 'stone's throw' away on the other side of Springburn. At this time there were around 200 light and 400 general repairs carried out on locomotives ranging from the Thompson 'A2' 'Pacifics' and 'B1s' to ex-NBR 4-4-0s, in addition to Gresley's 0-6-0s of 'J38' and 'J39' classification and 'K2', 'K3' and 'K4' 2-6-0s, not forgetting several tank classes. A similar number of heavy carriage repairs were undertaken, but light repairs totalled nearly six times as many. Just under 9,000 repairs were carried out on wagons annually.

BR continued the LNER's practice of placing small orders for containers and wagons at irregular intervals. The first were twenty-four Type 'S' in 1954 for the transport of miscellaneous goods from the port at Glasgow and elsewhere in Scotland to the various islands via ferry. In 1956 400 Type 'A' containers were produced; these were 7ft 6in long by 7 feet wide and 8 feet in height with a capacity of 4 tons. In addition, a small number of experimental containers of an open type were built at the works. In 1962 forty-four Type 'BP' container wagons were constructed for the movement of bulk powder, with a capacity of 1½ tons.

In the early 1960s Cowlairs was one of several BR workshops engaged in converting old carriage underframes to flat wagons for holidaymakers to take their motor vehicles with them on their travels. The capacity of these was 10 tons and several services were offered around the country, including connections with ferry ports for people venturing to the continent and Ireland. A total of eighty were reconditioned at Cowlairs, and the process spread to the growing number of redundant steam locomotive tenders, which were transformed into snow ploughs. The works also built three brake tenders mounted on bogies and

Gresley 'V4' Class 2-6-2 No 61700 *Bantam Cock* is seen at Cowlairs on 7 April 1957, shortly after withdrawal in March. The engine was later scrapped at Kilmarnock. *Bill Reed*

weighing 35½ tons; as diesel locomotives were introduced to freight services, many of which were still unfitted, the braking power was totally inadequate, necessitating this makeweight to be provided.

Cowlairs and Gorton were involved in trials to adapt welding for the repair of locomotive boilers for the LNER, and the process was reported by the *British Railways Magazine: Eastern Region* in 1948. Standard practice for this operation had previously been for a patch to be used or the entire plate replaced, both being costly and time-consuming. The use of welding was said to not only save on these two points but also increase the life of the boiler by up to a third. The first step was for the damaged portion to be cut out and the area surrounding it to be bevelled. Silver/phosphorus welding rods were used to improve the joint between the old and new pieces of copper. The weld was later checked for soundness using an X-ray device.

During the mid-1950s the next generation of locomotive engineers was being prepared in a new pre-apprenticeship training school that opened in Glasgow. For the boys given a place, this was a full-time endeavour with 27 hours given over to practical work and 12 hours to the theoretical side. The qualification gained was said to be a good step towards being accepted at Cowlairs, St Rollox or the other engineering establishments in the city for a full engineering apprenticeship. However, the mid-1950s was a difficult period for this career path in the city as the shipyards were losing business at an alarming rate and the NBLC (only a short distance from Cowlairs) was gambling on the new diesel locomotives with the result that the poor designs built at great expense bankrupted the firm. With two BR workshops serving the Scottish Area from the same locality, the closure of one was inevitable given the position of the business. Unfortunately for 2,000 employees at Cowlairs, this proved to be their workshops. The rundown of the facilities occurred in the second half of the 1960s and the final closure came in 1968; the site had been cleared by the early 1970s.

Reid 'N15' Class No 69144 stands at Cowlairs Works, also on 7 April 1957. *Bill Reed*

2
Darlington

The Stockton & Darlington Railway (S&DR) was just over 25 years old in the early 1850s. The company had experienced a dip in fortunes at the time after becoming over-extended financially through committing to the leasing of lines in the Middlesbrough area. A move into the empire of 'Railway King' George Hudson had fallen through due to his disgrace. Fortuitously for the company, iron ore was subsequently discovered in the region and the exploitation of this mineral increased traffic healthily.

Shildon was the location of the company's locomotive workshops at this time and, while being a suitable place at the start of the company's existence – on the western extremity of the 25-mile-long line – the placement of the facilities was not ideal after several expansions had occurred. This growth also meant that new motive power would be required together with spacious facilities to keep it in working order.

Towards the end of the 1850s the S&DR took steps to bring new workshops into existence and bought 33 acres of land in Darlington, which was in a generally advantageous position for the company, for just over £9,100. This plot was on the north side of Darlington North Road station and on the western side of the North Road. To the south-west of the station the company had already installed Hope Town Carriage Works in 1853, while to the west there was also the Hope Town Foundry of W. & A. Kitching (later becoming the Whessoe Foundry Co) and to the east was the South Durham Iron Works – subsequently the home of the Darlington Forge Co.

Locomotive Engineer William Bouch was charged with planning the facility and, after investigating many locomotive works around the country, he wisely thought that the provision of space for the present requirements alone was foolhardy, specifying that the shops should be large, but capable of further expansion when the need arose. Bouch calculated that some 16 acres would be required by the end of the century and the Board was happy to consent to this provision and his plans in general.

A feature of these would be for much of the apparatus for driving the machinery – commonly placed overhead in many workshops of the period – to be installed below the floor, allowing much more natural light to illuminate the interior of the building.

After the scheme was checked by a third party, the Board gave final approval and tenders were invited for the work. These were submitted both for the whole job and for individual portions, and the latter quotes came in more than £1,000 cheaper. Several firms were issued contracts and work began later in the year, being completed during 1862. At this time the machinery was fitted and the shops were ready to open on 1 January 1863.

The Erecting Shop was divided into three sections, with the outer two forming the repair bays, while the inner was used for housing the machinery. Long brick walls supported the roof and there were tall arches built into them allowing the men to pass back and forth. At the

The original Erecting Shop at Darlington when in use as the Wheel Shop.

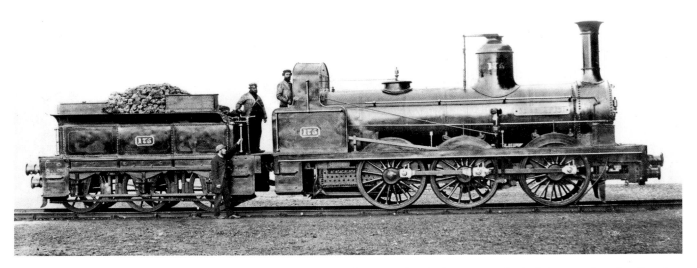

No 175 *Contractor* was the first locomotive to be built at Darlington; the design was typical of that used at the time by the S&DR for its freight traffic.

top of the roof were a number of ventilators to keep the air fresh. There were travelling cranes in the two outer portions of the Erecting Shop obtained from Sampson & Moore, and these were worked by manila ropes, which were capable of lifting a locomotive of 30-40 tons weight in around 6 minutes. The flooring was of timber and the walls were painted white, while the equipment was a lavender colour.

The machinery was driven by a large steam engine with a cylinder 22 inches in diameter with a 3ft 1in stroke. The boiler pressure was 60lb per sq in and exhaust steam was used to preheat the feedwater close to boiling point. The shafting for the machinery was between 4½ and 5 inches in diameter, fitted with metal couplings and running in iron plummer blocks with brass bearings. The belting departed from leather, which was traditionally used, and was made of wool supplied by Whitehead & Bros of London. This type was said to be much more durable than leather and a fraction of the cost.

Just before the works was completed, the S&DR and North Eastern Railway (NER) entered negotiations for a takeover of the former by the latter. This had to be ratified by Parliament and authorisation was given in early 1863, the formal takeover occurring at the end of July. Interestingly, the Board of the S&DR was given a certain amount of freedom to continue running the lines formerly controlled by the company, including the motive power requirements. Bouch was retained and continued to oversee Darlington and Shildon workshops. There appears to have been little interference from Edward Fletcher, the Locomotive Superintendent of the NER, and the first design to be built at Darlington was an S&DR-type 0-6-0 for goods traffic. More than three-quarters of the 158 engines forming the company's stock was made up of this type at the time of the takeover and there were no new passenger locomotives for several years subsequently.

No 175 *Contractor* was the first locomotive built at Darlington in October 1864, and was a continuation of the long-boiler type favoured by the S&DR. The boiler was 14 feet long, had a diameter of 4 feet and worked at 130lb per sq in pressure; there were two cylinders of 17-inch diameter by 24-inch stroke. Several other examples were built at Darlington to the late 1860s, when a modification to the design was made, and these new locomotives were classified '1001' by the NER. The driving wheel diameter was increased to 5ft 0½in from 4ft 11in of the earlier engines, the boiler pressure was increased by 10lb per sq in and the stroke of the piston was lengthened by 2 inches.

Bouch followed his reliable 0-6-0s with the unreliable '238' Class 4-4-0s. These had 7ft 1in driving wheels, 17-inch by 30-inch cylinders, and 13-inch-diameter piston valves that were made from solid brass. No 238 was the first out of the shops in December 1871 and was followed by a further nine up to 1875. These engines later had to be rebuilt as 2-4-0s and were more successful in this new guise, lasting in employment until the early 20th century.

In keeping with Bouch's expansion plans, several additions were made on site during the early years as well as the installation of new and modern equipment. In 1868 a roundhouse was built and this had space for twenty-four locomotives; nearly ten years later a second roundhouse of similar design was completed. Following the first roundhouse was the Smiths' Shop on the south side of the Erecting Shop in 1873. This contained thirty-six cast-iron hearths, 5 feet in diameter, with water-cooled tuyeres, which were 10 inches in diameter with a 2½-inch-diameter blast nozzle. The air was supplied by a Lloyd's fan 5 feet in diameter and a flue 4 feet in diameter. Smoke was carried away from the hearths by an underground system, to be discharged into the atmosphere by a chimney located on the far north-east corner of the works.

Two large hammers of 500lb and 300lb were used for smiths' work, the design being of American origin and built by Collier of Manchester. These were different from those normally used as the drive came from a belt rather than

During the early years very few passenger locomotives were built at North Road, but one – seen at Whitby – was Fletcher 'BTP' Class 0-4-4T No 1033, the first of twenty-five class members erected there between 1877 and 1880.

steam. The power was obtained from a 4-foot-diameter cross spring attached to a small fly wheel and return crank, which had the advantage of greater regulation of the weight required for the blow.

Another new addition was a chuck lathe, which had the distinction of being the first to be fitted with two chuck plates. The largest one was of 10-foot diameter and the smaller of 5-foot diameter, these being used to bore tyres. The machine was able to run at two speeds, so two different jobs could be undertaken at once and the plates could also be fixed together for heavier work to be performed. The former was the lathe's major advantage, as boring one 5-foot-diameter tyre took 3 hours and required the machinist's constant attention; with two tyres running, the worker was more productive. Bouch was involved in the design, and Massey Bromley and Scriven & Holdsworth of Leeds carried out construction of the 40-ton machine; the total cost was £1,400.

The year 1875 marked the first turning point for Darlington Works. Bouch was taken ill during the year and spent much of the time away trying to recuperate, but unfortunately he passed away in 1876 and William Younghusband became Works Manager, Darlington. The S&DR Board was also disbanded at this time and the area was brought under the greater control of the NER and Locomotive Superintendent Edward Fletcher. In the meantime the works played host to the celebrations for the fiftieth anniversary of the formation of the S&DR in September 1875 and locomotives were displayed in the Erecting Shop. The last Bouch design was also built and this had a slightly longer wheelbase than had hitherto been employed.

The first Fletcher engine to be built at Darlington was No 1050, which was the first of six 2-4-0s for passenger traffic. They still incorporated S&DR features, such as the standard cylinder size of 17 inches by 26 inches, and detail fittings, but these were perhaps a smaller version of his '901' Class express passenger locomotives. Following in

A total of six batches of '398' Class 0-6-0s were built at Darlington, and No 617 was part of the penultimate lot of ten engines completed during 1881.

No 369 was the first of the second batch of McDonnell 0-6-0s erected at Darlington in 1884.

1877 was the well-known 'BTP' Class 0-4-4WT; the first was No 1115, being accompanied by another seventeen up to 1880. An 0-6-0WT variation on the type was built in 1881 – No 124 – and a further eleven would be erected to 1882 with the standard features of the 'BTP' Class.

More Fletcher designs were built at Darlington up to his retirement in 1882, many of these being of the 0-6-0 '398' Class, which had 17-inch by 24-inch cylinders, Stephenson motion and slide valves, a 4ft 3in-diameter boiler with a 17sq ft grate area, a working pressure of 160lb per sq in, and 5-foot-diameter coupled wheels. A total of 325 of the class were built, almost split evenly between the company's shops and outside contractors; for much of the NER's early existence the company relied on firms to augment the locomotive building programme. The final Fletcher design built at Darlington was a series of four 2-4-0s in 1882.

Alexander McDonnell was Fletcher's successor and came to the position after eighteen years as Locomotive Superintendent of the Great Southern & Western Railway of Ireland. During this time he had greatly improved the methods employed in the company's workshops at Inchicore and standardised many components used by the locomotives. This was part of the reason why he was selected for the position on the NER, as the company's expansions had brought in a large amount of diverse stock that put greater stresses on the repair facilities at Gateshead, Darlington and York, coupled with the closure of many smaller repair centres from the absorbed railways. Unfortunately, McDonnell was not welcomed by the men in the North East and he did his popularity no favours by removing some of the Fletcher features that he did not find desirable. McDonnell's first design was for an express passenger 4-4-0 that was similar to Fletcher's

'901' Class but did not perform as well. This was followed by the Class '59' 0-6-0, of which a large proportion were erected at Darlington. The first – No 497 – was completed in September 1883, and the locomotives were generally similar to the '398' Class but with several slight detail modifications. The '59' Class turned out to be less capable than its predecessors and, with the increasing animosity towards McDonnell, he resigned during 1884, with many of the tasks set at his appointment remaining unfulfilled.

While the company pondered over his successor, General Manager Henry Tennant was appointed as head of a committee to oversee locomotive matters. The first task of this body was fulfilling the need for express passenger locomotives, and for these a return was made to the Fletcher 2-4-0 type. The first of ten – No 1463 – was constructed at Darlington in 1885.

The committee was soon redundant after the appointment of T. W. Worsdell, who left the Great Eastern Railway to move north. He had gained a good grounding in England before spending time in America at the Altoona Works, but was not particularly successful with his designs on the GER. As Gateshead was the company's principal works at the time, the first Worsdell design emerged from there in early 1886. In June Darlington released to traffic No 14 of the 'B1' Class for local freight duties. This had an 0-6-2T wheel arrangement and two 18-inch by 24-inch cylinders with Joy valve gear; the driving wheel diameter was 5ft 1¼in. A compound version of the design, with a high-pressure cylinder 18 inches by 24 inches in diameter and a low-pressure cylinder of 26 inches by 24 inches, was later built in numbers at Darlington, and of the class total of fifty, thirty-nine were from the works. Worsdell developed the compound arrangement in conjunction with the German locomotive engineer August von Borries,

Tennant 2-4-0 No 1466 poses between duties with driver, fireman and officials at York station.

and the system later found favour on several European railways. Also built at this time were two batches of Class 'C' compound 0-6-0s based on the Class 'B1' engines and totalling thirty-five. Other classes built at Darlington to Worsdell's designs were the 'E' 0-6-0T (120 from 1887 to 1895) and 'G' 2-4-0 (twenty between 1887 and 1888).

T. W. Worsdell retired in 1890 and was succeeded by his brother W. Worsdell, who had been with the NER since 1883 as Assistant Locomotive Superintendent. Over the next twenty years Worsdell, with the help of his assistant Vincent Raven, General Manager G. S. Gibb and Chief Draughtsman W. M. Smith, was able to modernise the NER locomotive stock by providing large and relatively powerful engines for the increasing traffic demands.

Darlington Works played a role in this transformation by erecting almost 700 locomotives over the period, or approximately thirty-five per year. However, this was still a supporting role to Gateshead, which would produce almost double the amount of engines, and this situation would not be overturned until the start of the 20th century. One of Worsdell's first moves was to abandon compound working, as well as making use of Stephenson's motion.

For the first few years of Worsdell's reign Darlington continued to build T. W. Worsdell's Class 'C' and 'E' designs, and the first new product from the works was the Class 'N' 0-6-2T No 383 in May 1893. However, this was similar to the 'B1' Class, just having slightly altered cylinder dimensions. Following this was an 0-4-4T light

The remit for the Class 'E' 0-6-0s was to perform shunting duties where necessary across the NER system. No 304, which was built as part of the first batch in 1886, is so engaged at York.

Like many engineers of the period, Worsdell favoured the 0-4-4T wheel arrangement for local services. No 1779 served in this capacity from June 1896 to November 1954.

passenger type; this was the 'O' Class and featured a standard 4ft 3in-diameter boiler with 15.6sq ft of grate area, working at 160lb per sq in; the cylinders were 18 inches by 24 inches and the driving wheels were 5ft 1¼in in diameter. Ten were built at Darlington in 1894, and these would be joined in service by a further 100 from the works. Also fitted with the above-mentioned standard boiler were the 'P' and 'P1' Class 0-6-0s, which were introduced for mineral and freight traffic before the turn of the century; of the total numbers, twenty and forty respectively were turned out by the North Road shops. In the early 20th century a version with a 5ft 6in-diameter boiler was built and classified 'P2', while the 'P3' had the same boiler but a slightly different firebox; thirty of both types were completed. They were designed to serve a change in mineral traffic as the company pushed towards higher-capacity wagons.

In the final decade of the 19th century the NER erected nearly 500 new locomotives, and because of this growth in stock the company required greater space to repair and maintain them. Expansion at Gateshead was out of the question; likewise at York the space did not exist for a change of roles from a repair establishment to a place of construction on any great scale. Here the foresight of Bouch came to the rescue of the NER, and Worsdell instructed Darlington Works Manager Ramsey Kendal, in partnership with Chief Architect William Bell, to plan the extension of the works at North Road.

There had been a large amount of expansion at Darlington in the mid-1880s when a new forge was built together with an extension of the Erecting Shop to the west

of the original building and a Tender Shop on the north face of these buildings. W. & R. Blackett of Bishop Auckland completed the work by October 1884 at a cost of almost £16,000. Prior to this work an old engine shed – built just before the works opened and outside the confines of the site – was converted to the new Paint Shop.

The new Erecting Shop was constructed along the north side of the 1884 extension and Tender Shop, being 508 feet long and 198ft 6in wide. The frame of the building was steel (provided by Messrs Butler & Co of Leeds) and was supported by the brick exterior. The roof was of glass, with the south side being a special green glass to reduce the strength of the sun in the warmer months, and supported by steel stanchions spaced at 36-foot intervals. There were three main bays for repairs that accommodated twenty-four locomotives each, and a smaller bay (25 feet wide) used as a special machine shop, tool fitting, brass finishing and grinding shop as well as accommodating some offices. There was one 70-ton overhead electric travelling crane serving the whole of the shops (supplied by Craven Bros of Manchester).

The engine pits were arranged on the stall system with suitable space all around for the work to be conducted, as well as allowing natural light to circulate. Visibility was aided by the provision of electric lights in the pits – in addition to forty-eight suspended above the shop, each having 1,500 candlepower – and there were also connections to the gas and compressed air supply; this was provided by Ingersoll Sergeant steam compressors to 100lb pressure. An 18-inch-gauge rail system was installed for the conveyance of materials to the pits on trolleys and

Darlington Works' New Erecting Shop comes to a brief standstill in the early 20th century for this view to be captured.

to the fitting benches on the south side of the building where the auxiliary machine bay was located. The latter was served by small lifting cranes and the machinery was powered by an electric motor driving shafting at 200rpm.

The Machine Shop was supplied with a large number of modern tools, such as lathes, etc, as was the Brass Finishing Shop adjoining. A separate space was provided for finishing and polishing and this was well-ventilated to keep the atmosphere free from dust. Young men would perform some of this work, which saw rough castings transformed before being used on a locomotive, in addition to older components being re-finished.

'BTP' Class No 1312 occupies the far berth while Worsdell 'P1' 0-6-0 No 2036 is about to be reunited with the coupled wheels in this scene captured in the New Erecting Shop.

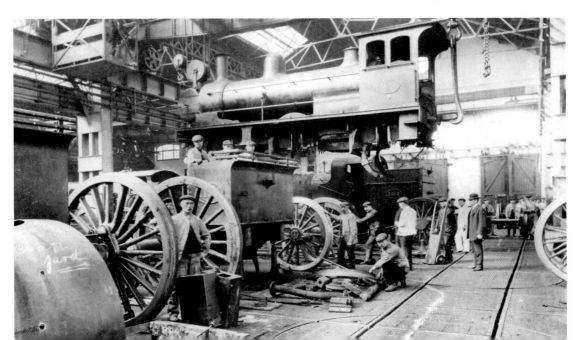

The Tinsmiths' Shop.

Electricity for the shops was produced on-site by three Willan's engines that were supplied with steam from locomotive boilers fired by a mixture of smokebox ash and coal, a reversible booster of the Lancashire Dynamo Co, and an accumulator of 110 two-volt cells made by Ashmore, Benson, Pease & Co. However, this was only a temporary arrangement and a modern system was later installed. During the winter months the water from the boilers was used to heat the workshops, afterwards returning to be fed back in.

With materials and construction costs, the work had cost the NER approximately £50,000, but the company gained one of the largest repair shops in the country. After the improvements the works were said to be able to handle some 500-600 locomotive repairs annually, which was a sizeable increase over the capacity of Gateshead. After the completion of the New Erecting Shop, the NER was able to close York locomotive works completely and concentrate the tasks carried out there at Darlington. Some of the men and machinery were transferred north, and towards the end of the first decade of the 20th century approximately 1,800 were employed in the workshops, which was a more than tenfold increase in the workforce since 1863.

The New Erecting Shop allowed a certain amount of reorganisation on site. The original Erecting Shop was refurbished for machining cylinders, pistons and general metalwork to other components, while the 1884 extension was reorganised for the bays to run from west to east rather than north to south. These were split in the middle and the northern half dealt with construction of new engines – an allowance of around thirty per year was given at the time – and the other half catered for minor repairs.

During all the building work locomotive construction carried on and twenty of the new Class 'U' 0-6-2T engines for goods duties were completed in 1902/03. These were similar to the Class 'N' but had 4ft 7¼in-diameter wheels. The 'P2s' were erected next and were followed by twenty 'T1' Class 0-8-0 heavy mineral engines, which were to be used on the South Shields to Tyne Dock line. These locomotives had slide valves, whereas earlier examples from Gateshead had piston valves. The latter were used on the next new type from Darlington, which was significant in being the first express passenger locomotive to be built there for a number of years. A total of ten 'R1' 4-4-0s were built between 1908 and 1909; they had 5ft 6in boilers working at 225lb per sq in with a 27sq ft grate, 19-inch by

Another view inside the New Erecting Shop, c1905.

26-inch cylinders with 10-inch piston valves operated by Stephenson motion, and, interestingly, a variable blastpipe that was 4¾ inches in diameter increasing to 7½ inches when working hard. The final product from the works under Worsdell was the 'V/09' Class 'Atlantics' – numbering ten – built in 1910. These varied only slightly from their predecessors, the 'V' Class, in having 19½-inch-diameter cylinders instead of 20 inches, and modified framing.

Vincent Raven succeeded Worsdell on 1 June 1910, taking responsibility for some 2,000 locomotives. However, one of the first matters requiring his attention was the movement of the Chief Mechanical Engineer's Department (the position's title had changed from Locomotive Superintendent under Worsdell in the early 20th century) from Gateshead to Darlington, later to be accommodated in new, dedicated (and decidedly palatial) offices a short distance south-west from Darlington Works on the Stooperdale estate. Accompanying the department were 1,500 men from Gateshead Works who were redeployed as part of the concentration of construction and repairs at North Road.

The Darlington Works site was not so extensive that all this influx of work, men and machinery did not cause a slight shortage of space. The NER looked again to the Stooperdale estate to provide space for a new Boiler Shop, Tender Shop and Paint Shop. The first two were located in one building placed between the main works site and the Stooperdale offices on the west side of the Barnard Castle line, while the third was situated to the north on the

Worsdell 'P2' Class 0-6-0 No 1159 pictured in almost new condition in 1904.

south side of the aforementioned route and the triangular junction of lines to Bishop Auckland. Both were erected between 1908 and 1910 at a cost of approximately £35,000.

The Boiler Shop was similar to the 1903 Erecting Shop, being 513 feet long, 219 feet wide and 35 feet between floor and roof spans. The structure employed a steel framework and outer brick walls for support. The interior was divided into four bays: two 60 feet wide for new construction and old boiler repairs (some thirty could be accommodated at once); a 30-foot bay containing the machine tools; and a 60-foot bay on the western side used

Worsdell's 'R1' Class 4-4-0s were redesignated 'D21' by the LNER after the Grouping, although No 1239 still carries the former class name, despite having the new company's initials applied to the tender, in this photograph taken at York.

The Paint Shop with Faverdale Wagon Works on the right. *K. Taylor collection, courtesy of J. W. Armstrong Trust*

for tender tank construction. On the eastern side of the building were several stores, the plate shed and general warehouse, these being served by a 3-ton overhead crane.

Several gas producers 8 feet in diameter and 9 feet tall were installed along the south-eastern wall of the shop to supply the four large gas furnaces – installed close by and opening into the building – used for heating the metal plates. There were three hydraulic stamping and flanging presses, the largest having a top working pressure of 300 tons and the others 250 and 100 tons.

A riveting tower was placed in the south-eastern corner of the new boiler section on the eastern side of the building and had a separate height of more than 50

feet to accommodate dedicated lifting apparatus and the upturned boiler. The hydraulic riveter had a maximum pressure of 65 tons and was capable of operating at reduced values. Another feature was a timer to ensure that the pressure was applied for a certain period to allow the task to be completed before the tool was removed.

Many of the heavier hand tools were driven by compressed air and the compressor had a capacity of 500 cubic feet of air per minute, being driven by a 105hp motor at 330rpm. Power to the small machines was supplied from 45hp motors to shafting 3 inches in diameter, then by belt to the apparatus. Some of the larger pieces of equipment were powered by dedicated motors,

Darlington manufactured these three flat wagons during 1917 to transport large naval guns forged in the factories of the North East.

such as the punching and shearing machine, which had a 22hp motor, the plate rollers with a 12hp motor, and the duplex radial-arm drilling machines – of which there were two – which had 10hp motors. Several were used for the four 25-ton overhead travelling cranes by Craven Bros, allowing forwards or backwards movement at a rate of 175 feet per minute. Several smaller cranes were purchased from Cowans Sheldon.

The hydraulic testing of boilers was also carried out at the shop and a set of three-throw hydraulic pumps was used for this purpose. Plungers were 3½ inches in diameter by a 12-inch stoke, and the electrically driven pumps were capable of delivering 50 gallons of water per minute at a pressure of 1,700lb per sq in. Pumps were from Hugh Smith & Co of Glasgow, which also supplied a number of the other hydraulic tools used at the works. For the test the boiler was filled with water from the mains to capacity, then, if there were no leaks, the hydraulic test began. Afterwards, some of the water was drained away and a fire was started to check the boiler under these conditions.

The arrangement of the shop was specially prepared to ensure that the materials entered the shop in one place and moved around in one direction from process to process until the boiler was completed and tested. The same arrangement was in operation in the tender section, where rollers, presses and other machine tools were located.

The 'Y' Class 4-6-2T for heavy mineral trains signalled the start of the Raven era and introduced the three-cylinder arrangement to the company's mainstream construction. The cylinders were 16½ inches in diameter by 26 inches stroke with 7½-inch piston valves, and were used in conjunction with a 5ft 6in-diameter boiler, working at 180lb per sq in. pressure, and 4ft 7¼in driving wheels. A total of twenty were built between October 1910 and June 1911. Another first for Darlington soon after was the erection of 4-6-0s to the 'S2' Class design. Generally similar to the earlier 'S' Class, they had a boiler diameter 9 inches greater at 5ft 6in, and the first seven built at Darlington between December 1911 and March 1912 used saturated steam, although the remaining thirteen were fitted with superheaters from new. The latter were of the Robinson type and had twenty-four elements $1^{3}/_{32}$ inch in diameter, which reduced the number of small tubes from 268 to 146. The last member of the class – No 825 – was experimentally fitted with Stumpf 'Uniflow' cylinders. These were arranged so that steam passed into the cylinder through the piston valve as normal but the exhaust went through a number of holes in the cylinder, with the aim of reducing condensation at the ports due to the temperature changes of the live steam and the exhaust.

Further freight engines were built in 1913. These were thirty 'T2' Class 0-8-0s, which utilised the superheated 'S2'-type boiler, 20-inch by 26-inch cylinders and coupled wheels 4ft 7¼in in diameter. Also constructed between 1913 and 1914 were the 'D' Class 4-4-4T engines for suburban trains

The boiler repair bay at Stooperdale, with the Machine Shop on the left and the area for new boiler construction on the right.

The new boiler bay at Stooperdale with a number of fireboxes being prepared.

The machine bay at Stooperdale looking south; note the large drills in use in the foreground and power obtained from pulleys connected to shafting suspended from the roof supports.

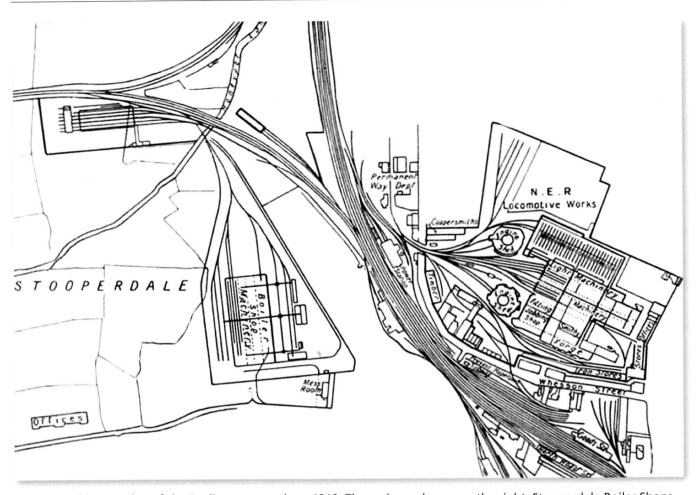

The general layout plan of the Darlington complex, c1910. The main works are on the right, Stooperdale Boiler Shops on the left and the Paint Shop at the top. Faverdale Wagon Works would later be established just to the west of the last-mentioned.

around the population centres of the North East. Twenty of these were erected with superheated boilers and cylinders with the same dimensions as the 'Y' Class.

With the electrification of lines around the Newcastle area proving a success in the early 1900s, Raven gained permission to electrify an 18-mile stretch between the marshalling yards at Newport and Shildon. Darlington Works was given the task of constructing the ten locomotives and this was all but completed during 1914 using electrical equipment from Siemens. The line opened

'A7' Class 4-6-2T No 9777 was not unusual in having three cylinders when pictured between 1946 and 1948, but as Class 'Y' No 1175 – constructed in January 1911 – the engine was in the minority.

during the following year and the locomotives proved to be quite successful.

Raven was soon dealing with other matters as he was given charge of Woolwich Arsenal after the outbreak of the First World War in August 1914. He was one of many men working for the company who served their country during the conflict by giving their expertise to armament production and other related activities. Raven's assistant, A. C. Stamer, took over in his absence and had the task of overseeing the continuation of the construction and repair of locomotives in the midst of difficult circumstances, as well as the reduced capacity of the shops due to the introduction of munitions work. In 1915 there was outrage at the shortage of shells for the men in France, and as a result a munitions factory was erected on the northern edge of the North Road site. Constructed at Government expense – the cost was nearly £41,000 including machinery – it was managed by the NER, which was expected to take over the facilities at the end of the conflict.

The NER was among the other railway companies of Britain in dedicating itself to the production of shells and other items, which were delegated to each workshop based on the suitability of their equipment to the order ready to be placed. This was done by the Railway Executive Committee, which was formed from several of the CMEs; the Chairman was the NER's General Manager, Sir Alexander K. Butterworth. Much of the work undertaken by all of the railway workshops involved 18-pounder high-explosive shells, 18-pounder shrapnel shells and 6-inch high-explosive shells. Reconditioning work was also undertaken on used projectiles.

Norman J. Lockyer was the Works Manager at this time (he held the position from 1909 to 1922) and he oversaw the output of 428,435 18-pounder high-explosive shells, 1,064,665 18-pounder shrapnel shells, and 134,876 6-inch high-explosive shells. Furthermore, 257,168 4.5-inch cartridge casings and 1,864,447 18-pounder cartridges were renovated. Darlington Works was successful in breaking the production targets during the conflict, as some 10,000 more 18-pounder shrapnel shells were manufactured than the quoted 5,000 per week. This also applied to the 6-inch shells, of which 1,000 more were made than the 250 originally agreed, and 30,000 over the 5,000 stipulated 18-pounder shells were refurbished. This latter work was performed in the aforementioned National Projectile Factory, where more than 1,000 women were employed in the total workforce of 1,250.

Women were an important addition to industry during this period and were successfully employed in a wide variety of roles. *The Engineer* of 11 January 1918 provided some figures relating to the amount at work: 500,000 were performing munitions work; 400,000 were in a role previously taken by a man; during 1916 a peak

Raven 'S2' Class 4-6-0 No 813 departs from York with a train from Leeds bound for Scarborough.

of 2,000,000 women were registered for work; nearly 10,000 women took munitions roles every week; and 1,000 new female recruits went into shell factories.

Females were said to perform their duties very capably and picked up the skills required quite easily. The manufacture of a 6-inch shell was quite labour-intensive as the rough shell forging received from another workshop had to be prepared, bored, counter-bored and faced. The shell was then turned to a finish and a thread made in the counter-bore before the inside was finely polished. The nose was then fastened on by a special cement. The body was then readied for the copper band to be added, which gave a good fit inside the gun barrel. The shell body was waved and serrated before the band, manufactured at York Works, was pressed in, then machined to a finish. The final process was for the base plate to be riveted in position.

Other work carried out at Darlington during the conflict included the construction of a mounting for a 6-inch anti-aircraft gun to a trolley wagon supplied by the Great Western Railway. Fifteen cradles and trails were also built for 8-inch howitzers and twenty for 6-inch naval guns. A total of 460 axles were made for 4.5-inch howitzers and these were sent for assembly at the Coventry Ordnance Factory. The NER also generously supplied locomotives – not just to the armed forces but to other railways. Fifty 'T1' Class 0-8-0s were sent to France, ten 0-6-0s travelled north to the Highland Railway, and a number were taken by the London & North Western Railway as well as Woolwich Arsenal for shunting duties.

New locomotive construction was naturally very restrained during this period, and only 'D', 'E1', 'T2' and 'Z' Class locomotives were completed. Twenty of the latter

from the North British Locomotive Company (NBLC) had started the class off in 1911 before further examples were ordered from Darlington. Thirteen were erected in 1914, nine in 1915, two in 1916, five in 1917 and one – fitted with Stumpf 'Uniflow' cylinders – entered traffic in 1918. Twenty 'T2s' were built in 1917 and ten in 1918, with a further fifty being purchased from Armstrong Whitworth & Co after the conflict came to an end.

Raven returned in 1919 and continued from where he left off with regard to locomotive design. A three-cylinder version of the 'T2' 0-8-0 – classified 'T3' – appeared at the end of 1919 with a modified boiler based on that used with the 'Z' Class 'Atlantics', having a larger superheater area and smaller grate area. Following closely behind this class and utilising the same boiler and cylinders were the 'S3' Class 4-6-0s, with 5ft 8in-diameter wheels, used in a mixed-traffic role. No 840 was the first to be built in December 1919 and was followed by a steady stream from North Road throughout 1920 and 1921, by which time there were thirty-five in service.

After the relative success of the Newport to Shildon electrification, Raven pushed for the conversion of the main line from York to Newcastle. While the plans were under consideration he was given permission to construct a prototype electric locomotive, and this emerged from Darlington in May 1922, having cost close to £30,000 – well over budget. The vehicle – No 13 – had six 300-horsepower motors supplied by Metropolitan Vickers and a 2-Co-2, or 4-6-4, wheel arrangement. Unfortunately, the plans were subsequently abandoned and the locomotive became a near permanent fixture in Darlington Works' Paint Shop for the next two decades.

Several NER electrics – Nos 10, 6, 5 and 13 – are seen in the Paint Shop. *Courtesy of J. W. Armstrong Trust*

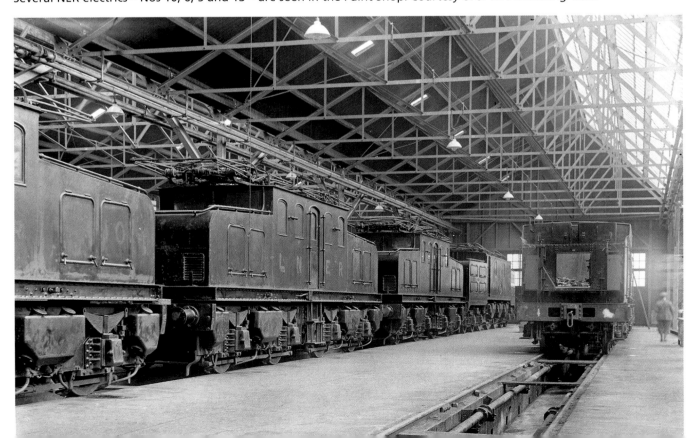

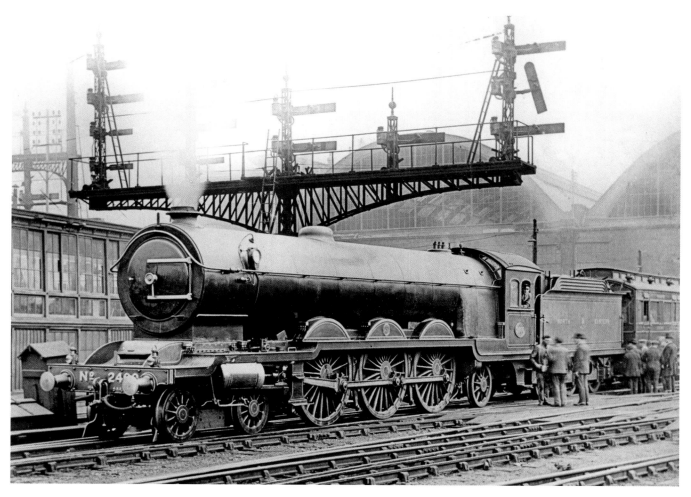

Raven 'Pacific' No 2400 is at King's Cross station to compete against Gresley's 'A1' Class in early 1923, with the ex-NER dynamometer car.

In early 1922 Darlington was authorised to build two locomotives with a 4-6-2 or 'Pacific' wheel arrangement, this partially being an experiment and reply to the Great Northern Railway, which was about to introduce a 'Pacific' engine for the express passenger services out of King's Cross. The NER 'Pacific' was based on the 'Z' Class, but with a larger boiler working at 200lb per sq in, a wide firebox and larger cylinders. Nos 2400 and 2401 were both completed before the end of 1922.

At Darlington the effects of the 1923 Grouping were not felt immediately as the NER placed several orders for its own designs before the event, leading to a continuity that was perpetuated by the LNER adding further examples. A start was made on building twenty 'S3' Class 4-6-0s in November 1922, completed in August 1923, to be followed by fifteen ordered by the LNER together with three Raven 'Pacifics'. The NER had also commissioned a final ten locomotives of the 'P3' Class, and these followed a recent batch in being fitted with Schmidt superheaters. Finally, the works constructed five 'H' Class 0-4-0Ts of a T. W. Worsdell design for shunting duties to replace the same number of withdrawn engines from the Hull & Barnsley Railway – absorbed by the NER just before the Grouping – of similar design that were withdrawn.

Late in 1923 the LNER placed work at Darlington consisting of fifty 'K3' Class 2-6-0 locomotives. The design had originated a short time earlier on the Great Northern Railway (GNR) and was chosen to be the standard LNER mixed-traffic engine of the foreseeable future. The class had three cylinders, Gresley's conjugated motion operating 8-inch-diameter piston valves, a 6-foot-diameter boiler with a thirty-two-element Robinson superheater, a tractive effort of 30,031lb and 5ft 8in-diameter coupled wheels. Modifications were made to the design, particularly to make the locomotive conform to the new composite loading gauge (the maximum height of rolling stock running within the new LNER system). The chimney was shorter and had a relatively austere appearance compared with the old design (the liner was also shorter to accommodate the change), the dome was noticeably squatter, and the whistle was placed lower down on the left-hand side in front of the cab. This latter was of the NER type, replacing the old-fashioned Ivatt style initially used on the GNR engines. A larger Group Standard tender was also designed at Darlington for the new engines, based on the 4,125-gallon tender used by the NER. The capacity was raised to 4,200 gallons of water and 7½ tons of coal, compared to the 3,500-gallon and 6½-ton capacity of the

Hydraulic pressure is used to force the driving wheels on to the crank axle of 'K3' No 2473.

GNR tenders. The design work necessary for the Group Standard tenders meant that they were not ready for the completion of the first engine – No 17 – in August 1924, and the third – No 32 – was the first to receive one. The two batches of twenty-five 'K3s' were completed by April 1925, and by that time a further order had been placed for ten, and these were built from August to December.

During 1925 the Institution of Mechanical Engineers visited the works and a summary of the layout appeared in the body's *Journal* during the year. Entering the site from North Road through the offices, the large mess hall was to the right and the main stores for the North Eastern Area to the left. In front was the first Erecting Shop, which had

been transformed into the Main Machine Shop and was in turn split into several areas for dedicated work to take place. Looking to the west the left-hand side of the shop was used for preparing wheels and axles, then behind was the Milling Shop for coupling and connecting rods. In the centre, as originally, there was a whole host of machine tools such as drills, saws, shaping machines, etc. On the right was the planing shop and behind were the larger tools for punching, slotting and boring.

Between the Machine Shop and the New Engine Bay was the Cylinder Shop. There the rough forgings were bored and finished before being set up with the motion on the frames, then being moved into the New Engine Bay. Many boring, drilling and tapping machines were present in the area. Accessed from the south end of this area was the Forge, Smithy and Spring Shop. The former utilised two steam hammers of 2 and 5 tons capacity, which received their steam from dedicated boilers and auxiliary locomotive boilers (supplied with heat wasted by the furnaces). Rivets and bolts were manufactured on site by dedicated machines.

Adjoining the west wall of the Forge were the Frame Shop, Coppersmiths' Shop and Brake Shop. On the northern end of this group was the Frame Shop, where alterations and modifications to old frames were carried out in addition to new frame construction, with a frame-slotting machine being present. The ready articles were then moved into the New Engine Bay where there were eight spaces for erection to take place; there was also room for repairs and two overhead cranes each of 60-ton capacity were ready for use in the two areas.

Between the New Engine Bay and the Main Repair Shop was a Machine Shop that could deal with the tasks required in both areas. Being relatively new, the area was

The second Gresley 'K3' to be built at Darlington is pictured near Croft Spa, c1930.

Above The New Engine Bay at Darlington Works. *K. Taylor collection, courtesy J. W. Armstrong Trust*

Below More new locomotives are being built in the Erecting Shop, but the odd one out is 'D49/2' Class 4-4-0 No 336 *Buckinghamshire* (later *The Quorn*), which was completed in June 1929. *K. Taylor collection, courtesy of J. W. Armstrong Trust*

little altered from when built. One important change was the door in the centre of the north wall, which allowed access to be gained to the old National Projectile Factory (320 feet long and 220 feet wide), then in use by several auxiliary machining departments. There was a section for making and repairing both small tubes and superheater tubes and a Grinding Shop. Benches were provided for working on the motion components and a jig was made available for setting these up before being fixed back on the locomotive under repair. Another area for making bolts and nuts was present, as well as space to build tools and jigs to help keep construction quick and efficient. Finally, there was the Brass Finishing Department where new castings – produced at the works at a rate of around 11 tons per week – and old items were made ready for fitting. An annexe to the building contained the accumulator for providing pressurised fluid for all of the hydraulic equipment used in the works. A place for the Artificial Limb Department was also found at North Road, serving the unfortunate employees who were injured in the line of duty.

Two old roundhouses were in use, one for stripping and sundry repairs and the other for new engines, and those refurbished, before they were taken on their test runs. The old straight shed (previously the Paint Shop) was in use as an electricity substation, taking the supply from the main Darlington Corporation supply. The total employment at Darlington during this time was 2,900.

In late 1924 and 1925 the final true NER designs were built at Darlington Works. The first was the 'T3' 0-8-0 – redesignated 'Q7' by the LNER – and ten were completed between March and May 1924. They were built to the new LNER loading gauge and possessed Gresley anti-vacuum valves behind the chimney. Constructed during the final two months of 1925 were five Worsdell Class 'X' 4-8-0Ts for shunting duties in NE Area marshalling yards, and these were virtually unchanged from the original design, apart from using Ross 'pop' safety valves.

Darlington Drawing Office was given the task of producing the first new Group Standard design in 1924/25. This was for an 0-6-0 goods type that would work in the NE, Southern and Scottish Areas and was officially referred to as 'J27 Modified', the designation being the LNER classification for the NER 'P3' Class. In the event this was a complete misnomer, as Gorton practice was favoured in the cylinder arrangement and Stephenson motion set-up (although slightly modified), and Doncaster's 4ft 8in diameter for goods locomotive coupled wheels was followed, as was the boiler design and use of a Robinson superheater. Features from Darlington included the smokebox, square firehole

A line of axleboxes await turning on the George Richards & Co Ltd lathes in the machine shop. *K. Taylor collection, courtesy of J. W. Armstrong Trust*

Coupling rods are milled on a machine supplied by Kendall and Gent.

and steam reversing gear. The tenders provided were of the 4,200-gallon Group Standard type as used with the 'K3s'. Although the new 'J38' Class 0-6-0s were to form a large new class, the purchase of a large number of 2-8-0s of Army origin from the First World War reduced numbers considerably to thirty-five, all built at Darlington between January and May 1926. The engines were allocated to the Scottish Area and this remained the case for the rest of their working lives, being employed on goods and mineral trains.

The 'J38s' were strong performers but did not have their numbers increased any further as a new design with slightly larger-diameter coupled wheels (5ft 2in) was deemed desirable. The 'J39' Class were also designed at Darlington and were quite similar to their predecessors, but with a slightly reduced boiler heating surface. In relation to this latter feature, for both the first batch and subsequently, construction was not carried out at Darlington but by outside firms. An initial order was for forty-four locomotives and these were turned out from North Road between September 1926 and September 1927. In total 289 'J39s' were built, of which 261 came from Darlington (the last in August 1941) with the remainder from Beyer, Peacock & Co in 1936/37.

From 1922 R. A. Copperthwaite had been Works Manager, Darlington, and had also overseen the management of the other workshops in the NE Area. From 1927 Copperthwaite was promoted to Assistant Mechanical Engineer, Darlington, under A. C. Stamer,

taking a wider view of locomotive matters in the area, and was succeeded at North Road by F. W. Carr, who had been Works Manager at York Carriage Works.

Gresley obviously valued the contribution Darlington Works had made to the stock up to this point as he entrusted the design of a new passenger locomotive to the Drawing Office in late 1925. This was later known

'J39' Class 0-6-0 No 1463 was erected at Darlington in March 1934 and is seen in the works' Paint Shop. *Courtesy of J. W. Armstrong Trust*

41

Well Trolley wagon No 155018 was built at Darlington in 1929 and had a capacity of 110 tons. Note that the vehicle was coded 'Weltrol N' by the LNER, but is displaying 'Weltrol L' in this image.

as the 'D49/1' Class 4-4-0, which had 6ft 8in-diameter wheels and was built for use in the NE and Scottish Areas. Darlington utilised the boiler of the 'J39' Class and based the three cylinders on those used by the 'Z' Class 'Atlantics', which were interesting in being cast as one piece rather than separately as was the case elsewhere. This had the advantage of saving weight and improving efficiency, but was costly to repair or replace if damaged or broken. Ties with the Stephenson motion were severed and Gresley's conjugated/Walschaerts motion for operating the centre valve was used, being different from standard GN practice in being positioned behind the cylinders, which improved inspection and reduced wear. The cab and bogie wheels were of the Darlington pattern, the latter being 3ft 1¼in in diameter spaced at 6ft 6in. The tenders were of the Group Standard 4,200-gallon design, but for the first twenty-eight locomotives ordered in April 1926 these were built at Doncaster Works to keep shop capacity within the limits at Darlington. The first twenty were completed between October 1927 and May 1928.

While the design work was in progress, Gresley decided that six of the locomotives would be fitted with Lentz poppet valves with oscillating cam valve gear. He had been attracted to the arrangement by several benefits, such as reduced wear compared with the piston type and greater accuracy of setting; earlier tests had been satisfactory enough to encourage further experience. The valves were patented, held by Davey, Paxman & Co Ltd, which liaised with Darlington on the design of the cylinders, steam chest and gear for these engines. The first was No 318 Cambridgeshire, built in May 1928, followed by the remainder up to August 1928. However, there were problems in service with this gear due to rapid wear of certain components, and the decision was taken to revert to the standard Gresley valve gear mechanism for the middle cylinder; this work was carried out on all the locomotives at Darlington in 1930.

The final two locomotives of the original order were reserved for another experiment, which was initially to be with compounding, but was subsequently made with rotating cams for the poppet valve gear. Using this mechanism was deemed more desirable by Gresley and a good deal of design work was put into the arrangement by both Darlington and Davey, Paxman & Co Ltd. As a result the first locomotive – classified 'D49/2' – was not ready for service until mid-March 1929. In the meantime a further eight engines fitted with piston valves had been built at

The 'Weltrol N' could take 150 tons if two cantilevers were used at either end. No 1, which was also built at Darlington, is depicted here.

The first 'D49' Class 4-4-0 locomotive, No 234 *Yorkshire*, was erected at Darlington in October 1927.

North Road, and the results with the rotary cam-operated poppet valves were suitable enough for a further fifteen to be ordered in December 1929 and twenty-five in October 1933, all being built at Darlington up to February 1935.

Gresley continued experimenting during the second half of the 1920s and the most famous – or infamous – locomotive of this type was the 'Pacific' fitted with a marine-type water tube boiler. No 10000 was completed at Darlington in November 1929, but the design work had been in progress there for several years. The boiler had also been in development since 1925, being produced by the shipbuilder Yarrow & Co, which had a good deal of experience with the type. Gresley employed the high-pressure boiler – 450lb per sq in – to try and achieve an economy in coal consumption, and necessarily employed compound working. Interestingly, Gresley met with representatives from the LMS to discuss the arrangement for the proposed fitting of compound equipment to a 4-4-0 – mentioned above in relation to the 'D49/2s' – as that company had a good deal of experience with three-cylinder compounds. Given that the 4-4-0s were not proceeded with and work on No 10000's cylinder arrangements was progressing at the time, an educated assumption would be that he told a 'white lie' to the LMS in order to gain the information he needed and to keep his project under a veil of secrecy. As result of the conference the decision was made to increase the number of cylinders to four.

With such a new and innovative design there were several

'D49/2' Class No 211 *The York and Ainsty* was one of fifty-six of the class fitted with poppet valves, with fifty using rotary cam valve gear. The locomotive is seen at Newcastle Central station. *Courtesy of J. W. Armstrong Trust*

Darlington assembled the frames for No 10000 and these were then sent north to Yarrow for the boiler to be mated to them. Afterwards North Road Works attached the remaining components.

outset. This pattern of time spent in traffic then returning to Darlington Works for repairs or modifications persisted until 1935, when Gresley (perhaps hastened by the Board) brought the cycle to an end. While the locomotive had performed well on occasions these were too few and far between to warrant further time and effort in trying to make them a regular occurrence. No 10000 had completed 90,000 miles when taken out of traffic and was stored in the Paint Shop for fourteen months before being moved to Doncaster for rebuilding. The unique boiler was duly returned to Darlington and was used at Stooperdale Boiler Shop until 1965, performing much useful work.

teeting problems, and Darlington Works was visited on a number of occasions in 1930 after the locomotive had performed a number of tests and had run on service trains. From August 1930 until January 1931 No 10000 was in the works while modifications were carried out to the regulator and the superheater, which proved troublesome from the

Darlington Drawing Office probably breathed a sigh of relief when the design work for the new 4-6-0 to run in the Great Eastern Area was given first to Doncaster, then the North British Locomotive Company, as several stringent specifications had to be met to allow the engines to run there. The NBLC built only ten of the 'B17' Class in 1928 before being snubbed in favour of placing orders at Darlington in 1928 and 1929. Between August 1930 and July 1931 seventeen were constructed, beginning with No 2810 *Honingham Hall* and ending with No 2836 *Harlaxton Manor*. As the NBLC engines had been in traffic for eighteen months, experience dictated that certain modifications had to be carried out and the later engines received altered spring arrangements, among several other things. Darlington would subsequently supply a further twenty-five 'B17s' up to June 1936, ending with No 2861 *Sheffield Wednesday*.

No 10000 departs from Leeds City station with a train to Newcastle in the early 1930s. The front end was specially designed and tested to help distribute exhaust away from the cab. *Courtesy of Yorkshire Post Newspapers*

'B17' Class 4-6-0 No 2812 *Houghton Hall* was the third member of the class built at Darlington in October 1930. The engine is photographed c1935 on Norwich station's turntable.

The West Highland Line also proved a constraining environment for locomotive operations through restrictions in axle loads. At the Grouping the motive power used consisted of 'D34' Class 4-4-0s, and as rolling stock had increased in weight the use of two engines often became necessary. Considerations had been given to a new powerful engine in the mid-1920s, but 'K2' Class 2-6-0s were sent north instead after being displaced from the Southern Area. Interest was revived in the mid-1930s and Doncaster designed a new locomotive in 1936, ordered from Darlington in October. No 3441 *Loch Long* appeared quickly and was ready for service in January 1937. The frames and cylinders (18½-inch diameter by 26-inch stroke with 8-inch piston valves operated by Walschaerts/Gresley gear) were similar to those of the 'K3', while the firebox was based on the 'B17' pattern and the superheater shared similarities with that fitted to the 'O2' Class. No 3441 worked the line with ease after arriving, although further examples were not forthcoming until ordered in February 1938;

While Darlington produced a large number of the LNER's standard classes, a specialised type was the 'K4' Class 2-6-0 for the Highland route in Scotland. No 3441 *Loch Long* put in twenty-four years of valuable service for the company and later BR.

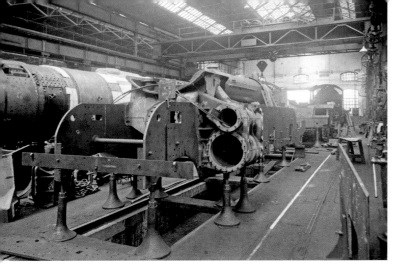

The seventh 'V2' Class engine of the first order to be placed with North Road is in the early stages of construction in the Erecting Shop on 3 July 1937.

The Kearns boring mill at Darlington with a monobloc cylinder casting loaded for machining.

The components for the built-up crank axle of the 'V2' Class before being joined together.

five were turned out from North Road between July 1938 and January 1939.

The Engineer of 11 February 1936 reported that Darlington Works had been the recent recipient of a large horizontal boring machine from H. W. Kearns & Co Ltd of Broadheath, Manchester. The equipment was not restricted to boring, despite the name, and could also perform surfacing, tapping, milling and drilling operations on cylinders, including the monobloc castings dealt with in the shops. The main table was designed with this latter role in mind and was 10 feet by 5 feet, also with a revolving table 7 feet by 5 feet. The process for machining the whole cylinder block took a total of 46 hours, but with only two settings, as work could be carried out on four sides simultaneously. A 25-horsepower motor drove the machine via belts and pulleys. A total of twenty-four speed settings could be achieved to suit the work, these ranging from 170 revolutions per minute to just 2. Sixteen rates of feed setting were split equally between boring and milling operations, these varying between eight and ninety-six cuts per inch.

Such a tool would become very useful soon after installation at the works. A new locomotive, which possessed monobloc cylinder castings and a 2-6-2 wheel arrangement, was shortly to be erected at Doncaster Works for express freight and passenger trains. The 'V2' Class was designed at Doncaster and, after the first – No 4771 *Green Arrow* – was built there in June 1936, a further four were completed up to November. Around the time of the pioneer's appearance an order for twenty-eight 'V2s' was placed at Darlington and the class would subsequently be produced in numbers, with the majority coming from North Road. The first locomotive to be constructed there was No 4776 in July 1937, the last being No 3695 in July 1944; 159 were built at Darlington out of a class total of 184, the remainder being Doncaster products.

The 'V2s' would prove to be Gresley's last new design to be erected at Darlington, but still to be considered are several classes that were modified under his authority between the Grouping and the early 1940s. This was done to improve the efficiency of both old and new types as technology, principles and tastes had changed relatively quickly over the early years of the 20th century, and in order to progress the design of the steam locomotive – both in terms of the individual parts and the sum total – even further. Gresley's design policy was one of continuous improvement based on experience, and he demonstrated this in his designs throughout his time as CME. Standardisation of components and interchangeability between classes of locomotive became increasingly important in order to minimise costs and improve availability of such standard parts.

At the time of the Grouping the former Hull & Barnsley Railway Class 'A' 0-8-0s were in need of new boilers, but with no spares available a new type was designed for them at Darlington. This had a slightly larger heating surface than the original and a 5lb per sq in higher boiler pressure. The first was fitted to No 2505 in October 1924 and the process continued up to early 1928.

Staff pose with 'V2' No 4834 in May 1939, with the engine fresh out of the Paint Shop. *N. Morgan, courtesy of J. W. Armstrong Trust*

The programme of re-boilering the 'J21' Class 0-6-0s (T. W. Worsdell Class 'C') with superheaters and piston valves was continued after 1923, having been started around the time of the outbreak of war. Later in the 1930s two modified versions of the superheater boiler were produced, in addition to further saturated boilers.

A similar situation befell the 'A8' Class 4-6-2T locomotives (Raven Class 'D' rebuilt from 4-4-4T) in the late 1920s when a new boiler barrel was rolled from one plate and fitted with a Robinson superheater with larger elements than the Schmidt type previously used. More variations on this theme were produced in the 1930s, being similar but with detail differences, and these were exchangeable between Classes 'A6-8' and 'T1'.

In the mid-1930s Class 'D20' 4-4-0s (Worsdell 'R' Class) began to receive boilers with an altered tube layout, increasing the number from 115 to 131, and a Robinson superheater. At the same time thoughts were turned to the cylinders, and No 2020 received 1¼-inch larger piston valves at 10-inch diameter with improved valve travel, as well as new axleboxes. Although the alterations took place in October 1936 the locomotive would remain the only one changed until 1942, and then only three more were dealt with before the task was discontinued.

The 'B16' Class 4-6-0s (Raven 'S3') were another class to benefit from the introduction of a boiler with a modified design, and the Diagram 49A perhaps had the most changes of those made during this period. A sloping throatplate was fitted to the firebox, making the length greater, but the grate area was just smaller and the number of small tubes rose from the original 102 to 156. Also, the superheater was of the Robinson type with more heating surface area, the boiler barrel was formed from two plates (formerly three), and the dome was situated a good deal closer to the cab than previously. Earlier in the decade the class had gone through a modernisation process encompassing components forming and associated with the chassis. Axleboxes and horn guides were changed and had improved lubrication, while the wheels and springs were given attention with the aim of making the riding better.

Gresley discarded the individual cylinders and replaced these with a cast monobloc encompassing all three cylinders. The valve events were improved, and Walschaerts conjugated motion was fitted to replace the Stephenson's link motion utilised by Raven. The cab was widened and lengthened and the running board was raised to clear the coupled wheels which dispensed with the splashers. No 2364 was the first to receive these features in mid-1937 and a further six would follow in 1939 and 1940.

The use of poppet valves was not restricted to the 'D49s' but spread to Raven's 'Z' Class 'Atlantics' (LNER 'C7'). No 732 received the 17-inch by 26-inch cylinders with valves operated by rotary cams in late 1933, and this operation also altered several other features at the front end. No 2212 was later changed in this manner as the 'Uniflow' cylinders required renewal, but no other locomotives of the class received the poppet valves. However, other 'C7' Class engines had been embroiled in several experiments involving feedwater heaters and boosters. No 2163 had the Dabeg system installed on the left-hand side of the boiler in early 1926, being driven off the rear crank pin.

The Gresley modernisation of Raven's 'S3' Class 4-6-0 is represented by No 2364.

This latter was one of the disadvantages of the design, as operation would not occur when stationary, which contributed to the decision to remove the apparatus in 1937. Another type fitted at Darlington was the ACFI feedwater heater, which was adopted by Nos 728 and 2206 in early 1928. This also had a number of flaws and was removed in the early 1940s.

Gresley had attempted to make beneficial use of the booster in the mid-1920s, but problems had been caused by the heaviness and bulk of this equipment being attached to the axle under the cab. The CME thought a solution to this problem would be to use a bogie instead, and articulate the engine and tender. The 'Atlantic' type was again chosen, being two of the 'C7' Class, and work on the arrangement began in 1926. By the time authority was gained and specialist firms engaged to design and build a suitable booster and an axle to drive on (in addition to a new boiler being provided), the conversion of the first locomotive, No 727, was not undertaken until mid-1931 and entered traffic in November, followed by No 2171 in December. These two engines were then classified 'C9'. The latter engine

gave persistent mechanical trouble in service and was in Darlington Works for several months having this rectified, but No 727 on the whole performed satisfactorily with the booster when in the hands of enginemen who could successfully operate the equipment. Unfortunately, the introduction of the 'A4s' and 'V2s' drastically reduced the usefulness of the Atlantics and the booster was removed after just five years.

A scheme affecting locomotives in the NE Area was the adoption of the vacuum brake as the LNER standard in 1928. The NER was with the Great Eastern Railway and Great North of Scotland Railway in using the Westinghouse air brake system, which was more expensive than the vacuum despite being quicker to operate. The modifications spanned several classes and hundreds of locomotives.

In 1933 F. W. Carr was redeployed and his assistant L. Farr succeeded him. There was another change at the end of the year when A. C. Stamer retired and was succeeded by Edward Thompson. The former had been with the NER for 32 years before the formation of the LNER and had overseen the NE Area from that event. The *LNER Magazine* of December 1933 commented:

Raven 'Atlantic' No 732 was fitted with poppet valves to achieve greater efficiency, but this was hampered by the design of the rotary cam motion, which did not allow enough variations in the cut-off settings.

'It is no exaggeration to say that Mr Stamer's retirement is an exceptional event, because he is one of the most popular and best-liked officers the North Eastern Area ever had. A walk with him through the busy railway shops or running sheds is an inspiration. It is immediately evident that he not only has a keen eye for all the equipment he controls, but he also has an intimate knowledge of the staff, having a kindly nod and a cheery word for either the black-faced fitter or the driver and fireman, hailing most of them by either their Christian names or nicknames.'

A number of tributes were paid to Stamer at formal gatherings in both Darlington and York, while perhaps the highest was from the men of the footplate and workshops who subscribed to present him with a clock as a mark of their esteem.

Thompson was in office up to 1938 and oversaw the construction of several classes at Darlington, together with the rebuildings and reboilerings of a number of others. Although instigated by Gresley and Bulleid, welding techniques were adopted in several workshops across the LNER, the NE Area included, with Thompson personally taking an interest in attempting to use welding to fabricate the rocking lever of the two-to-one gear in the Gresley conjugated motion. This piece was forged in the standard arrangement, which increased the weight and contributed to problems of wear always associated with the motion's use. The new component comprised four sections welded together with a centre bush, and this proved to be much lighter without loss of strength compared with the original design. Unfortunately, the joints could not be completely checked for soundness and the part could not progress to be tested in service.

A project that came to fruition just after Thompson left in 1938 was the delivery of three boilers with welded boiler barrels from Babcock & Wilcox. These were to the 'J39' Diagram 97 design and also had the tubeplates welded in position before the firebox, which was of the normal riveted type, was put in place. These boilers were in use for just over twenty years and there were no problems arising from their construction during this time.

After the death of Gresley in 1941 Thompson was promoted to CME and A. H. Peppercorn became his assistant, being transferred from the post of Mechanical Engineer, Darlington. There were also a number of movements in and out of the Works Manager's Office during this period, with R. A. Smeddle taking over from L. Farr in 1936, being himself succeeded by L. Reeves when assuming the title of Mechanical Engineer, Darlington. The tenure of Reeves only lasted for a year before G. C. Gold took over as Darlington Works Manager until the end of the war.

Thompson was in a difficult position when he took over, not only following Gresley, who had left a great legacy and strong ideas with regard to locomotive design, but also the Second World War was causing labour and material shortages with workshops again being taken over for the war effort. One of the new CME's first tasks was to produce a mixed-traffic locomotive with a wide route availability. Gresley had provided a design before his death but this was not proceeded with and Thompson brought his own ideas to fruition.

The main thrust of these was that the number of cylinders would be reduced from three to two on all but the most powerful express engines. Standardisation was also a key theme, in addition to keeping maintenance requirements to a minimum. Doncaster Drawing Office was given the job of producing the plans and this began in late 1941, coming to an end in mid-1942. The boiler was based on the 'B17' Class Diagram 100 (classified Diagram 100A) and the type differed in being slightly shorter between the tube plates, and having a longer firebox, a larger grate area and a higher boiler pressure at 225lb per sq in; the boilers shared the same heating surface figures. The two cylinders were also of an old pattern, being based on Gresley's 'K2' Class 2-6-0s, and were 20 inches by 26 inches with 10-inch-diameter piston valves operated by Walschaerts motion.

With the rearmament programme beginning towards the end of the 1930s, the LNER built two wagons capable of transporting large gun barrels for the Royal Navy. No 231274 is the second of the pair built at Darlington in 1938.

Thompson 'B1' Class 4-6-0 No 8301 was in service for just short of twenty years, working in the main from sheds in the GE Area, and was scrapped at Doncaster.

The boilers were ordered and completed at Doncaster Works, then sent north to be finished at Darlington. The works received an order for ten of the new 'B' – later 'B1' – Class 4-6-0s in August 1942 and the first, No 8301 *Springbok*, was built by mid-December. The remaining nine did not leave North Road as quickly; four were built in 1943 (from June to December) and five in 1944 (February to June). Due to the war, these were the only 'B1s' in traffic for a time and were allocated to the GE and Scottish Areas. The next order was placed at Darlington in May 1944 for thirty 'B1s', and these were constructed from

November 1946 to December 1947. The forty Darlington locomotives were the only members of the class (apart from a lone NBLC example) to have the honour of carrying the 'Antelope' series of names.

Thompson also envisaged a powerful mixed-traffic 'Pacific' locomotive as part of his standard designs and, following on from the 'P2' Class rebuilds, he gained authorisation to change the last four 'V2s' in hand at Darlington from 2-6-2s to 4-6-2s. The main reason for this change was to gain experience from the minor differences possessed by the two designs. The cylinders of the new

Twenty years elapsed between the construction of the Raven 'Pacifics' and the Thompson 4-6-2s. No 3697 (later *Duke of Rothesay*) was the second and is pictured at King's Cross shed during 1946.

Thompson 'B2' Class 4-6-0 No 1671 *Royal Sovereign* stands in the locomotive yard at King's Cross station.

engines – later classified 'A2/1' – were slightly larger than those of the 'V2' at 19 inches in diameter; they also used bigger piston valves, 10 inches in diameter. The boiler was quite similar to the 'A2/1' and 'P2' rebuilds, but differed in the firebox dimensions as the former had a 41.25sq ft grate and the latter 50sq ft. The four locomotives were turned out from Darlington between May 1944 (No 3696) and January 1945 (No 3699).

Darlington was again involved in armament production during the Second World War – with more than 1,000 men and women employed on this task – but locomotive production (utilising a workforce of nearly 2,500) was more pronounced and even included a large number of LMS-designed 8F Class 2-8-0s for freight duties. At the start of the conflict the War Department chose the type to be the standard to be used by the forces before a simpler version was produced. The railway companies were approached tby the Railway Executive Committee to build the 8Fs in late 1941 and agreed to do so, but declined to take any into stock, only considering them to be under loan for the duration of the conflict. Orders were then placed at several workshops including Darlington, which received two, one in January for twenty engines and the other in July 1943 for a further ten. Construction began in February 1944 and continued through to August 1945, with the pioneer – No 8500 – being the first product of North Road to possess a Belpaire firebox. Surprisingly, the LNER declared in 1943 that the company would pay for 100 8Fs, while in the event

only sixty-eight were built. Brighton Works was involved in the task and Darlington originally had forty-three to build, although twenty were later transferred to Doncaster for erection. This order was started after the REC engines were completed, and construction ceased in October 1946. All these engines were later transferred to the LMS.

During 1944 Thompson also restarted the 'B16' rebuilding programme, but with a few more changes, and the new engines were then placed in class part three. The main new features were left-hand drive and three sets of motion for the valves serving the three cylinders, in addition to improved valve events. No 922 was the pioneer and a further eleven locomotives followed up to the end of 1945. Only another five took part in the conversion before the programme was discontinued in 1949.

Before the end of the Second World War Darlington took responsibility for maintaining the 'B17' Class 4-6-0s from Stratford and Gorton. During this period two engines were experimentally fitted with 'B1' Class Diagram 100A boilers, initially working at 180lb per sq in, later being raised to 225lb per sq in. Thompson went further by having a total of ten 'B17s' rebuilt with two cylinders, 'B1' bogies and a raised running plate, these becoming the 'B2' Class. No 2871 *Manchester City* was the first to emerge from North Road in August 1945, and No 2844 *Earlham Hall* was the last in March 1949.

The final new Thompson design to involve Darlington was the 'L1' Class 2-6-4T. The prototype was constructed

Darlington's most unsightly product in more than 100 years was perhaps the London Midland Region's Class 4MT 2-6-0. No 43098 simmers in the grime of Leeds City station on 12 December 1952. *Courtesy of Yorkshire Post Newspapers*

at Doncaster, then, after rigorous testing, further examples were ordered from several sources, including North Road, which had twenty-nine put in hand during November 1945. The locomotives were eventually produced between January and August 1948, taking the numbers 9001-9012/69013-69015/67717-67730 and having some slight detail differences from the other members of the class, which were bought from the NBLC and Robert Stephenson & Hawthorns.

After Thompson's retirement, A. H. Peppercorn succeeded him and continued to a degree the locomotive policy his predecessor had begun, until able to modify some of the features that were proving problematic and perpetuate those that were successful. This was true of the 'A1' Class 'Pacifics', which were in the midst of the design process when Thompson left office. The 'A1' type was to follow the lead of the rebuilt Gresley 'Pacific' No 4470 *Great Northern* with an 'A4'-type boiler and staggered cylinders. Eventually this was revised for the new engines to use the 'A2'-type boiler and a more traditional front-end arrangement. An order for twenty-three 'A1' 'Pacifics' was placed at Darlington in January 1947, and these were produced between September

1948 and July 1949, being numbered 60130 to 60152. These engines could generally be distinguished from their counterparts erected at Doncaster as North Road Works had used countersunk rivets for the cab and tender, creating a much neater appearance.

Darlington received a request for a further ten 'B1s' in November 1947 and these were completed between July and October 1949. The final ten class members were also built at Darlington, but British Railways authorised them in 1949 to appear in 1950. The final LNER order to be fulfilled was interesting in being of NER origin. The locomotives were of W. Worsdell's 'E1' (LNER 'J72') 0-6-0T Class for light goods and shunting duties, and a total of twenty-eight were ordered as part of the 1946 building programme, but deferred until 1949, when, over three years, the engines started to appear. Nos 69001-69028 were true to the original design and only differed in minor detail appointments.

At nationalisation 3,548 people were employed at Darlington Works (the female war workers were dismissed at the end of 1945), and almost 1,500 locomotives were maintained there. Approximately three weeks were spent inside the repair shop for heavy attention, and the engine was out of traffic for more than a month. A. H. Peppercorn remained Mechanical Engineer for the North Eastern and Eastern Regions and L. Hinds was the Works Manager, having taken over from G. C. Gold in 1945.

While the workshops were busy completing the final LNER orders, British Railways was formulating the locomotive construction policy for the coming years. This turned out to be a standard series of engines that could work all over the country with minimal maintenance requirements. BR also saw fit to utilise the capacity of its inherited workshops, and Darlington was engaged to construct forty-two (later reduced to thirty-seven) Ivatt Class 4 2-6-0s of LMS origin. These had two 17½-inch by 26-inch cylinders supplied by steam from 10-inch piston valves operated by Walschaerts motion; the boiler, with a twenty-four-element superheater, had pressure set at 225lb per sq in, 23sq ft grate area and 5ft 3in-diameter coupled wheels. As an aid to maintenance the engines were provided with self-cleaning smokeboxes, high running plates to give full access to the motion and wheels, rocking grates and hopper ashpans, and to help the footplatemen the cab possessed a back incorporated into the tender design for when running rearwards. The locomotives – Nos 43070-43106 – were built between August 1950 and April 1951 and went into service on the North Eastern and Eastern Regions.

Shortly after the latter date Darlington began to produce a smaller version of the Class 4MT. These were Ivatt Class

2MT engines originating from Crewe in 1946 to replace a number of life-expired 0-6-0 types running for the LMS, and were built to perform a similar role in the former LNER territories. They had two 16½-inch by 24-inch cylinders, a grate area of 17.5sq ft, a boiler pressure of 200lb per sq in, a tractive effort of 17,400lb, and 5-foot-diameter wheels. A total of thirty-eight Class 2MT 2-6-0s were erected between June 1951 and March 1952.

After these were put into traffic work began on the first BR Standard locomotives from North Road Works. The Class 2 2-6-0s were in fact little different from the aforementioned class, as the design more than adequately fitted the requirements for the power classification. There were only slight detail modifications such as a different chimney, an altered cab to allow greater route availability, and a BR-type top feed and regulator. The first batch of ten were in service on the Western Region by April 1953 and the other fifty-five class members emerged from Darlington in four orders completed from December 1953 to November 1956, being spread across the London Midland, Scottish and NE Regions.

Built concurrently with these engines were a large number of diesel-electric shunting locomotives with an 0-6-0 wheel arrangement. The initial examples followed a design that was also a product of the LMS, being based on a number of prototypes introduced in the mid-1930s. A total of thirty-six Class 11 shunters emerged from Darlington between March 1952 and January 1953,

Another engine built for the LMR was Ivatt Class 2MT No 46495, which is seen here at Rugby on 14 October 1963. *Bill Reed*

BR Standard Class 2MT No 78000 is in the Erecting Shop on 11 February 1952. *Courtesy of J. W. Armstrong Trust*

Class 10 diesel shunters in the Erecting Shop on 3 September 1957; the Blackstone engine is prominent.

The construction of the new diesels required the adoption of fabrication techniques, including welding, which was relatively new to the works. *I. H. Hodgson, courtesy J. W. Armstrong Trust*

possessing an English Electric six-cylinder engine and main generator with two traction motors. The Class 11 type provided inspiration for BR's ubiquitous Class 08 shunters, of which a total of 996 would be constructed. From this number, 220 came from Darlington – the first was completed in August 1953, numbered 13060, and the last (No D4192) was taken into service during August 1962, averaging just over twenty-four locomotives a year.

A slight variation on the 08 Class was produced at Darlington in 1959 with a different gear ratio to allow higher speeds to be achieved. Ten of the twenty-six comprising Class 09 came from the works, the others being manufactured at Horwich. Another deviation from the 08 theme was the Class 10, which had a six-cylinder four-stroke Blackstone engine rated at 350 horsepower, the same as the 08, in addition to the tractive effort of 35,000lb, and a top speed of 27mph (surpassing the aforementioned by more than 10mph). Only six of the 146 locomotives in the class were not the product of Darlington, and they were completed in the space of four years from No D3478 in January 1958 to No D4094 in June 1962. Interestingly, these locomotives were soon considered expendable because their engine differed from the 08s, and they were withdrawn between 1967 and 1972; No D4094 was condemned in August 1968.

The LMS's 2MT 2-6-0s served as the basis for a Class 2MT 2-6-2T design, and large numbers were built around the time of nationalisation. Therefore R. A. Riddles prudently decided that the same arrangement should be made for the tender and tank versions of the Standard Class 2MT. Although the first twenty class members were to be erected at Darlington, in the event they were produced at Crewe Works during 1953. Four years then elapsed before the next, and last, batch of ten were constructed, these coming from Darlington. The tenth engine, No 84029, also turned out to be the last of approximately 2,269 steam locomotives to be built at the works on 11 June 1957.

After the announcement of BR's Modernisation Plan and Pilot Scheme for diesel locomotives, Darlington was seen as being low down in the hierarchy of workshops that could contribute examples. Nevertheless, an order for twenty Type 2 locomotives – later Class 24 – was placed with North Road in early 1958, and these appeared in the Eastern and North Eastern Regions between February 1960 (No D5094) and January 1961 (No D5113). Soon afterwards the Sulzer engine was modified to produce slightly more horsepower – 1,250 at 750rpm, compared with the 1,160 of the Class 24s – and the traction motors were redeveloped. The new components were then fitted to fresh orders for similar Type 2 locomotives, later Class 25, and a total of sixty were built at Darlington. The pioneer of this batch was No D5151 in April 1961, and No D7597 was the final example in August 1964, also proving to be the last locomotive to be erected at Darlington Works.

Even though there had been several alterations to the site to accommodate the construction and repair of diesel

Boilers receive attention in the Stooperdale Boiler Shop. *K. H. Cockerill, courtesy of J. W. Armstrong Trust*

locomotives in 1961, a year later the British Transport Commission announced that a third of the workshops were to close, among these being North Road together with the Stooperdale Boiler Shop. Darlington carried on maintaining the steam fleet as the numbers were depleted and welcomed several classes that had hitherto been infrequent visitors or strangers to the shops, such as ex-LMS designs and the Gresley 'A3' and 'A4' 'Pacifics'. During late 1965 and early 1966 the works were run down, the machinery removed under the supervision of the last Works Manager, J. Brown, and the 2,500 employees dispersed. The final repair was undertaken in January 1966 and Darlington North Road officially closed on 1 April 1966 after 103 years of tireless service.

Darlington still had plenty of work to perform in 1965 despite the run-down of the steam fleet. Worsdell 'J27' No 65880, Peppercorn 'K1' No 62004 and 'WD' 2-8-0 No 90503 are visible. *A. R. Thompson, courtesy of J. W. Armstrong Trust*

Above The entrance to Darlington Works is closed and the buildings and land are for sale in this image, which was captured in the late 1960s. A supermarket and industrial estate have since been built on the site. *Courtesy of J. W. Armstrong Trust*

Below The interior of the New Erecting Shop prior to demolition. *Courtesy of J. W. Armstrong Trust*

3

Doncaster

Several schemes were considered for a railway line between London and York in the early 1840s before the Act for the Great Northern Railway was given Royal Assent on 26 July 1846. Subsequently, the line opened in a number of stages from August 1848 until the terminus at King's Cross was ready for traffic on 14 October 1852. The first locomotives were 2-2-2s, with 5ft 6in drivers and 15-inch by 20-inch cylinders, bought from Sharp Brothers of Manchester.

As the first phase of route construction centred around Boston, the company's first engine and carriage repair shops were located on the west side of the Spalding line (north of the junction to Sleaford) and were of temporary construction until the installation of permanent facilities in the early 1850s. The Erecting and Machine Shops were placed at the north end of the site and were 205 feet long by 86 feet wide. The former occupied the eastern half and had two tracks running the length of the building, while the latter took the western side for the smiths and turnery. Further west of these was another building, 215 feet by 43 feet, housing the stores and another two tracks for work to be carried out.

These shops were never intended to be a permanent base of operations for the company's locomotive and carriage maintenance. At the time that the GNR's Act was approved, the Mayor of Doncaster wrote to the company's Board inviting them to establish the workshops in the town. Similar proposals were also received from other places on the line wanting to benefit from the employment opportunities that this would bring. However, Doncaster had the upper hand because the GNR Chairman, Edmund Beckett Denison (also MP for the West Riding), was a resident of the town and had been instrumental in having the line penetrate the western side, rather than bypassing the area altogether. Locomotive Engineer Edward Bury produced plans for shops at Doncaster during his brief tenure (1848-50). His successor, Archibald Sturrock, was less enthusiastic, claiming that the town's position was not ideal, being at the northern end of the GNR system. He

Edmund Beckett Denison (1787-1874) was the driving force behind establishing the GNR.

argued the case for locating the works at Peterborough, which was central to all the company's lines. However, Denison was able to convince the other Board members that Doncaster was more advantageous, given the proximity to the foundries in Sheffield and coalfields in Yorkshire. In 1851 final approval was given for land to be purchased for the erection of the new workshops. A contemporary report noted that in Doncaster the decision was met with enthusiasm and the local church bells were rung 'until the wild ear ran giddy with their joy'.

A site of 28 acres was chosen on the western side of Doncaster station, near the banks of the River Don. William Cubitt and his son Joseph – together with Sturrock – then proceeded to produce plans for the workshops – initially on 11 acres – which consisted of Erecting Shop, Boiler Shop, Turnery, Smithy and Carriage Shops, at an estimated cost of £45,000. In March 1852 tenders for the work were advertised and in May were awarded to Messrs Arthur and George Holme of Liverpool – the task scheduled to end on 31 March 1853. This date proved to be unattainable and in May 1853 Cubitt reported to the Board that the shops were nearly ready and that 'Nothing remains to be done except such as office fittings, baths, machine fixing, completing tanks and such matters.' A steam hammer, cylinder boring machine and two large lathes were also reported to be in position and ready for work as well as the stationary steam engine being prepared for testing. In June the Smithy accepted the first group of workers, who were transferred from Boston with their families, and all 700

employees had arrived by the end of the year, with a further 249 engaged from Doncaster.

The influx of people caused a demand for housing and this was satisfied by the company, which by the end of the 1850s held £200,000 of property in Doncaster; some of the houses achieved £8 per annum rent. There was also the question of providing a suitable place of worship for the workers and Denison was a particularly strong advocate for the GNR to provide such a facility. A minority of shareholders disagreed and when an Act for the project was presented to Parliament they successfully blocked the Bill. Denison was not deterred and, together with likeminded directors, he raised the necessary funding through subscriptions and donations, which totalled £6,195 2s 7d. Construction was carried out by Mr Wilson of Grantham for £4,511 to the design contributed by Denison's son (also named Edmund), who was an amateur architect. The foundation stone was laid by Denison on 24 September 1857 and consecration by the Archbishop of York occurred during the following October.

A short time earlier St James's School had been opened to educate the workers' children and provisions were made for nearly 500. The company paid the £1,200 construction costs and made an annual donation to the running of the school; this was augmented by a Government grant. The school also hosted religious services until the opening of the nearby church.

Locomotive work at Doncaster was initially confined to repairs, as the GNR bought engines from the trade, and the same was true for carriages and wagons. At first

The first works buildings are seen here in the later years of the 19th century. Visible on the right are the Offices, Upper and Lower Turneries and the Carriage Shop, and on the left the Boiler Shop and part of the Erecting Shop.

Brass finishers with some of their wares pose in front of Stirling 'Single' No 93, which was built at Doncaster in December 1879.

these were of firms' proprietary designs. Sturrock soon put forth his own specifications based on the practices of the Great Western Railway, where he had previously been employed. However, he was often hampered by the Board, which was reluctant to anticipate future traffic requirements and was slow to react when they began to press. The insubstantial permanent way also served to limit the capacity of the locomotives and Sturrock sought to circumvent this by providing power to the tender by an ingenious, albeit quite flawed, system.

In 1866 Sturrock announced his intention to retire at the relatively young age of 50. Several people were interviewed, including Patrick Stirling, who had recently been rejected for the position of Works Manager (subsequently taken up by John Shotton). Sturrock recommended Stirling to the Board and he was made Assistant Locomotive Engineer until Sturrock retired on 1 October, then taking charge with the stipulation of a three-year probationary period.

At the time of this appointment there was an expansion taking place at Doncaster as the locomotive stock had reached more than 460. The Erecting Shop, which originally had fifteen berths on each side of the building, divided by a central isle to accommodate a steam-powered traveller for moving the locomotives

around, had another six bays added to the west end. Close to the southern side of the Erecting Shop was the Boiler Shop, and the area between them was put to use by providing a covering and installing machinery, such as slotting and drilling machines in addition to several hand-operated 35-ton cranes. The Boiler Shop was also extended by demolishing some interior dividing walls and adding to the southern side of the building, thereby doubling capacity; the machinery was updated through the provision of a riveting machine.

A new Brass Foundry was built on land a short distance away from the Boiler Shop to the south-west, and the structure contained twelve crucible hearths. Another shop to be brought into use (between the Smithy and the Erecting Shop's western ends) was the Spring Shop, which had two furnaces and twelve hearths for work to be carried out. Even further to the west of the main shops was the Forge, which had three steam hammers and four furnaces. A method was devised for using the waste heat from the furnaces to power the boilers supplying steam to the hammers. By the River Don a gas factory was erected with thirty-five retorts and two 60-foot by 20-foot gas-holders to provide fuel for up to 6,000 lights; the cost of this facility was £5,850. Finally, extensions were made to the Carriage Shops.

No 18 was not only the pioneer Doncaster locomotive but was the first of the highly capable Stirling 0-4-2s, of which 154 were built to 1895. The engine was withdrawn in January 1903.

Prior to his arrival on the GNR, Stirling had been Locomotive Engineer with the Glasgow & South Western Railway (G&SWR) and had overseen the construction of Kilmarnock Works for contributing his designs to stock. With this in mind, and with the extensive additions at Doncaster, Stirling was in a strong position to argue a case with the Board for constructing new locomotives at the works, and the idea was agreed upon. The first was an 0-4-2 locomotive based on a recent rebuilding programme of old engines. Three were initially authorised for mixed traffic work, having two inside cylinders of 17 inches by 24 inches, a 4ft 0½in-diameter boiler working at 140lb per sq in. and 5ft 7in-diameter wheels. The pioneer was No 18, which entered traffic on 3 January 1868. The type proved quite capable and a total of 104 were built at Doncaster (with modifications) to 1895.

Following closely behind was a batch of six 7-foot 2-2-2 locomotives, beginning with No 6 in March 1868 and ending with No 14 in August. These were quite different from Sturrock's earlier 'single' engines in being much simpler of construction and components, and signalled a general shift in locomotive practices on the GNR. At the same time Stirling had also ordered several 6ft 6in 2-4-0s from outside contractors, but these featured standardised components with the two aforementioned types and an 0-6-0 design, which also appeared in 1868. Initially, these latter were also bought by the company, while Doncaster built fifteen between 1869 and 1873. Rounding off 1868 were three nominal rebuilds of 2-4-0s to 0-6-0STs with

5-foot-diameter wheels, standard cylinders and boilers.

Stirling was formally appointed Locomotive Engineer in September 1869 and, to show the Board that its faith was well founded, the next new locomotive out of Doncaster was 4-2-2 No 1. The design had been in development during Stirling's time with the company and he drew on his previous experience with powerful 2-2-2s built for the G&SWR by adding outside cylinders to allow for large 8ft 1in driving wheels. The thinking of the time deemed that a large wheel diameter was vital for providing good adhesion for the transfer of energy from the cylinders to the rails. Stirling was initially dubious about providing a bogie at the front end because of the cost, even though the riding would be improved. In order to determine the best course of action he borrowed an outside-cylinder GER 'Single' and compared the performance with a GNR 'Single' on the main line. Even though the former was more satisfactory, there was evidently the need for a bogie as one was soon provided for the new design. No 1 was constructed at Doncaster in April 1870 (taking works number 50) and the engine was evaluated in service before further examples were built, many having detail alterations after experience or due to changes in traffic conditions. In all, fifty-three 'Singles' were erected at Doncaster between 1870 and 1895.

Another powerful design followed in 1871 for mineral traffic, with an 0-6-0 wheel arrangement. The two inside cylinders measured 19 inches by 28 inches and were unusual in being cast together, rather than singly, with a

Doncaster's first 'star' express engines were the Stirling 'Singles'. No 48 was the 150th engine to be built at the works in October 1874 and was in service until November 1908.

flange to connect the pair, and were served by one steam chest. The boiler was of 4ft 5in diameter with 1,352sq ft of heating surface working at 140lb per sq in. Only six of these specialised engines were built between 1872 and 1874, as it was soon realised that the trains the class were expected to haul – around fifty-five wagons or more than 600 tons – could not fit in the sidings provided. This left the locomotives working standard loads and nullifying their existence, but their employment was prolonged until the early 20th century.

Stirling continued to meet the requirements of the GNR throughout the 1870s, producing several classes in numbers, including 0-4-4WTs for suburban traffic, 0-6-0s for goods, 2-4-0s and 0-6-0STs. Many of these had standard cylinders and other features, and were simple but robust in construction. An investigation into the locomotives of the company was made by the Board during this period, finding that the quality of the stock had increased a good deal under Stirling. In 1877 the average age of the stock was six years and the mileage accumulated during this period was 154,383, or an average of 25,730 per year. At the end of Sturrock's tenure the figures had been, respectively, eight years, 162,977 and 20,372. This improved reliability allowed the company to earn more money than its immediate rivals. For instance, in 1876 each locomotive brought in an average of £5,000, while the NER's engines earned £4,471. The GNR also boasted lower maintenance costs, at £220 per engine in 1876, falling to £197 in 1877, while the NER's figures were £288 and £280 respectively.

Towards the end of the 1870s eminent engineer John Ramsbottom inspected Doncaster Works on behalf of the Board and reported back that space was rapidly diminishing and expansion would soon be necessary. This advice was taken and schemes set in motion, the first being the extension of the Gas Works, followed by an Iron

Foundry to the west of the forge on the extreme boundary of the site. Between the two latter buildings the space was filled during 1882 by the new Boiler Shop, and a new stores was also completed. In the original main block a reorganisation took place and a tender construction and repair shop was formed.

The Wagon Shops originally housed in this part of the works were removed at the end of the decade to Doncaster Carr, a short distance away to the south and on the western side of the main line, also being near the locomotive shed. H. Arnold was given the contract and the work was completed in 1889, costing more than £25,000. The shops were split into two sections capable of holding approximately 200 wagons each: one had seven tracks for new construction to take place with associated tools being provided, while the other area had fifteen roads

The interior of the Iron Foundry in 1912, with a steam-powered overhead crane.

A variety of GNR wagons are lined up outside Doncaster Carr Wagon Works ready for attention.

dedicated to the repair of the stock. The new Wagon Shops had the distinction of being the first at Doncaster to be lit by electric lights. A platform was also provided so the workmen could be transported from the station to the site. The space left behind was filled by the carriage department, which also took over two large new buildings along the northern perimeter – the West Carriage Shop and North Carriage Shop.

Another stage to the enlargements was the addition of the New Erecting Shop in 1891 on the north-eastern side of the Forge. There were five roads, a central one for finished engines to exit and two for construction purposes, which could accommodate five locomotives

A scene captured inside the New Erecting Shop.

each, giving a total capacity of ten. The New Erecting Shop was necessary because the width of the bays in the original Erecting Shop was becoming too small to hold the engines. Repairs continued to be carried out there on those engines that could still fit in it.

The Engineer visited Doncaster Works in 1892 after all this work had been carried out and some of the more salient details presented in a special issue on the GNR dated 16 December are as follows. The Pattern Shop was located in the extreme western corner of the site and produced new examples, in addition to repairing and modifying those already in use in the shops. The building also housed several cabinetmakers, who crafted furniture, etc, for the company's stations and offices, and several tools and machines (some made at Doncaster Works) were present for the production of these.

Conveniently located nearby was the Iron Foundry where sixty men and boys were at work in well-lit surroundings. There were two cupolas employed on alternate days and these were loaded in the building, but in a section partitioned off to make the space more comfortable for the workers. A steam-powered overhead travelling crane transported the cupolas and the finished articles, the heaviest of which were two cylinders cast together (mentioned previously) at 24cwt, while the single cylinders generally weighed 15cwt. The cylinders were always cast on end, the molten metal running from the back end to the front. A simple moulding device was used for setting the sand and was principally used for small items such as brake blocks and carriage axleboxes. The apparatus almost doubled the amount of moulds produced by a man in a day. The casting of brass was also performed in a shop, which had ample natural light.

Several furnaces lined one side and these were at a height for the crucible to be manoeuvred easily.

The Boiler Shop measured 300 feet long by 100 feet wide, with the west side occupied by various pieces of machinery, such as those for planing, drilling, shearing, punching, rivet-making, etc. Double riveted joints for the boiler plates were favoured and to perform this task a hydraulic riveter was supplied by Messrs Fielding & Platt of Gloucester. The article suggested that even the best hydraulic riveters could not match the finish of those done by hand, but was still of a high quality nevertheless. An accumulator was used to supply hydraulic pressure at 1,500lb per sq in and the apparatus was located in the shop, also being used by the hydraulic flanger. This was a new addition, located in an adjoining smaller structure. The mechanism of the flanger consisted of a ram of 16-inch diameter and four smaller cylinders, each with a 6-inch-diameter ram and housed beneath the floor. The rams pushed the platform with the metal sheet upwards and forced contact with the die (of several types made at the works) supported above to create the desired shape. The sheet would then be removed to an anvil a short distance away where any imperfections would be hammered out. The process of producing a plate, including

heating, was just under 2 minutes and the cost had not yet been calculated but was expected to be below the 17s 6d paid for performing the process by hand; flanging copper tubeplates cost 10s 6d for the two.

No internal caulking was allowed by Stirling due to the relationship established between this method of boiler construction and boiler explosions. Caulking of the exterior was practised and pressurised air tools were used for this. A machine was present for the manufacture of copper stay bolts and this was almost as old as the works. The article related a story that a firm had made representations to replace this model with a new and improved one, duly dispatching a salesman to the Boiler Shop Manager. Upon arrival the former was quite aghast to see the old machine churning out many bolts much more quickly and efficiently than the new type. When he enquired which company had produced such a machine the reply came that his own firm had supplied the apparatus!

The boilers were not tested hydraulically but through steam, and only to a pressure as high as 180lb per sq in. The reason given was that high-pressure tests could lead to damage of the boiler, and using steam made the tests under working conditions, which were more reasonable. Two overhead travelling cranes were used in

A group of blacksmiths pose for the camera around the turn of the 19th century; note the young age of the boys at the back.

Two foremen keep a close eye on proceedings in the Machine Shop.

From the opposite end of the Machine Shop we see a number of axleboxes being worked on.

Much of the space available in the Lower Turnery is occupied by machinery and the belts to drive them. Despite this, there appears to be plenty of light entering the shop, which was a key consideration of the time.

the Boiler Shop and these ran on square shafting, which was protected by means of an arrangement resembling a trough. Operating conditions in the shop meant that soot and dirt would congeal with the oil on the runner, affecting the movement of the crane.

Heavy work was performed in the Forge and a large drop hammer was used for some parts, although wheel centres were no longer made in this manner and were cast instead. Buffers were made in the shop; they started out as a ball of metal before being given several heavy blows to form the piece. Drawhooks were also forged, the process taking some 7 or 8 minutes. A Greenwood & Batley nut-making machine was present, as was a bolt and rivet machine.

In the Smiths' Shop many of the smaller items used on a locomotive were manufactured at forty double hearths, then being moved to one of the shop's eighty anvils, which were arranged close by. There were also five small steam hammers placed centrally in the building. One of the items made utilising the above tools was draw chains, the iron bars for which were heated in the hearth before being bent to shape and finished under the steam hammer. This apparatus was used for a number of other accessories, and steel templates were on hand to make sure the dimensions were correct. Up to four men worked at the steam hammer, under the watchful eye of the foreman, and they were paid according to the amount of components they produced during the week. As far as possible employees were kept on the same jobs and in the same groups to keep productivity high.

Facing Doncaster station was a long two-storey building that housed several offices and the Upper and Lower Turneries. The latter was located on the ground floor – employed 160 – and contained tools such as a planing machine by Smith, Beacock & Tannett, as well as a gap lathe by the company, two double boring machines, one by Craven Brothers and the other made by the works. The former also supplied a planing machine to finish the valves and ports of the two cylinders made as one casting. These required a specialist tool due to the narrow opening through which access was gained at the front of the cylinders. Slide bars were ground on an emery wheel that could either spin, rock back and forth or move from side to side. Old and new crank axle lathes were in use, the latter being easier to operate, and there were a number of headstock lathes for turning wheels and tyres.

Directly above was the Upper Turnery, with more than 220 people at work there, a quarter of them being brass finishers. The tools were driven by shafting running the whole length of the shop and powered (together with the tools in the Lower Turnery) by a two-cylinder beam engine from J. Carmichael of Dundee. A cutter was in use for making tapering cotter holes, as was a double emery cutter machine for working with case-hardened metals, and a heavy screwing machine cut big square or V threads. Materials could be moved between the two Turneries via a trap door.

A single-rail travelling crane from Craven Brothers was used in the Machine Shop to move materials or items to the necessary tools. One of the largest was the wheel lathe from Smith, Beacock & Tannett, and the 8ft 1in-diameter wheels of the Stirling 'Singles' could easily be fitted on for turning, the face plates being of 8ft 10in diameter. Another tool was the six-spindle nut-tapping machine, and there was also a stud, bolt and pin lathe.

Next door was the Tender Shop. This had a frame drilling and slotting machine that had been there before the shop had changed uses. The maximum size of plate that could be worked was 26 feet by 3ft 10in, and to increase efficiency at least four plates were dealt with in one operation. A milling machine was another tool not specific to the work conducted in the shop, being used to cut the forked end of the coupling rods used by certain types of locomotive. The cutting head was of 19-inch diameter with forty-four radial pieces of steel to shape the fork, and this part was made on site as the example sent by the manufacturer was not up to the required standard.

There was a dedicated room to house the carriage wheel-balancing apparatus, which was relatively new as the practice had hitherto been shunned by many. All of the carriage wheels were dealt with on the machine and the operation was quite simple to perform. There was a wrought-iron frame plate on each side of the wheel, and half brass bearings, resting on spring supports, were used to carry the wheels. A rope suspended from the ceiling was then slung underneath the axle and pulled taut for the wheels to be spun as fast as they were meant to travel in service. The operator marked the wheel to find the heaviest point, then added small pieces of cast iron to create a balance. The heaviest additions did not exceed 2lb.

The Tin Shop carried out the production of all the company's signal and locomotive lamps, as well as those used in stations, sheds and yards; carriage lamps had been redundant since the introduction of gas lighting. In the Spring Shop the pieces of metal bought in to the required size were tested three or four times under the steam press to make sure they were satisfactory before installation. A space was provided for the reconditioning of boiler tubes. Once removed from the boiler the tubes were cleaned in a rotating drum filled with sand, then inspected. If still in good condition, their ends were removed and they were stored for use in smaller boilers. Those damaged were flattened and sent to be scrapped.

Construction of carriages was carried out in a large area with several roads, and the bodies were erected on trestles over these. When nearly finished, the body was lifted and placed on the wheels – eight being favoured at the time, although not as part of bogies. All the machine tools were dedicated to woodworking (being located in the southern corner of the shop) and driven through a locomotive-type engine. The tools were of the type expected in such a place – circular saws, band saws, planing machines and drills. A direct-acting gang-saw, dating from 1870, contained as many as fifteen circular saws and was used for cutting panel boards, etc.

Brute force is used to manoeuvre this wheelset.

1st and 3rd Class carriages of various vintages have been lifted off their wheels for attention in the Carriage Repair Shop.

The Wagon Shops at the Carr had electric lighting as the town's gas supply did not extend that far. Messrs Hammond & Co supplied the necessary electrical equipment and this originally consisted of three continuous current dynamos with an output of 300 volts and 56 amperes. Two of these machines were used to supply the eighty-four lamps fitted in the shops. Another dynamo provided 130 volts and 120 amperes. The dynamos were driven by specially designed engines from John Fowler & Co of Leeds, which had single cylinders 10 inches in diameter with a 20-inch stroke and cast-iron pistons. The crank shaft was 5 inches in diameter and the flywheel 6ft 3in in diameter. The engines were set in concrete foundations and the steam was provided by locomotive boilers. A total of four of these engines were at work and cost 2.1d each to run.

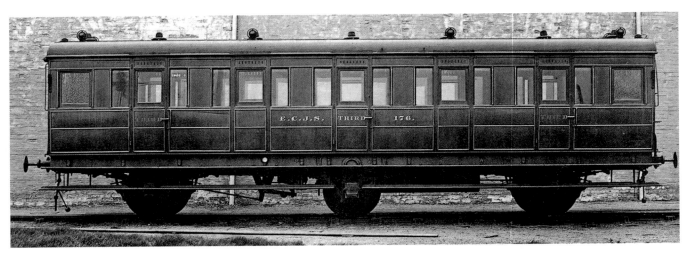

East Coast Joint Stock carriage No 176 was one of sixteen built to the Diagram 20 design between 1889 and 1891. There were five compartments seating six each and all were connected to toilets at each end by a corridor.

At this time there were 3,000 people employed at Doncaster Works. Mr Shotton was the Works Manager, having held the position for 26 years, with Patrick Stirling Jr as his Assistant for some of this period.

E. F. Howlden was responsible for carriage construction during Stirling's period of office, which not only encompassed the GNR stock but that of the East Coast Joint Stock (ECJS). The majority of the GNR carriages were built at Doncaster but in some instances orders were placed with the trade. This was partially due to the burden placed on the carriage works in having to meet the needs of the ECJS, as the NER and NBR shops did not contribute many examples until the 1890s and 1900s.

At the start of the 1870s the GNR was producing four-wheel carriages of several types, then in 1871

An aerial view of Doncaster Carr Wagon Works in about 1950.

the company built a six-wheel composite coach for express service, followed by several for the ECJS. Shortly afterwards Doncaster was among the earliest railways to build sleeping carriages for service in Britain. Another new feature was bogies, and these were introduced at the same time as the above, the first being a composite carriage seating forty. This was evidently successful, as a further three were built in 1876 and a similar arrangement was used for a saloon constructed for the use of the Prince of Wales. Stirling attempted to introduce carriages with four axles instead of two four-wheel bogies, as the construction costs between the two types differed by £500. However, the riding qualities were not of the same standard, so only a few examples were completed.

In the early 1880s the three companies concerned agreed to have 110 new carriages built for the ECJS, and an order for forty-eight of them was placed at Doncaster. During this period Stirling also produced an innovative design for a coach with a 'side gallery', or corridor, running the length of the vehicle allowing communication between the compartments and toilets installed at either end. The first was No 87, having four 1st Class compartments, one being reserved for the use of ladies, and mounted on six wheels. The carriage was successful and was perpetuated the following year, with the type being mooted for inclusion in the ECJS.

The GNR wagon stock was not particularly varied during Stirling's reign and mainly consisted of open wagons of 9-ton capacity. A portion of these was constructed at Doncaster while the remainder were bought – or loaned – from the trade. More than 1,000 covered vans for goods were in service at the end of the 1880s; some had been built by the GNR, while the remaining types covered a quite varied range of uses from ballast and timber to cattle and horses.

Stirling continued to meet the needs of the company's traffic until November 1895 when he sadly died in office. His successor had already been discussed and several eminent locomotive engineers had been approached for

Built at Doncaster in about 1910, this Ballast Brake Van was used for permanent way maintenance as a means of transporting workmen to the area under attention.

their opinions on the matter. The final choice was H. A. Ivatt, then Locomotive Engineer of the Great Southern & Western Railway of Ireland, and he was appointed to take up the role from 1 March 1896. As Stirling's locomotive policy was sound there were few major changes to be made, the main one being the adoption of a steam dome for the boilers of all new designs and the extension of this policy to older types where practicable. Ivatt's primary task was to provide suitable modern designs as and when the traffic demanded. Around the time of Ivatt's appointment, D. E. Marsh became Works Manager as Mr Shotton had also died.

Both passenger and freight services required reinforcements after Ivatt's arrival and he chose to tackle the former initially by developing Stirling's 2-4-0 type. The first change was the adoption of a bogie at the front end to provide greater stability, followed by a larger boiler – of 4ft 5in diameter working at 170lb per sq in. – affording a greater reserve of power. The first was No 400, which emerged from Doncaster in December 1896, and the engine was the pioneer 4-4-0 on the GNR. After settling in, the locomotive was deemed a success and a further ten were ordered and built during the following year. Later classified 'D2', a total of fifty-one would be completed up to the turn of the century.

Ivatt utilised some of the features of the 4-4-0s for his next design, which was a 4-4-2T produced to handle suburban traffic in the West Riding, the two classes

Ivatt 'D1' Class 4-4-0 No 1373 was erected at Doncaster in November 1900 and was in traffic until November 1948.

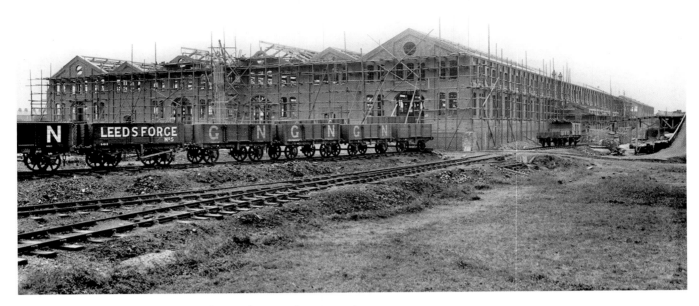

The Crimpsall Repair Shop in an advanced state of construction.

sharing boiler and cylinder dimensions. The first ten were built at Doncaster between 1898 and 1899 and performed their duties creditably, enough for a further fifty to be erected at the 'Plant' for service on similar trains running around London.

As the 1890s progressed the need for a new express engine became pronounced and Ivatt's appointment delayed the preparation of a suitable design. A larger boiler was necessary and this reduced the size of the coupled wheels, also adding another pair. The resulting 4-4-2 'Atlantic' wheel arrangement was a first for the GNR – and for any British railway company – the type having originated in America around a decade earlier. No 990 (later named *Henry Oakley* after the GNR General Manager) had two cylinders of 18¾-inch diameter by 24-inch stroke, slide valves operated by Stephenson motion, a 4ft 8in-diameter boiler with 1,442.2sq ft of heating surface, and pressure set at 175lb per sq in; the grate area was 26.75sq ft and the 6ft 7½in-diameter coupled wheels produced a tractive effort of 15,640lb. Again, Ivatt had the locomotive tested thoroughly in traffic before committing to further examples, and ten subsequently appeared

Behind the Crimpsall was the Tender Shop.

The paint shop was on the western side of the works. From the 1930s the building also housed the works' compressed air equipment for the various tools.

during 1900. Another batch of ten was built at Doncaster in 1903, while a lone four-cylinder 'Atlantic' had appeared the previous year and proved to be a disappointment, being rebuilt some ten years later.

During 1898 Ivatt decided to extend the use of the 'D2' 4-4-0 design to express work, and for this he provided a new boiler, which was of 4ft 8in diameter with a greater heating surface for both the firebox and tubes. Five were erected initially in 1898 and were followed by sixty-five more up to 1909, the type latterly being classified 'D1'.

Before Stirling's death a start had been made on providing 0-6-0 goods locomotives. Ivatt soon modified the boiler design to include a dome for a batch completed by Dübs & Co in 1897/98, and several other small alterations were made at this time. That company also built a further forty-eight up to 1901, as Doncaster was too busy to take them in hand (Kitson & Co also contributed twenty-five), although the 'Plant' was able to squeeze out fifty between 1898 and 1900. The works' capacity problems, exacerbated by a strike during 1899, caused the GNR to look to America during that year to fulfil traffic requirements, with twenty 2-6-0s being bought from Baldwin.

After the turn of the century space became sufficient in the New Erecting Shop for Ivatt to commence building a prototype 0-8-0 for heavy mineral trains between Peterborough and London. No 401 was in traffic for February 1901, being fully evaluated before fifty-four more were ordered. The class carried a similar boiler to that of the 'Atlantics', although larger cylinders were fitted.

The alleviation of the pressure on the workshops was

largely due to a new Repair Shop, Paint Shop and Tender Shop being erected on vacant land nearby known as the Crimpsall meadows, and the Repair Shop would take this name. H. Arnold & Son was employed on the building work, which eventually cost £250,000. The Crimpsall Repair Shop had four bays 520 feet long by 52 feet wide (served by two 35-ton overhead travelling cranes) and combined could accommodate 100 locomotives. There were also two smaller bays 520 feet by 30 feet used by coppersmiths and fitters to carry out machining and minor boiler repairs. A rail system – of 18-inch gauge – was present inside and outside the shops for the transport of materials. The men were provided with compressed air for powering hand tools, in addition to electricity for some of the machines and the lighting, while heating was provided by hot water pipes.

The Wheel Shop was positioned on the western wall of the Repair Shop and measured 292 feet wide by 60 feet long. There were several lathes in operation and these were driven by a bank of electric motors arranged along the western wall. Two tracks in the shop were for the movement of the wheels, and apparatus was present for their manipulation. Behind the Wheel Shop was a large area devoted to the storage of wheelsets. The Tender Shop was also at the back or west of the Crimpsall and had two large repair bays and a smaller bay for machine tools. The two areas for the work to be carried out possessed three tracks each and were served by two overhead cranes; stripping took place in the centre lane. Total capacity for the shop was thirty-two tenders. The Paint Shop was on

Ivatt 'Large Atlantic' No 251 – certainly worth a moment of contemplation.

the eastern side of the site and consisted of eight roads with shallow pits, each being able to hold five engines.

While these developments were taking place Ivatt advanced the design of his 'Atlantics' by producing a new boiler that was 10 inches greater in diameter than the original type. Additionally, a wide firebox was supplied to provide more heat for the water in the boiler. Again, Ivatt built an engine for testing – No 251 – before any construction on a larger scale; after the pioneer was erected in 1902, the next would not be seen until 1904. From then a further ninety would leave Doncaster, while one locomotive was built as a four-

cylinder compound and another of the same type came from Vulcan Foundry.

Ivatt made a slight error in introducing an 0-8-2T design for London suburban services in 1903, as the engines proved to be too heavy and were rejected by the Civil Engineer. However, the type was perpetuated and found work on coal trains around West Yorkshire and Nottinghamshire. The local services in London received new motive power later in the decade when Doncaster turned out fifty-six 'N1' Class 0-6-2Ts, despite being not much lighter. Both classes shared components with others; the 0-8-2T with the 0-8-0 mineral locomotives and the

The first 'N1' Class 0-6-2T is pictured shortly after construction in April 1907. Those following had a small number of detail differences.

The body of Composite dining saloon No 3039 is on the traverser outside the Carriage Shop in 1906. The coach was used in Gresley's 'Sheffield Stock' of the same year.

0-6-2T a boiler similar to the 'D1' 4-4-0s. The 'N1' Class also gave rise to fifteen 'J21' Class 0-6-0 goods engines completed at Doncaster in 1908.

At the turn of the century several railway companies experimented with using a small steam engine attached to a carriage for running on branch lines in order to save money. The GNR entered the arena in 1905 with two built at Doncaster, these being 0-4-0ST locomotives with 10-inch by 16-inch cylinders, a 4ft 0½in-diameter boiler working at 175lb pressure and having a tractive effort of 4,455lb. The carriages were 43ft 11in long and 8ft 10in wide, and had an elliptical roof, a four-wheel bogie at the rear end and five compartments, seating thirty-six 3rd Class passengers and ten 1st Class. The coaches were the first from the new Carriage & Wagon Superintendent H. N. Gresley, who arrived during that year from the Lancashire & Yorkshire Railway (L&YR); another new employee was F. W. Wintour, who became Works Manager.

Up to the mid-1890s the GNR was still constructing six-wheel coaches, but from then an effort was made to switch over to bogie stock and both six-wheel and four-wheel varieties were used. In mid-1897 Ivatt was instructed by the Board not to build any more six-wheel carriages, and for nearly ten years all new stock generally conformed to the practices of the time, although a departure was the adoption of the buckeye-type coupler. After Gresley's arrival the new stock no longer had the clerestory roof, which was replaced by the elliptical type, and the six-wheel bogies were abandoned in favour of the four-wheel type based on those used by the L&YR, which Gresley subsequently developed into the standard for many years afterwards. The first carriage proper from Gresley was Composite Corridor No 2977, built at Doncaster at the end of 1905 and followed by several Open 3rds and Brake 3rds. Soon afterwards his mark was felt on the ECJS as the new GNR outline was adopted for forty carriages erected

An articulated composite triplet set in the works yard .

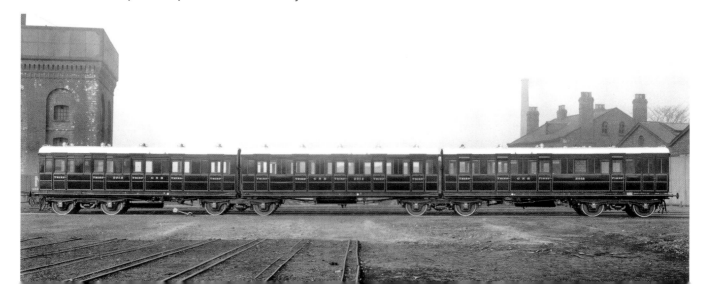

War work being undertaken in the Carriage Shop.

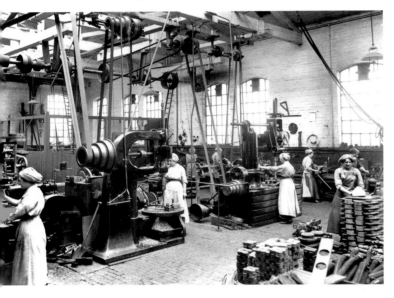

Women war workers in the Drill Shop of Doncaster Carr Wagon Works.

at Doncaster in 1906/07 to replace old six-wheel coaches in the fleet. A statement of intent was the 'Sheffield Stock' completed in 1906 and comprising a Brake 1st, Composite dining car, Open 3rd and Brake 3rd, all having steel underframes and electric lighting. This pattern was replicated for the carriages turned out in the following year for the King's Cross to Newcastle trains.

As there were a large number of six-wheel carriages in GNR stock – at the turn of the 19th century there were approximately 1,700 – the finance, or will (some were still not very old), was absent for a wholesale replacement with bogie coaches. Gresley made an experiment of removing the axles from the body and mounting a pair of bodies on a bogie at each end with one being shared in the middle. The first modifications of this kind were made to ECJS six-wheel corridor coaches Nos 202 and 206

in early 1907 and proved quite successful, riding much more comfortably than the original arrangement. A large number of conversions followed, mainly being articulated twins, but there were a number of triplets, quadruplets and even quintuplets formed at Doncaster.

Superheating locomotives was carried out by a number of railways all over the globe in the early 1900s and the GNR joined in at the end of 1908 when 0-8-0 No 417 received the Schmidt type with eighteen elements of the 'long loop' type. This reduced the number of small tubes to 104 and the boiler pressure was also lowered to 160lb per sq in., but was later increased to 170lb per sq in. Another improvement to the locomotive at this time was the substitution of slide valves for piston valves, which were more reliable and less prone to wear. Ivatt was evidently satisfied as five were subsequently built in this condition during late 1909 and the apparatus spread to other classes, including 4-4-0s and 0-6-0s.

Ivatt retired on 16 September 1911 and his position passed to H. N. Gresley, who was considered rather young (at the age of 35) for the appointment. Nevertheless, he had impressed Ivatt, and the Board had no hesitation in allowing this transition. O. V. S. Bulleid, formerly a Premium Apprentice at Doncaster, returned the following year to become Gresley's Assistant, while Edward Thompson was given responsibility for the Carriage & Wagon Department.

Gresley inherited modern and capable stock that required few additions at the time. His first product was a continuation of the 0-6-0s that Ivatt had introduced shortly before retiring, and these locomotives had only slight detail modifications from the earlier examples. Ninety-five were erected at Doncaster between 1911 and 1922. However, one type lacking from the company's ranks was a suitable mixed-traffic design and, again, Gresley was bold in adopting the 2-6-0 wheel arrangement, which was little used in Britain at the time. Furthermore, outside Walschaerts valve gear was employed, the 'H2s' being the first class in the country to do so. The cylinders were 20 inches by 26 inches with 10-inch piston valves, and the boiler shared features with the latest superheated boilers fitted to the Ivatt 0-8-0s. No 1630 went into traffic for testing in 1912 before another nine followed in 1913. Later, a larger 5ft 6in-diameter boiler was deemed necessary, and twenty, classified 'H3', emerged from Doncaster with this in two batches during 1914 and 1916; thirty-five were also built by contractors.

Gresley had only been in office a short time when the Ivatt 0-8-0s started to become overwhelmed by the demand for coal in London. Soon a 2-8-0 was on the drawing board to provide some relief and this followed the pattern of the 'H3s' with large boiler (fitted with twenty-four elements), with enlarged cylinders of 21 inches by 28 inches. No 456 was at work by the end of the year and another four emerged from Doncaster in 1914, but further production was stifled by the outbreak of war. Twenty Class 'J23' 0-6-0Ts for the West Riding were also built before the conflict took hold.

In the run-up to the commencement of the First World War Doncaster Works had experimented with using diesel engines to produce the electricity to be used on site. In 1910 a Carels Frères vertical four-stroke engine with three cylinders was installed and this generated 350 horsepower at 190rpm for all the electrical equipment in the Crimpsall Repair Shop. The type proved to be quite successful and as a result of the cheap price of oil at the time a second engine was purchased. However, a subsequent rise in price saw this saving reduced.

At the Wagon Works a gas producer was put in use, being fed from the large amount of the shops' wood-shavings, etc. Crossley Brothers supplied all of the apparatus necessary and this consisted of a producer 9 feet in diameter by 21 feet high, and an engine of 175 horsepower coupled to a 100-kilowatt generator; there was always an adequate reserve of power. The Campbell Gas Engine Co Ltd later supplied more equipment of the same type, the wood consumption of the whole plant being 2¾lb per brake horsepower. The advantage of using wood rather than coal was that there was very little maintenance necessary to the producer and the plant was seldom shut down for this reason. The sawdust and wood pieces were collected by a network of ducts that deposited the material in hoppers that were later conveyed to the plant.

War work was soon being undertaken at Doncaster and in 1915 part of the Tender Shop was turned over to reconditioning 18-pounder cartridge cases. During the following year the Lower Turnery was also similarly

Women varnish 6-inch high-explosive shells at Doncaster.

employed on 6-inch high-explosive shells. Initially, apprentices were placed on these tasks and were producing 10,000 per week, but before long women were employed, often on 12-hour shifts, including weekends, and the rate increased to 50,000; the percentage of rejection was only 0.17. At the end of the war Doncaster had supplied 124,236 6-inch shells, 56,100 fuses and 43,000 adapters, and had renovated 4,267,093 18-pounder cartridge cases – with an additional 138,000 for the Admiralty. The

East Coast Joint Stock Brake 3rd No 324, which was built at Doncaster in 1902, is given a thorough clean during the First World War.

workshops also made several components for shipping to other locations for final assembly; these included 150,000 noses for 6-inch shells, 128,000 base plates for 6-inch shells, 47,000 noses for 4.5-inch shells, 50,000 rifle bodies and 6,000 rifle noses, 4,000 tank links, 3,100 screw coupling nuts, and 15,000 various parts for gun carriages.

Doncaster had the task of assembling parts for several different kinds of guns, such as fifty 18-pounder and 13-pounder anti-aircraft cannons mounted on vehicles, while cradles and pedestals were machined for small- and large-calibre weapons. Miscellaneous items included thirty-one naval searchlights, converted for use on land, 750 ambulance stretchers, and 913 general service wagons. At the end of the war Gresley praised both the general staff and the female employees for the high standard of work they had carried out under difficult circumstances. He was awarded a CBE for the manner in which he had overseen the shops.

Gresley had found time in between his many duties for the war effort to think about future traffic requirements and his policy towards this. During the early years of the 20th century both passenger and freight trains had continually increased in weight and this was exacerbated by the war. Many railway companies introduced three- or four-cylinder locomotives to increase the power available and Gresley was no different, favouring three cylinders for a number of reasons, including a more uniform tractive effort, less coal consumption and increased mileage between general repairs. In the case of three cylinders separate sets of valve gear usually had to be supplied, but Gresley developed a system – similar to that fitted to four-cylinder locomotives – where the outside valve gear operated the valve for the centre cylinder.

Towards the end of the war Gresley was able to build his first three-cylinder engine, and 'O2' Class 2-8-0 No 461 appeared from Doncaster in March 1918. The locomotive was otherwise generally similar to the earlier 'O1' Class

2-8-0s and under test was found to be more economical in coal consumption, allowing the valve gear to be adopted for future construction. However, as applied to No 461 the motion was quite complicated and was simplified before being fitted to the new 'H4' Class 2-6-0s. Ten of these locomotives were introduced from Doncaster in 1920/21 and – at 6 feet in diameter – possessed the largest boiler yet to be used on a British locomotive.

Both the 'O2s' and 'H4s' served as a means of testing various of Gresley's ideas before the introduction of his last GNR design. Despite superheating many of the Ivatt 'Atlantics' during the war years, they were becoming unsuitable for the principal express trains and a new type was needed. Gresley turned to American practice for inspiration and developed a 4-6-2 'Pacific' locomotive with the aim of hauling trains well over 500 tons at 50mph. No 1470 *Great Northern* was constructed at Doncaster in March 1922, followed by a second engine, No 1471, in July. The two locomotives had three cylinders of 20 inches by 26 inches with 8-inch-diameter piston valves operated by the conjugated motion, a 6ft 5in-diameter boiler working at 180lb per sq in, a thirty-two-element superheater, a 41.25sq ft grate and 6ft 8in-diameter coupled wheels.

After the benefits of articulation had been realised for the older coaching vehicles in stock, attention was turned to producing new articulated carriages. The first were twin sets consisting of an Open Brake 3rd and a side-corridor Composite (ten 1sts, forty-eight 3rds), and these appeared in 1915, with further examples being completed up to 1919. The body length was standardised at 49ft 3in and the outer bogies were the 8ft 6in GNR pattern while the inner bogie had an 8-foot wheelbase. In 1917 similar twins were built for 1st Class passengers, and in 1922 twin 1st Class sleeping cars were erected for the ECJS. The bodies were 56ft 2½in long (total weight 61t 17cwt), they had twenty compartments, a toilet and an attendant's room, and were decorated simply in teak and mahogany.

Gresley's 'A1' 'Pacific' No 1470 *Great Northern* as built in 1922.

The Leeds quintuplet set of 1921.

Rounding off post-war carriage construction at Doncaster was the quintuplet set of 1921 for the mid-morning/early-evening King's Cross to Leeds service. The running gear was the same as outlined above and the set was formed of a Brake 3rd, a 3rd Class diner, kitchen, 1st Class diner, and Brake 1st. Seating was for 128 passengers and the total weight was 118t 3cwt. The kitchen was notable for being the first to employ electricity for cooking, and the apparatus, which was either charged at stations or by batteries charged by axle dynamos once under way, was designed by Bulleid and J. Stone & Co.

Under Gresley the wagon stock generally consisted of 9-ton open goods wagons, 15 feet long with a 9ft 6in wheelbase and four wooden planks forming the sides; the design was also adapted for coal traffic. As time progressed the capacity was raised to 10 tons and after the war a new 12-ton open wagon was ordered in numbers from contractors. The next most numerous type was the covered goods van of 8-ton capacity, which was 18 feet long and had a 9ft 6in wheelbase.

At the Grouping Doncaster Works was responsible for 1,358 locomotives, 2,522 carriages and 30,029 wagons and vans. With a staff of approximately 4,000 and relatively modern facilities, the shops were well-equipped to meet the new company's needs for the immediate future. However, this work would have to be undertaken without the direct oversight of Gresley as, soon after his appointment as Chief Mechanical Engineer of the newly formed LNER, he moved his office to King's Cross, accompanied by Bulleid and several others.

'Goods Break' vans of 10-ton capacity like this had been superseded by examples of 20-ton capacity by the time of the Grouping.

Gresley's first LNER 'Pacific' was renumbered 4472 and named *Flying Scotsman* for the British Empire Exhibition. The engine is pictured at King's Cross station.

Before the GNR's existence ended, the company ordered a further ten 'A1' Class 'Pacifics', the first being No 1472, later No 4472 *Flying Scotsman*, in February 1923, and the last No 1481 in September 1923. This latter was the first of the twelve 'Pacifics' then in existence to be modified for the new loading gauge and subsequently had its height reduced further at Darlington Works in 1924. The pioneer LNER 'Pacific' was tested against the NER's 'Pacific' during 1923 and the former was deemed sufficiently superior for more 'A1s' to be ordered. Doncaster received an order for twenty locomotives while North British was

No 3946 was part of a batch of Gresley 'O2' Class 2-8-0s built at Doncaster after the Grouping. The locomotive is given a caution signal from Cemetery signal box on the main line during June 1932.

engaged for the same number, the batches entering traffic, respectively, between June 1924 and July 1925 and August and December 1924. The Foundry at Doncaster soon had an increased workload as the decision was taken to name the majority of the class after racehorses, and the task was carried out from April 1925, taking just under a year to complete. The plates turned out to be quite fragile and replacements began to be fitted in early 1926 with an improved design that offered more support.

In January and February 1923 Doncaster was asked to construct a total of fifteen 'O2' Class 2-8-0s. These were also cut down to fit the new loading gauge and had built-up crank axles instead of the forged type used on their predecessors. Nos 487-495 and 3496-3501 were turned out from October 1923 to June 1924 and all were soon allocated to Peterborough New England shed, where they remained for many years; all would receive their repairs at Doncaster. Produced concurrently with this class were ten 'J50' (GNR 'J23') Class 0-6-0Ts, equipped with boilers salvaged from several redundant classes.

The Carriage Works was also busy fulfilling GNR orders while Bullied, who took charge of carriage matters immediately after the Grouping, determined the standard features for the new LNER stock. Twin Brake 3rd articulated coaches were completed for several local services around the system, while for the long-distance trains articulated twin sleeping carriages were put into service. A programme of replacing the suburban trains out of King's Cross had begun after the war and new quadruplet sets had been designed for these, with two formations being coupled together to form the eight-carriage sets. Two were finished in 1923 and eight appeared in 1924. Some were to the GNR design, while others had modified LNER standard details that increased the weight slightly. A major project in 1924 was the construction of five triplet restaurant carriage sets, two for the 'Flying Scotsman' and the others for general Anglo-Scottish services. Seating was for both 1st and 3rd Class and the cooking equipment was powered by electricity.

The Wagon Shops were employed on much new construction, with 2,500 high-sided open wagons being built in the two years after the Grouping, in addition to a number of cattle wagons. A large order for 12-ton covered good vans was fulfilled to Diagram 16, having frames 17ft 6in long and a 9-foot wheelbase, and fitted with automatic vacuum brakes. Moreover, refurbishment work was carried out on fifty 45-ton quadruple bolster bogie wagons bought from the War Department as surplus.

In 1925 a century had elapsed since the opening of the Stockton & Darlington Railway and celebrations to mark this event were planned to take place, including an exhibition of rolling stock and a parade of both new and old locomotives. Much of the national and international railway community was to be in attendance for the gala and Gresley wanted to make an impression, not only for his own reputation, but for that of the LNER as a progressive and modern railway. Of the two new designs scheduled to be present, one was designed and constructed at Doncaster. This was the 'P1' Class 2-8-2 'Mikado' locomotive that was to be used in service for heavy coal trains on the main line and was necessarily the most powerful freight type in the country at the time. Much of the design was based on the 'A1' 'Pacific', the two classes sharing the same boiler, while the motion arrangement was similar to that used by

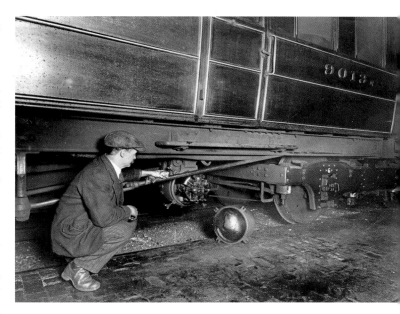

The dynamo of 'Flying Scotsman' kitchen carriage No 9013N is inspected shortly after the Grouping.

the 'O2' Class. An unusual feature was a booster, which was supplied to assist the locomotive when starting, and this was obtained from America. Two engines were built, No 2393 – the first – in June 1925, just in time for the centenary in July, with No 2394 following before the end of the year. Both locomotives cost approximately £10,000 each to complete.

After the excitement of this project, Doncaster Works settled down to more mundane, but equally as important, projects such as the construction of the Group Standard 'N2' Class 0-6-2Ts for use in Scotland. These had left-hand drive, improved suspension and larger-diameter axle journals. Given similar treatment was the 'J50' 0-6-0T

Gresley 'P1' Class 2-8-2 'Mikado' No 2393 is pictured at the head of a coal train during the late 1920s.

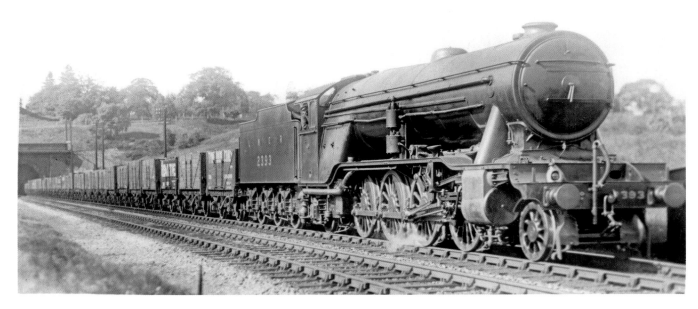

'A3' 'Pacific' No 2580 *Shotover* stands on the turntable at King's Cross station, with driver and fireman posing in the connection for the corridor tender. The engine completed the first non-stop 'Flying Scotsman' to London in 1928.

design, and several batches totalling thirty-eight were built at Doncaster between 1926 and 1930. In addition to the above alterations, the class received Ross 'pop'-type safety valves, under-footplate injectors and steam brakes. These locomotives were distributed around the LNER system.

Several of the standard carriage types were erected at Doncaster from the start of the second half of the 1920s and the works continued to produce twin articulated 1st Class sleepers as the demand for this service was growing. The wagon works was employed again on building 12-ton good vans, but in this instance the 250 built only had manual brakes. Replacement fish vans for life-expired examples were also constructed at Doncaster to Diagram 23, numbering nearly 200; these had exposed bodywork framing, sliding doors and connections for steam heating. A 23-foot-long version, totalling fifty examples, with a 14-foot wheelbase was also produced at the Carr. The LNER continued to place orders at Doncaster for 10-ton cattle wagons up to 1930, and 265 Diagram 39 vehicles were built together with 565 to Diagram 40, although these were relatively similar in all but details. Furthermore, several vans for departmental use (fully equipped with machine tools) were turned out during this period, as were 250 12-ton sleeper wagons for the Permanent Way Department.

Gresley's 'Pacifics' were not completely satisfactory during their early years as the coal consumption was high, which was subsequently attributed to the valve gear setting not being set at the optimum level. Doncaster

Drawing Office had attempted to put this right but fell short, and Gresley's technical assistant, Bert Spencer, subsequently completed the task. No 2555 *Centenary* was the pioneer in March 1927 and the remainder of the class were altered as they went into Doncaster for general repairs. Around the same time Gresley decided to increase the working pressure of the 'A1s' to 220lb per sq in. and this required a new boiler, which also contained a larger superheater with forty-three elements rather than thirty-two. Five were ordered initially from Doncaster and fitted to Nos 4480 *Enterprise*, 2544 *Lemberg*, 2580 *Shotover*, 2573 *Harvester* and 2578 *Bayardo*. The first two were altered at the works in 1927, while the other three had the diagram 94HP type fitted at Darlington in 1928. Under test the high-pressure locomotives – classified 'A3' – were found to be hardly different from the 'A1s'. Nevertheless, Gresley was convinced by the merits of the application and ten new 'A3s' (featuring the valve gear modification) were ordered from Doncaster in August 1927, beginning to appear a year later with No 2743 *Felstead*.

The improvements to the 'Pacifics' came just in time for the introduction of the non-stop 'Flying Scotsman' train during the summer season, which travelled between the English and Scottish capitals (392.8 miles) in 8 hours 15 minutes. For a change of crews to occur approximately half-way without stopping, Gresley came up with the ingenious solution of inserting a small passageway in the tender, allowing the men to pass from the footplate

A triplet restaurant set – consisting of Restaurant 1st (16481), kitchen (16482) and Restaurant 3rd (16483) – for the 'Flying Scotsman' of 1928.

to the train. Doncaster Works Manager F. H. Eggleshaw recounted some of the details of the construction to the *LNER Magazine* in 1928. The staff were said to be quite pleased to have been given the task over the other workshops, but were a little apprehensive at the short timeframe given for the completion of the tenders. The Forge and Foundry sprang into action immediately and moved the parts to the Tender Shop as soon as they were ready, while supplies from outside were rushed in as fast as possible. Soon the frame plates, horn blocks, drag boxes, frame stays, springs, spring brackets and central couplers were being assembled in a bay, while the tank was fabricated separately before being placed on the frames. The body was then mated with the wheels and removed to the Paint Shop for the livery to be applied – this process being given the shortest amount of time possible. After the tender was weighed and tested, coupling to a specially selected locomotive took place. The first (No 5323) was ready in early April – some fifty days since the order had arrived – and was coupled to No 4472 *Flying Scotsman*. Mr Eggleshaw goes on to say that many of the staff at Doncaster gave up their lunchtime on 1 May to see the fruit of their labours pass through the station, blocking many of the roads in the process. A testament to the workmanship and general standard of construction is the fact that of 125 trips run during the season, or nearly 100,000 miles, only one failure occurred, and this was due to a faulty lubricator.

New carriages were built for the 'Flying Scotsman' and these comprised an articulated set of 1st diner, kitchen and 3rd diner with decoration by Charles Allom. This was a departure from standard practice in containing little polished wood, being painted instead, and luggage racks were replaced by a small closet at the end of the carriage. Bench seats were substituted by padded chairs in 1st Class, and 3rd Class was made more comfortable. A Brake 3rd was also built, containing a compartment for the enginemen to wait in or retire to. Two novelties of the train were a hairdresser's compartment and a ladies'

The interior of the 1st Class restaurant of the 'Flying Scotsman' triplet.

retiring room, both being fitted into a 3rd Class carriage constructed during 1924 at York. While the latter was not very successful, the former ran for several years – perhaps giving an indication of the riding quality of the carriage and the standard of the permanent way!

The 'Plant' received a request for twenty 'K3s' to be erected in 1929, and these incorporated several modifications over the earlier engines. *Locomotives of the LNER Part 6A* notes that some of these were not to Darlington's liking, as the works was allocated the locomotives for repairs, being put to use in that area. For example, the chimney cowl and liner were altered to improve draughting and this was done partially in line with practice at North Road by fitting a cone, but this was different and therefore non-standard. However, the inconvenience was short-lived as a new chimney arrangement was introduced ten years later, replacing the earlier types. Darlington was also kept in the dark over Doncaster's method of fixing such defects as cracked frames, and an afflicted engine was delayed for several months for the transfer of information to occur.

The last new Gresley design before a pause was built at Doncaster in September 1930. The 'V1' Class 2-6-2T was produced for suburban traffic, initially in Scotland and London, having three 16-inch by 26-inch cylinders (cast as a monobloc) fed by 8-inch piston valves operated by Walschaerts/Gresley motion, a 5-foot-diameter boiler with a total heating surface of 1,609sq ft working at 180lb per sq in, and a grate area of 22.08sq ft; the coupled wheel diameter was 5ft 8in. No 2900 was the earliest example, and twenty-seven more followed up to December 1931; a further six were ordered, although these did not appear until 1934/35 due to the Great Depression and the financial hardships endured by the LNER as a result. This was not only felt in the locomotive department – the carriage and wagon arms of the works were also hit and output dipped dramatically between 1931 and 1933.

Gresley was more than happy to show off Doncaster Works to the Institution of Locomotive Engineers during 1927. He personally conducted small groups taken from the party of 150 members, many of whom had come from countries across the globe. Also on hand to answer any questions were Works Manager F. H. Eggleshaw; Assistant Works Manager G. A. Musgrave; Carriage & Wagon Works Manager A. H. Peppercorn; Wagon Works Manager W. H . Brown; former Works Manager, then Assistant Mechanical Engineer Southern Area, F. Wintour; Mechanical Engineer, Doncaster, R. A. Thom; and Chief Draughtsman W. Elwess.

In an article produced for the *LNER Magazine* in 1930, R. A. Thom described the recent reorganisation that had taken place at Doncaster Works, particularly at the Crimpsall. He began the piece by quoting the LNER Chairman William Whitelaw, who at the Annual Meeting of the company had made interesting remarks about the reduction in repairs carried out in the workshops, specifically related to those for locomotives:

'The reduction in our locomotive stock has been rendered possible by the great improvements which we have made, in recent years, in our workshops, whereby we are now able to repair and turn out locomotives from our shops in a much reduced time; at December 31, 1929 we had 564 engines under or awaiting repair, showing a decrease of 60 on the previous year's figure, and of 207 as compared with two years ago. Six years ago we had 932 engines under or awaiting repair at the end of the year, or 368 more than at present.'

Thom commented that approximately 1,300 locomotives were repaired by Doncaster at the time and prior to the reorganisation 100, and sixteen tenders, were squeezed into the Crimpsall at any one time. The time spent at the 'Plant' averaged sixty working days and over this period six or seven engines were attended to by one fitting gang that was under the supervision of a chargehand. The process started with a partial strip before the wheels were removed and the task was completed. All the parts were sent away for refurbishment and renewal

Members of the Institution of Locomotive Engineers pose with a 'Pacific' after their visit to Doncaster in 1927; Gresley is in the centre with R. A. Thom on the right and O. V. S. Bulleid on the far left.

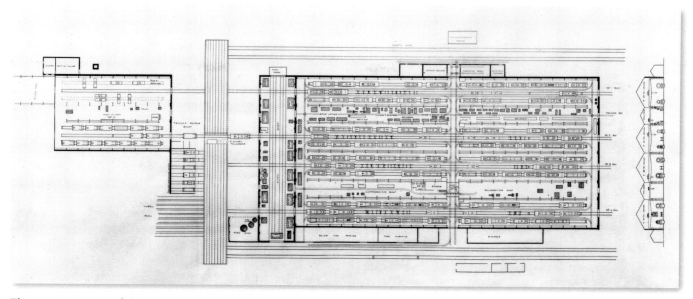

The arrangement of the Crimpsall Repair Shop before the reorganisation was implemented.

and returned as quickly as possible to be reused on the same engine. Thom says that this was done as far as practicable, although delays often occurred as a result of parts being sent out of the Crimpsall to the different shops in the main site.

An improvement was suggested and implemented whereby the number of engines accommodated at any one time was reduced to thirty-six (twelve each in three bays). One bay in both the Crimpsall and Tender Shop was turned over for component repairs to be carried out and staff were transferred in to these areas to stop items being moved out of the building. No 1 Bay in the Crimpsall was half turned over to tender work and half to wheeling locomotives. Stripping took place outside the building on a dedicated road and eight locomotives could

be dealt with. Care had been taken for several of the most important classes to be provided with boilers, cylinders, motion, etc, from a well-stocked spares pool to ensure that the engines re-entered traffic promptly.

As soon as the locomotives were on the stripping lane any repairs necessary to the boiler were ascertained first so that this could be carried out or the replacement arranged, as this work usually took the longest time. The brick arch and firebars were removed so a firebox inspection could take place, then the fittings in the smokebox were taken out. The next stage saw the motion dismantled and cleaned in a dedicated shed, and the final phase was for the tubes to be cleared from the boiler. A traverser moved the locomotive to the required bay, where it was lifted off its wheels and moved by crane to a spare berth. All of the

After the changes the Crimpsall was not so congested, even with tenders now being admitted – the Tender Repair Shop is now occupied by the Boiler Repair Shop.

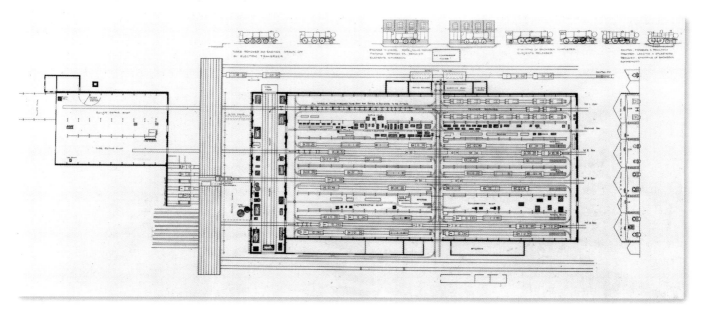

A view inside the Crimpsall taken during GNR days.

components that had been removed were deposited in a dedicated space at the head of the bay where they were refitted as necessary. After assembly the engines had a base coat of paint applied before moving over to the Paint Shop for finishing.

Another aid to speeding up the repair process was a set of several new machine tools, some of which were placed in the Wheel Shop, which also received a new travelling crane. In the Tender Shop the road taken out of use for the originally intended purpose became a place for boiler repairs to be performed, which also encompassed fixing defects on flues and tubes. The new system and rationalisation of the work had reduced the time spent under repair to just twenty-seven working days.

In 1932 Doncaster began construction on the first Group Standard batch of 'O2' Class 2-8-0s. A delay of nearly ten years had occurred because the LNER had purchased a large number of War Department 2-8-0s at a good price in the mid-1920s. The 'O2s' were similar to the GNR series but had several changes made to bring them up to date, including new motion, improved valve events, a new cab with left-hand drive, and steam brakes. Production began with No 2954 and finished in April 1932, followed by seven taking the same numbering series, which ended with No 2437 in March 1934. All sixteen were dispatched to March shed for freight workings in the GE Area.

Gresley began the design process for his next new locomotive in early 1932, as the Running Department had requested a powerful locomotive to work the heavy trains over the mountainous route between Edinburgh and Aberdeen. The 'Pacifics' working the services at the time were limited to no more than 500 tons and, following the introduction of new sleeping carriages, train weights often exceeded this in the summer months. The proposed locomotive went through several design permutations, although the use of eight coupled wheels (of 6ft 2in diameter) in a 2-8-2 'Mikado' formation and the 'A3'-type boiler were constants in the thinking process. The final plans saw three cylinders (cast as a monobloc) provided with poppet valves operated by rotary cam valve gear, an ACFI feedwater heater introducing a pre-warmed feed into the boiler, a V-shaped cab front to reduce glare at night, a Kylchap double blastpipe and chimney, and a smokebox incorporating smoke deflection. No 2001 Cock o' the North was the most powerful passenger locomotive in Britain when sent into traffic during May 1934 and was subsequently followed by a second – and more conventional – 'P2' Class locomotive, No 2002 Earl Marischal.

No 2001 was the star attraction at the Doncaster Works Open Day of 26/27 May 1934. No 4472 Flying Scotsman and Beyer Garratt 'U1' Class locomotive No 2395 were also on hand to help the staff raise money for the Doncaster Infirmary and several railwaymen's charities. As

Standing in front of No 2001 Cock o' the North (left to right) are R. A. Thom, Mechanical Engineer, Doncaster; E. Windle, Chief Locomotive Draughtsman; J. S. Jones, Assistant Works Manager; F. H. Eggleshaw, Works Manager; the Paint Shop Foreman; unidentified; the Erecting Shop Foreman; and two chargehand fitters.

'A4' Class 'Pacific' No 2509 *Silver Link* hauls an ordinary express at New Southgate.

many as forty exhibits were present in the Crimpsall Repair Shop's sidings for the curious, and workers generously gave their time to explain items to the uninitiated. At the event's opening ceremony Mr Ronald Matthews of the LNER Board praised the work carried out at Doncaster, adding that the members of the Board were especially pleased with the manner in which this was carried out by the employees. Over the weekend the exhibition drew in approximately 40,000 people and raised nearly £1,000.

Doncaster Works would see *Cock o' the North* quite frequently up to the end of the year as several modifications were made due to a number of flaws in the original design, in addition to many tests being carried out. At the end of the year the engine was prepared for a visit to the Paris-Orleans Railway testing station at Vitry-sur-Seine near Paris and spent several unhappy months there due to several mechanical problems. No 2001 was in the works for two months after returning and re-entered service for the summer season of 1935.

Gresley had high hopes for the features used on *Cock o' the North* and intended to incorporate them into future designs. Plans were made during 1934 to introduce a new high-speed train between King's Cross and Newcastle, and for this a new locomotive was planned. This initially resembled the 'P2' but soon evolved after experience with the engine to take on the form of the 'A3' Class. A subsequent development was the addition of streamlining to the locomotive in order to reduce the air resistance, which was quite an advanced undertaking at the time.

The plans for the running plate were not arrived at scientifically; Gresley sketched them out on a piece of paper and the fitters in the erecting shop followed this – unsuccessfully – until he explained a drawing of the correct shape to be produced.

Four 'A4' Class 'Pacifics' were built initially. The engines had 18½-inch by 26-inch cylinders with Walschaerts/Gresley motion operating 9-inch-diameter piston valves, a boiler with a total heating surface of 3,325.2sq ft working at 250lb per sq in pressure, a grate area of 41.25sq ft, and 6ft 8in-diameter coupled wheels. The locomotives had an unusual silver-grey livery, the right shade being adopted after the works shunter tested several schemes. No 2509 *Silver Link* was completed in early September 1935 for the new train, which commenced running at the end of the month; both met with every success and the former set the speed record for steam on the maiden run. The remaining three engines were in traffic before the end of the year.

The Silver Jubilee of King George V occurred in 1935 and to celebrate this occasion the LNER chose to name the new train after the event. A set of carriages was provided in addition to the 'A4' Class and these were quite different from what had been built at Doncaster previously. The seven carriages, which had only been ordered in early 1935, were built using steel body panels (covered in Rexine, an artificial leather) over the standard teak frame; steel was a relatively new addition to the materials used in construction. To reduce the weight and improve comfort,

Doncaster built relatively few members of the 'V2' Class after the first five. No 4771 *Green Arrow* is pictured at Doncaster shed pre-war.

articulation was employed and the formation was split into three sets – two twins of Brake 1st, 1st, 3rd, Brake 3rd and a triplet restaurant. The carriage interiors were also devoid of wood and the decoration was in several colours of Rexine.

The 'V2' Class 2-6-2s were also to be derived from the 'P2' Class, then the external appearance of the 'A4s' was to be applied, but this idea was discarded, the new locomotives only taking the mechanical specifications. The frames, springs, piston rings, superheater and cab were all based on the 'A4' arrangement. The three cylinders were 18½ inches by 26 inches with 9-inch piston valves, the total heating surface was 3,110.74sq ft, the grate area 41.25sq ft, the working pressure 220lb per sq in, and the coupled wheels 6ft 2in in diameter. No 4771 *Green Arrow* left Doncaster in June 1936 and immediately became a success with fast freight and passenger services alike; Nos 4772-75 were built between August and November.

A Kearns horizontal boring machine was bought for use at Doncaster, and a monobloc casting is being milled here.

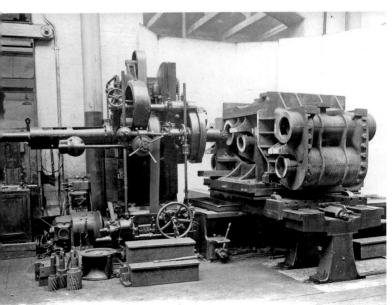

With *Cock o' the North* proving a disappointment and *Earl Marischal*'s performance being generally superior, an order at Doncaster for another four 'P2s' was completed at Doncaster in 1936 to the latter's specifications. One difference was the appearance. As the exhaust from the piston valves of No 2002 had caused smoke to drift, Gresley saw fit to apply the front end of the 'A4s' to the 'P2s' – perhaps also appropriating some publicity in the process – and both Nos 2001 and 2002 were later rebuilt in this manner; *Cock o' the North* also had the poppet valves and feedwater heater removed. The last engine, No 2006 *Wolf of Badenoch*, incorporated an altered boiler with a longer combustion chamber than had hitherto been used. When 'W1' Class No 10000 was rebuilt at Doncaster in 1937 the engine was also fitted with this boiler type and was streamlined like the 'A4' Class.

On 10 June 1936 members of the Institution of Mechanical Engineers were treated to a tour around the workshops, again being conducted by Gresley, in addition to LNER Chairman William Whitelaw. The visit was part of a summer expedition made by the Institution to places of interest in Yorkshire, with a particular emphasis on the LNER's infrastructure, as Gresley was President of the Mechanical Engineers for the year. The *LNER Magazine* reported on the day:

'There was much favourable comment upon the remarkably efficient organisation and the up to date machinery being used. The members were particularly interested in the specially designed "Kearns'" boring mill on which the castings for the three cylinders – standardised on the LNER by Mr Gresley with some 470 engines fitted with the arrangement – are machined.'

The guests were also treated to the spectacle of a boiler being riveted and the firebox throatplate being forged. Before luncheon was served the group was led to the Paint Shop yard where a selection of locomotives, including Nos 2509 *Silver Link*, 4472 *Flying Scotsman*, Ivatt 'Atlantic' 4420, 2003 *Lord President* and 4771 *Green Arrow*, were stationed for inspection. After the excited crowd – of

A busy scene in the Carriage Shop under GNR auspices: Open 3rd No 3047 from the 'Sheffield Stock' is in the foreground.

approximately 170 people – had scrutinised these engines thoroughly, a photograph with *Silver Link* was taken to capture the day for posterity.

The *LNER Magazine* also carried an interesting feature in the September 1936 issue as part of the 'My day's work' series, with Mr J. Stocks, a carriage painter at Doncaster, giving some details of his job. The various tasks, such as painting, varnishing and renovations, were the responsibility of a particular gang, which was set to a specific place, like the bogies, side panels or roof. Mr Stocks was attached to the gang that applied the numbering and lettering to the coaches. First, the transfers were tacked, rubbed lightly, then covered with a coat of varnish and left for a few hours. The application was performed after the

Chief Engineer's Saloon No 900580 was built at Doncaster in 1936 and had steel panelling. The carriage survived in service well into the 1980s and has subsequently been preserved.

Above The old Weigh House with scales by Sam Denison & Son of Leeds.

Below The new Weigh House and the weighing devices arranged in a central pit.

panels had been rubbed down with a pumice stone, and while the transfers were damp they were sponged and leathered to complete the process.

The gang had the responsibility for producing the destination board fixed to the roofline of the carriage. As a timesaving measure the places most often served by the company were 'pounced' (a fine powder dusted over a stencil), while others were applied by lettering pencils. The painter then went over these in black paint using brushes that were referred to according to their size in relation to birds, the smallest being a 'lark' and the largest a 'goose'; a Mahl stick and palette rounded off the tools necessary. The lining of the carriages was applied by a long-haired pencil covered in paint in the centre of the moulding, which kept the line straight. A record of all the processes through which the carriage had gone during its latest shopping was marked on the side before the vehicle left the shops, together with the date and the works' code NE 458.

A description of Doncaster Works from the time of the Institution of Mechanical Engineers' visit in 1936 later appeared in the *Journal* of the organisation, and this included details of several recent rationalisations of the various shops. A new central drawing office had been formed to bring the draughtsmen dealing with locomotive, carriage and wagon matters for the whole company under one roof for a free exchange of ideas and practices. A large space was provided in the main office building and arranged in three sections: the north end was occupied by carriage and wagon draughtsmen, numbering around thirty; in the centre there were a group of offices for the heads of the three departments; and the section at the southern end housed the locomotive drawing office, with up to thirty-five employed. The offices were also occupied by the Works Photographer, and rooms were taken by models and drawings – this latter being fireproof.

In 1932 the original Tender and Erecting Shops were converted into the Main Machine Shops. All the machinery was transferred from the Upper and Lower Turneries, including those for brass machining and finishing, and was placed in the western end of the central steam traveller bay. Another section of the shop was arranged to contain all the tools necessary for machining motion components, such as precision grinders, milling machines and turret lathes. The Kearns boring mill was in a dedicated bay with other tools for machining crank axles and axleboxes. The frame cutting and milling tools were still located in the shop and included rollers, slotting and drilling machines and an oxy-acetylene cutting plant. There was also a certain amount of assembly carried out, with the horns, brackets and stays affixed before transfer to the New Erecting Shop.

The Boiler Shop was equipped with a new hydraulic flanging shop, containing three hydraulic presses and three furnaces fed with oil fuel. The largest press had a capacity of 750 tons and a 10-ton overhead travelling crane served the shop. A dedicated building had been erected for tube repairs, and handling had been reduced to a minimum through the installation of several appliances. The tubes were first sorted into batches and examined, those rejected being dropped through a trap door. The tubes cut down for use in smaller boilers were belled and annealed, then stacked, while those continuing in the same type of boiler moved to wait their turn in the electric butt-welder. There were two of these machines, one for dealing with small tubes up to 2¼ inches in diameter, the other superheater flues with a diameter up to 5½ inches, and the time taken to complete the welding process was between 10 and 20 seconds for both. The Wheel Shop could claim up-to-date lathes, drilling and grinding apparatus as well as a 400-ton hydraulic wheel press. Sensitive instruments were used for checking the balance, diameter of tyres, wheel centres, crankpins and axles.

The Carriage Shops were arranged on the progressive system whereby the work flowed in one direction. Raw logs were cut down in the sawmill and the wood then passed to the adjoining Body Shop, which had four lanes for new construction to be carried out. Located to the east was the Carriage Repair Shop. This possessed three tracks on the west side for maintenance and two for heavy work that required the body to be separated from the wheelsets; the total capacity was fifty carriages. Along the southern ends of these five roads was the machine tool bay, with lathes and balancing apparatus for attending to the wheels. Two 20-ton overhead cranes served the lifting bays and 2-ton cranes were used in the machine bay. The average heavy repair was said to take twenty-six working days.

In 1935 a new Weigh House was built in the Crimpsall Repair Shop yard near the Paint Shop. This location was advantageous as making sure that the axle weights were correct before the locomotive was sent into traffic was an important procedure. A. H. Peppercorn explained to the *LNER Magazine* the background to the installation of the Weigh House:

'A few years ago the decision was made that the weighing machines at both Doncaster and Darlington were inadequate for the large engines in use on the LNER and after investigation the CME decided that the design which incorporated a separate weighing machine or individual machine for each wheel, had many advantages over the existing type of table, affording greater accuracy, sensitivity and speed of manipulation. Subsequently Messrs Ransomes & Rapier of Ipswich were contracted to design the new machines and the one at Darlington was installed in 1934 and at Doncaster in 1935.'

The Weigh House was arranged with a pit – 58 feet long and 4 feet deep – running almost the full length of the building, bordered by a pair of rails and containing the weighing equipment. Entry could be gained from both ends and the provision for natural light to enter was generous. There were fourteen separate devices forming the weighing machine, seven on each side, and each had a capacity of 12 tons. The weighing units worked on the steelyard system whereby two arms, one short (supporting the weight of the object) and the other long (resting on

A closer view of one of the individual weighing machines.

a pivot), were out of balance until a weight on the latter brought the pair into balance. With the arrangement at Doncaster the steelyards were connected to each other, which allowed the actual weight of the locomotive to be determined, in addition to displaying the weight supported on each unit. When each individual unit was balanced the springs were adjusted to carry the right weight by turning the nuts on the screwed spring links either tight or loose. With the weight distribution correct, the locomotive rested evenly and level on the springs. When in traffic this allowed the power to be transmitted smoothly and the riding was relatively free from disturbance.

The concrete floor of the pit was perfectly level to ensure great accuracy for the equipment. Each unit was mounted on four wheels, which ran on rails laid in the ground, to allow adjustments to suit the wheel arrangement and spacing of the locomotive under scrutiny. Electric lights were provided for each device and these were set to illuminate the steelyard arms. The part supporting the locomotive's wheel was formed of a substantial metal guide with the top edges inclined upwards from each side to a central ridge, where two 6-inch-diameter rollers were held. Screws positioned these to a point where both were just touching the tyre flange, then the rollers were finely positioned to be completely level. The assembly was then moved upwards to form greater contact, the amount of upwards force necessary being a quarter of a ton. All the

The observation cars used as part of the 'Coronation' sets are under construction in the Carriage Shop – note the wooden roof, while the side panels are metal.

units then took the weight of the locomotive and were raised simultaneously so that they stood just above rail level. The lift was performed by a 5-horsepower motor driving gearing and shafts connected to each unit. The average time taken to weigh a locomotive was 2 hours.

After the success of the 'Silver Jubilee' service, Chief General Manager Sir Ralph Wedgwood sought to introduce another high-speed train, and in this instance the route was King's Cross to Edinburgh. In the meantime another batch of 'A4s' had been ordered from Doncaster (totalling seventeen, later increased to thirty-one), and five of these were specially chosen to haul this train – named the 'Coronation' – when launched for the summer season. Again new coaches were built and these were inspired by the 'Silver Jubilee' set but with modifications after experience gained in service. Perhaps the main one was for all the stock to have a centre aisle with seats positioned on either side and for the restaurant cars to be dispensed with, meals being served at passengers' seats. The set consisted of four twin articulated sets: Brake 3rd/3rd; 3rd/kitchen 3rd; 1st/1st; and kitchen 3rd/3rd Brake. The final item in the formation was the striking 'beavertail' observation carriage, the shape of its end derived by wind-tunnel testing. Construction was the same as the 'Silver Jubilee' apart from the Rexine coating to the steel panels, as this was found to cause corrosion. The interior still used the material and there was a liberal employment of aluminium for the detail fittings.

For passengers travelling between King's Cross and Leeds another new high-speed service was devised and named the 'West Riding Limited'. This was introduced for the start of the winter timetable in 1937 and the coaches provided had the same specifications as the 'Coronation' apart from there being no observation carriage, and the internal decoration was of a different scheme. A fourth

'A4' 'Pacific' No 4491 *Commonwealth of Australia* is ready to leave King's Cross station with the 'Coronation'.

set of carriages was also built to act as a standby should any mechanical faults occur or if maintenance needed to be carried out.

The final new train introduced from Doncaster before the war was erected for the 'Flying Scotsman' in 1938. The two sets consisted of fourteen carriages: Brake 3rd, Composite, 3rd, Composite, 3rd, Buffet, 3rd, triplet Restaurant (slightly longer than the standard), 1st, 3rd, and 3rd Brake. The exterior panels and frames were of teak, double glazing was employed and pressure ventilation used. The interior followed the pattern of the high-speed trains by using Rexine and several shades, including red, blue and peach, contrasted in the different sections. A demonstration of the train was arranged for the press, and to catch their attention the LNER arranged for Stirling 'Single' No 1 to be restored together with coaching stock previously used with the 'Flying Scotsman' in 1888, and this work was carried out at Doncaster.

At the start of the 1930s the construction rate of new wagons was affected and slowed down considerably before improving before the end of the decade. Forty-five 10-ton meat vans were built in 1930, with steel underframes, at a cost of £187, as well as seventeen 8-ton refrigerator vans and a further thirty the next year. During the same period 299 Diagram 64 20-ton brake vans were built, as well as twenty express goods brake vans. With the introduction of containers for the transport of goods and merchandise Doncaster built several variants, including thirty-nine of the BC Type for moving bicycles, fifty of the BD Type, and 200 BK Type containers for furniture removal. During 1938 500 of the small H Type containers were completed and these had the advantage of being able to fit in the standard open wagon and did not require a specialised carrier like the others.

In 1936 Doncaster Wagon Works was busy with an order for 200 12-ton open wagons with a 10-foot wheelbase. Then the following two years saw 700 more completed, but these were fitted with automatic brakes for fast freight services. The stock of single bolster wagons had fallen at this time and replacements were constructed during the year, numbering 100.

The final batch of twenty 'V1s' was completed at the 'Plant' between July 1938 and February 1939. In the meantime a decision had been made to increase the

A 'Coronation' carriage under construction in early May 1937.

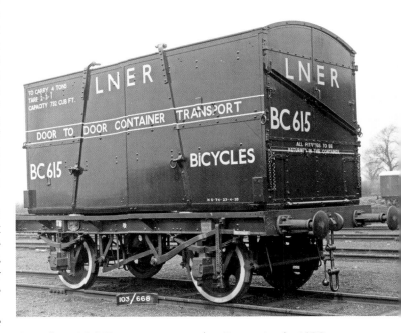

Container BC 615 was constructed at Doncaster in 1936 for the movement of bicycles.

The loss of cattle traffic allowed a number of cattle vans to be converted to container flats as the LNER pushed this new service in the early 1930s. No 150692 was built at Doncaster in 1927 and converted in 1936.

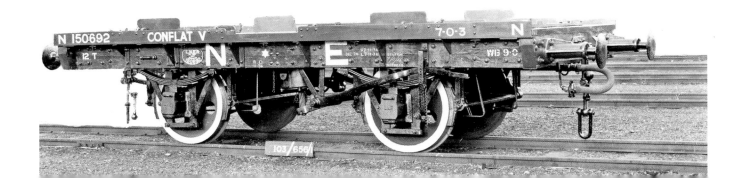

Gangs of men are engaged in erecting wagons at Doncaster Carr c1920 under the supervision of Foreman George Parkin.

No 6701 was completed at Doncaster in August 1940 and was fitted with electrical equipment from Metropolitan Vickers. The body rested on two four-wheel bogies and each axle was driven by a motor; all four could produce 1,740 horsepower continuously.

At the end of the decade there was a growing need for an engine that was not only powerful but also had a wide route availability. Work on this project began in the Doncaster Drawing Office during mid-1939 and soon took the shape of a smaller 'V2' Class 2-6-2. Two were ordered in early 1940, although due to wartime material shortages they were not ready until February and March 1941. No 3401 *Bantam Cock* was the first; it had three cylinders 15 inches by 26 inches with 7-inch piston valves, a 5ft 4in-diameter boiler with 1,799.9sq ft of heating surface and pressure set at 250lb per sq in, and 5ft 8in-diameter coupled wheels. No 3402 was unique in receiving a steel firebox partially fabricated using welding and possessing a Nicholson thermic syphon to improve water circulation and heat transfer.

Early in 1939 an agreement was reached between the workers in the Locomotive, Carriage and Wagon Departments and the LNER for the provision and administration of a Motor Ambulance Fund. The employees evidently felt that there was a need for a vehicle – with a building for storage – to transport them to hospital if serious injury occurred in the shops, or if they fell ill and needed to be taken home. Although instigated at Doncaster Works, the ambulance was available to anyone employed by the LNER in the district. More than 3,400 staff signed up to the Fund and allowed sixpence to be taken out of their pay every quarter for the upkeep of the vehicle and facilities. An incentive for the scheme was that family members were also entitled to use the ambulance and the benefit was retained into retirement. The vehicle

working pressure of the boiler to 200lb per sq in and another ten engines, classified 'V3', were ordered, being built between September 1939 and April 1940. When boiler renewals became necessary the 'V1s' received the Diagram 102HP type fitted to the 'V3s'. A total of sixty-three of the eighty-two class members carried that boiler during their lifetime.

In the mid-1930s Gresley and the LNER decided to experiment with electrification, and the route chosen was the old GCR Wath to Manchester line, which penetrated the difficult terrain of the Pennines. Like the NER before, the 1,500 volts DC overhead system was adopted and Gresley was tasked with preparing a prototype locomotive.

No 6701 outside the Paint Shop with the exterior panels removed to show the arrangement of the internal components.

The result of the accidental Carriage Shop fire that occurred early in the Second World War.

was supplied by specialist firm Wilson & Stockall Ltd and was powered by an Austin six-cylinder engine that generated 18 horsepower.

A number of new machines were installed at the 'Plant' during late 1939/early 1940. One of these was a milling machine from James Archdale & Co Ltd of Birmingham, which could perform several different aspects of the process. The items most commonly milled included pony truck centres, bogie stretchers and axlebox keeps. A wide range of feeds between ¾ and 27 inches per minute could be set, as well as the speed – 16 to 160 revolutions per minute. A special feature was the ability to move from the starting position or to the next milling area very quickly. The spindle was used in partnership with a flywheel to reduce chatter, vibrations and deflections. The motor driving the machine was housed within the bed of the apparatus.

James Bennie & Sons Ltd of Glasgow supplied a laminated spring press with a capacity of 270 tons. This was designed for use with steel bars 6 inches wide by ¾ inch thick, and a number of other tasks could also be completed, such as trimming the bars to the right length, forming the ends and pressing out holes and slots. Several tools were required for these and the machine allowed for all the processes to be carried out on one plate at a time or for a batch to go through each. Springs were produced for all three departments at Doncaster.

When Thompson came to power in 1941 there was some reorganisation of the Locomotive Department. The major one was the movement of the CME's office from King's Cross to Doncaster, which was partially the result of the war and of Thompson being settled in the town at the time. The distinction of separate Mechanical Engineers being responsible for the three main areas of the LNER (Scotland, North East and Southern) was abandoned and replaced by five posts styled after the workshops at the centre of the district – Doncaster, Darlington, Stratford, Gorton and Cowlairs. A. H. Peppercorn took the first-mentioned and was also made Assistant CME in partnership with D. R. Edge, who had been given the same position under Gresley after Bulleid's departure in 1938. H. Harper was placed in charge of the head office and E. Windle was made Chief Draughtsman. D. D. Gray was appointed Head Locomotive Draughtsman and F. Day Head Carriage Draughtsman.

The first task Thompson required Doncaster to carry out was the reconstruction of Robinson's GCR Class '8A' (LNER 'Q4') 0-8-0 tender engines as 'Q1' Class 0-8-0T locomotives. The former class was due to be scrapped if war had not broken out and, as there was a need for shunting engines – 'J50s' had been ordered – to save materials the decision was made to rebuild, which displaced tenders that could be refurbished for use with new stock. No 5058 was the first to be modified at Doncaster in June 1942 and much of the original material was retained, although a new cab and water tanks and bunker had to be fabricated. A further three appeared during the next twelve months before the water capacity was increased and the coal space reduced for the final nine conversions.

Thompson's design policy consisted of reducing the number of classes, which were mainly of pre-Grouping origin, to just ten. The main feature of these was that standard components would be used wherever possible to reduce and simplify the maintenance burden on both

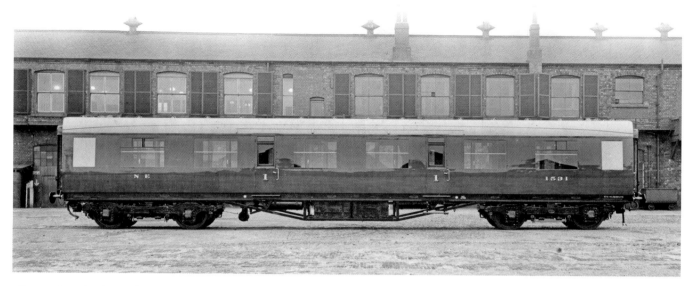

Above Standard 1st Class corridor carriage No 1531 in 1945.

Below The new feature for post-war corridor stock was the transverse corridor.

the works and the sheds. As the war was in full swing Thompson was unable to make much impact immediately and had to be content with producing prototypes to refine his thoughts. A mixed-traffic 'Pacific' was envisaged for future requirements and the CME decided that the 'P2s', which had been under-utilised and had experienced some minor mechanical problems, should prove the test case. No 2005 *Thane of Fife* was taken into Doncaster first and had its cylinders replaced, three sets of Walschaerts valve gear fitted, and the boiler cut down before emerging in January 1943. Thompson was evidently satisfied with the subsequent performance as in September 1943 authorisation was granted to rebuild the remaining five 'P2s', and this was achieved in 1944. A similar type was planned for express passenger traffic and a locomotive with 6ft 8in-diameter coupled wheels was chosen to be rebuilt in 1945. No 4470 *Great Northern* was that engine and, together with new 10-inch piston valves and independent motion, received an 'A4'-type boiler working at 250lb per sq in.

Doncaster was not very active in the construction of new carriages during Thompson's tenure, partly because the Main Carriage Shop burned to the ground on Saturday 21 December 1940 and would not be resurrected until later in the decade. In 1945 two prototypes for future 1st and 3rd Class requirements were constructed with steel body panels secured to teak frames and standard underframes. The interior was the main departure from Gresley's stock as aisles were provided between sets of compartments to ease the congestion when entering or alighting at stations. The interior decor was muted with cream walls and polished woods.

War work was again placed at the 'Plant' and the Carriage Department helped to construct ambulance trains right at the start of the conflict for both home and overseas use. Four-inch high-angle naval guns were constructed by the locomotive shops, in addition to gun mountings for tanks, anti-tank gun carriages, gun baseplates, breech rings for

Gun mountings under construction at Doncaster in 1943, while locomotive work continues in the background.

6-pounders, anti-aircraft searchlights, bodies for Valentine tanks and components for Horsa gliders. Women were again very helpful in assisting with the many varied processes going on during this period. Peter Grafton in *Edward Thompson of the LNER* gives an interesting story relating to one of the tasks carried out by the female staff and how an improvement was affected. Lady Matthews, wife of the LNER Chairman Sir Ronald Matthews, was visiting Thompson one day when she noticed women degreasing locomotive frames. This was done using an agent spread over the plates and the accumulated detritus removed by hand. Lady Matthews suggested that the lot of the staff might be made easier by rinsing the frames instead with water. Thompson agreed and procured hoses for the job.

A special project carried out in early 1945 was the conversion of a 1st Class sleeping carriage into an armour-plated saloon codenamed 'Bayonet' for use by General Eisenhower when he was travelling in Britain and Europe. Doncaster also built fifty of Stanier's 8F Class 2-8-0s between 1943 and 1945.

A number of railway companies had experimented with the use of locomotives with diesel engines for shunting duties before the war. In 1944 the LNER entered the fray

No 1592 was a 1st Class sleeping carriage rebuilt at Doncaster for the use of General Eisenhower as the Second World War came to a close.

The interior of the set, which also included No 1591, and was given the codename 'Bayonet'.

with No 8000, the first of four 0-6-0s fitted with an English Electric six-cylinder engine developing 350 horsepower, a 200kW main generator and two traction motors with a continuous rating of 115 horsepower.

The first new 6ft 2in Thompson 'Pacifics' – later classified 'A2/3' – were authorised from Doncaster in mid-1944, numbering fifteen, and were followed by the

same amount in early 1945. The design of these engines was slightly modified to incorporate a longer boiler and firebox combustion chamber, with large metal-plate smoke deflectors also being fitted. The initial batch was built between May 1946 and September 1947; the boilers were supplied from Darlington. No 500 *Edward Thompson* had the distinction of being the 2,000th locomotive to be erected at Doncaster Works.

In the event the second order was changed as Thompson retired during mid-1946 and was replaced by A. H. Peppercorn. There had been problems with excessive strain around the smokebox with the varieties of 'A2' 'Pacific' and to eliminate these the front end was shortened. Several other minor changes were made before the first, No 525 *A. H. Peppercorn*, was completed in December 1947. While the remaining 'A2s' were in the course of construction, Doncaster began work on the 'A1' Class 'Pacifics', which followed this lead, and a total of twenty-six were completed, taking numbers 60114-129 and 60153-162.

There was a move to use steel for new wagon construction after the war and Doncaster Carr assisted in this project by producing the timber floors for a large number built by an outside firm. With the end of the conflict, surplus rail vehicles became available and the LNER took advantage by purchasing thirty-eight 'Warwell' wagons built for the transportation of tanks. In 1947 these were renovated at Doncaster into 30-ton six-bolster wagons. Additionally, seventeen became 80-ton 'Flatrol'

'A2' 'Pacific' No 500 – later named *Edward Thompson* – creates an impression in the works yard.

Above A. H. Peppercorn and his staff pose in front of the last 'Pacific' built for the LNER just before nationalisation – 'A2' No 525 *A. H. Peppercorn.*

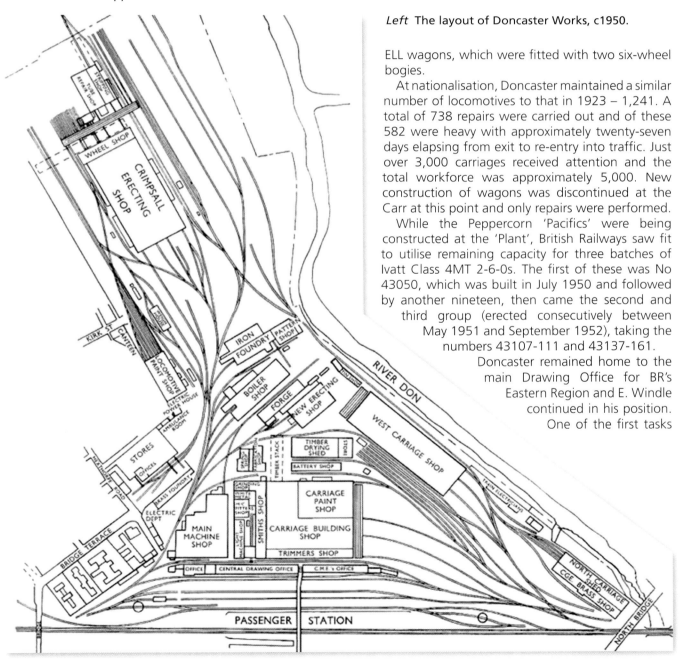

Left The layout of Doncaster Works, c1950.

ELL wagons, which were fitted with two six-wheel bogies.

At nationalisation, Doncaster maintained a similar number of locomotives to that in 1923 – 1,241. A total of 738 repairs were carried out and of these 582 were heavy with approximately twenty-seven days elapsing from exit to re-entry into traffic. Just over 3,000 carriages received attention and the total workforce was approximately 5,000. New construction of wagons was discontinued at the Carr at this point and only repairs were performed.

While the Peppercorn 'Pacifics' were being constructed at the 'Plant', British Railways saw fit to utilise remaining capacity for three batches of Ivatt Class 4MT 2-6-0s. The first of these was No 43050, which was built in July 1950 and followed by another nineteen, then came the second and third group (erected consecutively between May 1951 and September 1952), taking the numbers 43107-111 and 43137-161.

Doncaster remained home to the main Drawing Office for BR's Eastern Region and E. Windle continued in his position. One of the first tasks

Above Plotting valve events in the Drawing Office.

Below The Drawing Office in the early 1960s.

was getting involved in the work needed for the new BR Standard classes. together with Swindon, Brighton and Derby, the office was delegated a specific type to produce. Doncaster was given the Class 5 4-6-0 and Class 4 2-6-0, in addition to components that were destined to be used on all the locomotives such as cylinders, crossheads, slidebars, coupling and connecting rods, and valve gear. However, free rein was not allowed and all designs from the Drawing Office had to be submitted to a committee and approved before specific plans were produced. The draughtsmen were also in constant contact with workshop foremen to pre-empt construction problems and rectify any that did occur.

E. S. Cox in *British Railways Standard Steam Locomotives* commented upon how the dilution of power from the Drawing Offices did not have a negative impact on the completion of the various tasks:

'I cannot pay too high a tribute to the manner in which both officers and men in the different offices faced and accomplished their new tasks. Broadmindedness and good humour lubricated all our contacts, and goodwill and co-operation were forthcoming in ample measure. Indeed, I do not recall a single sour note during the while of this hard slogging work in what was for many an unfamiliar medium.'

The design for the Standard Class 5 followed closely that of Stanier's Class 5 built for the LMS in large numbers during the 1930s and 1940s. The boiler was very similar, together with the frames, although the thickness of the plates was slightly increased and the coupled wheels were increased in diameter by 2 inches to 6ft 2in. Derby Works monopolised construction duties until 1955 when Doncaster built twenty-five (Nos 73100-124) followed by seventeen (73155-171) for the Eastern and North Eastern Regions in 1957. Interestingly, the first batch marked the discontinuation of Doncaster's tri-note whistle, as they were liable to sound uncontrollably on this class and were replaced by a standard type. There were also several other minor detail differences between Class 5s built at the 'Plant' and elsewhere.

As soon as the last LMS Class 4 had been built, Doncaster moved on to produce the BR Standard version, which was considerably lighter than the former, giving a broader sphere of operation. The boiler was based on the LMS version and several features, such as the motion, were the same as those used by the Standard Class 5s. Horwich Works erected the first twenty in 1952 and these were followed by five from Doncaster between December 1952 and January 1953. The 'Plant' continued to build these from October to December 1953 and in several batches subsequently up to 16 October 1957, when a total of seventy engines had been put into service. The last was No 76114, which was also the final steam locomotive to be erected at Doncaster; the final tally was 2,228. *British Railways Standard Steam Locomotives Volume Two* gives the average cost of the final batch from the works as £20,648, while those completed at Horwich at the same time were priced £22,083. There had been a considerable increase of some £4,307 from the first lot.

Rounding off Doncaster's involvement with the

The staff of the Weigh House are pictured in 1957 with BR Standard Class 4 2-6-0 No 76114, which was the last new steam locomotive built at the works.

The remains of the Dynamometer Car ordered by the LNER in conjunction with the Rugby Testing Station project after the Carriage Shop fire of 1940.

construction of the Standard classes was an order for ten Class 4 2-6-4Ts in 1953. These were destined for the Scottish Area, taking numbers 80106-115, and were fitted with water scoops, tablet-catchers and modified superheaters.

The new Carriage Shop in course of erection in July 1948.

In 1947 the task of building a new Carriage Shop began, to replace the one that had been destroyed by fire at the start of the war. A steel frame was used and a tall central bay was incorporated for the installation of two overhead gantry cranes of 25-ton capacity, which allowed carriages to be lifted over each other. The whole workshop comprised Sawmill, Joiners' Shop, Trimming and Upholstery Shop and areas for Fabrication and Assembly. The final LNER coaching stock built under BR – also being the last teak-framed carriages from Doncaster – comprised several Travelling Post Office carriages, 3rd Class Brakes, 1st Class restaurants, sleeper 3rds, semi-open Composites, lavatory Composites and a Dynamometer Car. The latter had been authorised under Gresley as part of the joint venture between the LNER and LMS for the construction of the Locomotive Testing Station at Rugby. The car was in the course of completion when it was damaged by the fire in the Carriage Shop and a replacement was begun just before nationalisation. When sent into traffic during 1951 there was no need for it at Rugby, and Darlington Works assumed responsibility.

Coaching stock was also standardised by BR. There were no major departures from the practices of the 'Big Four' at the time and bogies, underframes and bodies had similarities to their predecessors. Doncaster Carriage

The interior of the new Carriage Shop, which was provided with ample space for lifting.

Shops first received an order from BR in December 1950 for five 1st Class restaurant cars (Diagram 16), ten kitchen carriages (Diagram 700), and forty 2nd Class corridor coaches (Diagram 146). The catering vehicles generally followed Gresley's LNER design and were fitted with anthracite cooking equipment. The stock was completed between May 1951 and November 1952.

At the end of 1949 the last CME of the LNER and current CME for the North Eastern and Eastern Regions of BR, A. H. Peppercorn, retired after an association with the GNR and LNER of nearly 45 years. He had begun his career at Doncaster in 1905 when taken on as a Premium Apprentice under H. A. Ivatt and was a contemporary with W. O. Bentley, who later left the railways and subsequently founded Bentley Motors Ltd. This demonstrates that, by and large, the training provided by the railway workshops was applicable to other areas of engineering and many of the students, either necessarily or by choice, followed this career path. Peppercorn represented the other side, whereby progression through the various levels could ultimately lead to the pinnacle of the profession. J. S. Jones, whose retirement was recorded in the *LNER Magazine* during 1955, had also been a Premium Apprentice at Doncaster in 1907 and went through several management positions during his career; these included Assistant Works Manager Doncaster during the early 1930s and later

Works Manager Gorton, then Dukinfield, during the war. Mr Jones ended his career as Assistant Locomotive Superintendent Eastern Region.

Peppercorn was fondly remembered by many of the

In the late 1940s and early 1950s the use of jigs was widely embraced for carriage construction as designs moved away from wood to metal, which required welding.

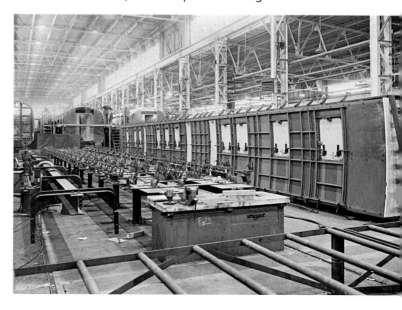

The much-liked A. H. Peppercorn is presented with retirement gifts from his colleagues in late 1949.

people he came into contact with in the various areas of the LNER. He was succeeded by J. F. Harrison, who had also been a Premium Apprentice at Doncaster, studying under Gresley in the early 1920s. He was made Assistant to Peppercorn in 1947 and in 1951 took over on the London Midland Region before replacing R. A. Riddles in 1958 as CME of BR, holding the post until his retirement in 1966. While at Derby Harrison tried to inject some Doncaster features into the design of the Class 8 'Pacific' No 71000 *Duke of Gloucester*, then under consideration, but these were rejected on cost grounds as well as being non-standard with the Class 7 'Pacifics'.

At the end of September 1953 Doncaster Works celebrated its centenary and several events were organised for the occasion. Over the weekend of the 19th and 20th an exhibition of locomotives, carriages and wagons was held, together with other entertainments for the 40,000 visitors who attended. One of these was a model railway constructed at the 'Plant', which transported 10,000 people over the two days. R. A. Riddles performed the opening ceremony, which was presided over by the Mayor of Doncaster, who was a former employee of the works, and the works Chaplain. An interesting follow-up to the open day took place on Thursday 24 September, when the public

was allowed access to the workshops while normal tasks were being carried out, and some 10,000 people enjoyed this rare treat. Transport to the open day on 20 September was provided from King's Cross behind the two surviving Ivatt 'Atlantics' – Nos 251 and 990 *Henry Oakley* – and this was an event in itself, drawing large crowds along the whole length of the line between London and Doncaster. The return journey that day was made behind pioneer 'A4' 'Pacific' No 60014 *Silver Link*, which was in the hands of the equally famous Driver E. Hailstone. A similarly popular special train was run between King's Cross and Leeds with the same locomotives the following weekend.

During the war years and the period following, the maintenance of locomotives reached a low ebb because of shortages of materials, loss of the workforce and the inability to entice new employees to the job. An example of how this situation affected the stock is given by the 'A4' Class. The average annual mileage of the engines in 1950 and 1951 was more than 56,000 and 52,000 respectively, and in 1956 more than 65,000 miles was achieved with around 70% availability. The Haymarket 'A4s', although outnumbered by their English classmates, ran higher average mileages over a twelve-month period. In the early 1950s the 'A4s' north of the border ran approximately

60,000-65,000 miles, then in the latter part of the decade the average went to more than 70,000 miles, with similar advances in availability. Because of improvements made, both generally and in specific areas of workshop and maintenance practices, mileages for many of the 'A4s' increased to nearly 100,000 miles, with high rates of availability and unbroken service on the principal expresses.

These increases were partly due to the addition of the Kylchap double blastpipe and chimney for all class members. The appointment of K. J. Cook as Mechanical & Electrical Engineer North Eastern and Eastern Areas in 1951 also played a part. Cook had been educated at Swindon Works and had risen to be the Works Manager there in 1937, then becoming the Mechanical & Electrical Engineer Western Region. Once at Doncaster, Cook set about improving workshop practice in order to increase the reliability of all the locomotives repaired there. One method introduced was optical alignment of the cylinders, frames and axleboxes in order to reduce stresses when running, either arising from the track or the movement of the valve gear. Cook argued that the greater the accuracy in the set-up of the axles on which the different parts moved, the lower the maximum stresses caused. A high standard of set-up would also lead to reduced tolerances, which in the Gresley 'Pacifics' had always been quite generous. The result of improving the latter was that the rate of wear and play in the joints of the motion would be much reduced, leading to higher mileages between repairs. Traditionally the centre lines of the cylinders and the lining-up of the axle centres from the former was achieved via fine lengths of wire that had been positioned by finding the centres through the use of callipers. Optical devices were pioneered for the process in the 1920s and were subsequently adopted by the GWR

No 60014 *Silver Link* – just one of Doncaster's famous engines – was on hand for the celebrations of the centenary of the 'Plant' in 1953.

and used at Swindon for many years.

In his paper delivered on the method to the Institution of Mechanical Engineers in 1955, Cook comments on the procedure and the background to its introduction at Doncaster:

'At the Mechanical Tool Exhibition in 1952 a British optical exhibit was noticed which appeared to be capable of development although at that time it had no reference to locomotives. The makers became very anxious to cooperate and quite quickly a method much simpler than the German, and capable of proceeding very much further in the quest for accuracy, was produced. It became known as the Auto-Reflection method, using instead of a collimator a reflecting mirror fixed parallel to and in line with a straight edge. The auxiliary apparatus and measuring rods are also much simpler.'

In addition to the optical alignment method of set-up, Cook brought the Churchward/de Glehn type of big end bearing from Swindon. Gresley's original 'marine' type bearing was made of two parts of bronze that had two sections each of white metal inserted $3/8$ inch deep into the bearing. The Swindon type was a continuous white metal surface set on to a brass surface and there were two gaps at the bottom and the top to allow felt pads to lubricate the metal; these had to be very carefully fitted or the component would fail. The bearing was cautiously machined to ensure the correct fit around the axle and the success of this new type was accompanied by vigilant maintenance and religious inspection every 12,000 and 24,000 miles. P. N. Townend – Shedmaster at King's Cross during this period – also notes that reliability was considerably improved by having the 'A4s' sent to Doncaster Works for their 36,000-mile inspection, when the motion, piston valves and cylinders would be comprehensively examined. This was done because a number of the components would have to be shipped to Doncaster for repair and the axleboxes had to come the other way, so for the ease of everyone concerned the task was delegated to the works.

The National Savings Movement was formed during 1916 as a way to augment capital for the war effort and for ordinary people to save money. However, the movement continued beyond 1918 and by the 1950s had around 7,000,000 members. The Railway Executive endorsed National Savings, and *British Railways Eastern Region Magazine* reported that Doncaster Works was the base for an Area Committee with the Works Manager as Chairman. Also mentioned was that there had been a recent increase in the membership at the works and the amount of money being saved. This led to the 'Plant' being used to publicise a campaign to initiate more people into the movement, both in Doncaster and further afield.

In April 1953 the Carriage Shops received a large order for 185 non-gangwayed stock to be used as part of suburban trains. These comprised eighteen 1st Class Open carriages, twenty-eight Open 2nds with lavatories, eight-nine Brake 2nd coaches, and fifty Composites with toilets. Two different lengths of underframes were used – 63ft 6in and 57 feet – and the length of the compartments varied as a result. This was more pronounced with the toilet-fitted stock, which was generally confined to the ER. The order was the only one placed as the Modernisation Plan was announced shortly afterwards and diesel multiple units (DMUs) gained favour for future construction.

Soon after the Modernisation Plan emerged, BR built fourteen prototype carriages for main-line trains in an attempt to gain a fresh perspective on the specifications and ideas being employed at the time. Private firms were invited to participate and Doncaster Carriage Works was given the honour of building from the plans produced by BR. Two were Open 1st saloons and these differed in seating arrangements, one having swivelling and partially reclining seats, while the other had fixed seats with tables positioned between the two rows of three seats. Another two were Open 2nd Class carriages with seating for either forty-eight or sixty-four, and the final pair were a Corridor 1st and a Corridor 2nd. These two differed from the standard by having a compartment removed and the free space distributed to those that remained to increase comfort. These new carriages were presented to the public for their feedback (also carried out while in traffic) at Battersea between 28 and 30 June 1957; also present were a number of new diesel locomotives, including the prototype 'Deltic'.

Accidents have been a part of workshop life since their inception. After the Second World War was there was a greater emphasis on health and safety in the workplace and this happened to coincide with an increased understanding of rehabilitation following serious injury. In early 1957 the Doncaster Rehabilitation Centre was opened to help those both moderately and severely harmed performing railway duties in the area. Under the direction of Dr J. Sharp Grant, Regional Medical Officer, Eastern Region, the facility was run by Medical Officer, Doncaster, Dr W. Turnbull on the eastern perimeter of the Crimpsall site. There was a particular emphasis on providing exercise that was controlled and restorative for the patient, while also re-establishing a sense of worth and productivity. To this end, machine tools were installed with special adaptors for the patients, in addition to filing and stamping being performed. Medical professionals at Doncaster Royal Infirmary and the patients' General Practitioners were also in constant contact with the centre to oversee and recommend treatments.

The general welfare of the workforce at the 'Plant' was overseen by Miss G. Ward, who had joined the LNER as a Woman's Welfare Assistant in 1943. She was one of several people employed by the ER to give help and advice to railwaymen and their families in matters concerning illness, death, personal problems, work-related issues, etc. Miss Ward spent much of her time travelling around the Doncaster area to visit men injured at work or with serious illnesses to see how they were and if they required any assistance.

While taking care of current employees, Doncaster was

Engineers of the future outside Doncaster's Apprentice Training School.

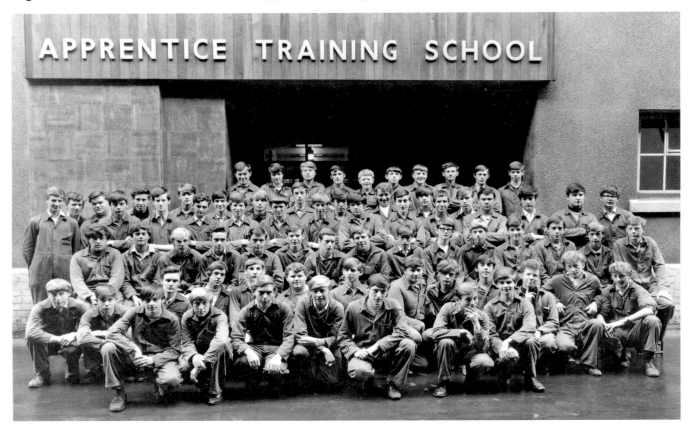

A new electric locomotive for the Kent Coast scheme is wheeled in the New Erecting Shop during 1959.

also looking to the future and offered a series of works courses to boys attending grammar school. The 'Plant' was one of just several places of industry that had arranged a programme for ten boys to sample a number of areas to give an idea of the careers available. At Doncaster there were presentations and discussions held before visits were made to the control room for the Woodhead route at Penistone and the engines sheds at Lincoln and Reddish.

Electrification of a number of suburban routes out of Liverpool Street station called for new electric stock to be ready for the opening during 1960. In the late 1950s Doncaster Carriage Shops were reorganised in order to construct the vehicles, and a bay in the Building Shop with two extra tracks taking four sets was turned over for the task, which also involved fitting the motors. Several of the tools associated with old methods of construction were dispensed with and new types acquired. One of these was a Loudon 4-foot wheel lathe; this allowed the tyres of wheelsets fitted with roller-bearing axles to be machined without having to remove the axleboxes – saving a good deal of time and labour. A total of nineteen four-carriage sets were built at Doncaster (with bogies from York) and the formation comprised Motor Coach, Trailer 2nd Open, Brake 2nd Open and Composite Open with lavatory. The

sets were also fitted for multiple working with other units.

Another line to be electrified was the former London, Tilbury & Southend route, which had previously been run by the LMS from the Grouping to nationalisation, then being transferred to the Eastern Region. Doncaster again received a portion of the contract for new vehicles, which were of a similar formation as the aforementioned electric stock; the works had to produce 112 Driving Trailer coaches and thirty-six Trailer Composite coaches. Seating was for nineteen 1st Class and 344 2nd Class; the former were seated in compartments while the latter had open accommodation with toilets provided. Special attention was paid to the suspension to make the ride as smooth and quiet as possible, with liners of asbestos and synthetic resin to reduce noise; the body sides and roof were similarly treated.

The first main-line diesels ordered for the ER arrived in the late 1950s and Doncaster had to inspect and perform trials with them before they could be accepted from the manufacturer for service. In the Crimpsall Repair Shops changes were made to accommodate them for when repairs would be required. Half of the bays were initially turned over to the diesels and the floor had to be lowered in order for the engines to clear the bodies when lifted

'A4' No 60009 *Union of South Africa* was the last steam locomotive to be repaired at Doncaster, and this group of staff was one of several that posed to mark the occasion.

out by the overhead cranes. Those in use were replaced during 1960, being nearly seventy years old, and two new 45-ton-capacity examples were fitted, with power provided by four electric motors; the span of each crane was 45ft 6in. A new area near the Pattern Shop was provided for the Fibreglass Shop, which made new parts for the diesel locomotives, in addition to replacing worn or broken sections.

A number of main-line electric locomotives were needed for several lines, including the Southern Region's main lines from London to the Kent ports. The twenty-four locomotives built at Doncaster ran off the third rail at 750V DC (rated at 2,300 continuous horsepower) and could also take power from the overhead cables that were used in some sheds and sidings. No E5000 was completed in December 1958 and the last, No E5023, in October 1960.

Another scheme saw the West Coast Main Line converted in stages between 1961 and 1965 to use 25kV AC overhead wires. The LMR called on the 'Plant' to erect forty locomotives, and a further sixty were ordered from contractors. All were generally similar and could develop 3,200 horsepower, with a top speed of 100mph. Details were left to the discretion of the manufacturers, and this mainly concerned the traction motors, which were supplied from several sources; Doncaster used British Thomson-Houston motors. The works also designed a new type of bogie for the locomotives, with frames formed from several sections welded together. Difficulty was encountered with expansion during the process, then cooling, which changed the dimensions, requiring an allowance to be provided in the plates when they were cut. The *British Railways Eastern Region Magazine* of 1962 announced that after the first – No E3056 – was delivered in August 1961, Doncaster received a letter from the Electrical Engineer of the LMR congratulating the men on producing a fine piece of machinery.

The last steam locomotive to be repaired at Doncaster Works was *Union of South Africa* in November 1963. The 'Plant' had kept the engine fresh for more than twenty-six years and more than 1.6 million miles. According to *Locomotives of the LNER Part 2A*, No 60009 held the record for the highest mileage achieved by an 'A4' between General Repairs, with 126,814 in twenty-one months

between 1950 and 1952. Many more famous engines – not forgetting the workhorses of the GNR, LNER and BR – had been kept in traffic over 110 years and as many as 40,000 repairs had been carried out. However, the works not only dealt with construction and repairs, but also scrapping of locomotives, and perhaps thousands were dealt with.

A constant between the steam and diesel eras was the works' Research Department, which included the Chemist and Metallurgist Department, carrying out various tests on components and materials from Doncaster, Stratford and firms supplying the shops. The facilities were located near the 'Plant' in a building formerly occupied by the town's workhouse, and Mr C. Dinsdale MSc was in charge of three assistants, A. Lockley, T. Evans and L. Hornsby. A special check was made of the welds performed in all of the shops at Doncaster by means of a 150kV X-ray unit, with even the most experienced welders coming under scrutiny from time to time. Broken components were also examined to ascertain the reasons behind the failure; this also applied to machine and hand tools. Several devices for testing were present, one being used to determine the strength of steel to be used in the works. Another piece of equipment used regularly was a projection microscope equipped with various lenses that enabled magnification up to 3,000 times.

With steam locomotives no longer maintained at Doncaster, several of the shops were converted for other uses. The Iron Foundry was fitted out for shot blasting to take place and to repair chains for heavy lifting as well as various types of cranes. The Boiler Shop became a Fabrication Shop and the Forge and Spring Shops were demolished. The work in the latter was transferred to the Brass Foundry, and the Tender Shop was reorganised for diesel locomotives to be stripped of various components before entering the Crimpsall. To the east of the latter a Test House was built in 1965, where two diesel locomotives could be accommodated simultaneously. The year also saw the end of new carriage construction and the return of the Wagon Works from the Carr. The North and West Carriage Shops were converted for DMU maintenance and a Test House similar to that built at the Crimpsall was erected between the two. The main Carriage Repair and Building Shops became the Heavy and Light Wagons

'Deltic' diesel locomotive No 9019 *Royal Highland Fusilier* in the Test House built on the north-west side of the Crimpsall site in 1965.

Diesel engines receive maintenance in the Crimpsall Repair Shop during March 1967.

Repair Shops respectively.

In 1968 BR split the Workshop Division from the main business and the new concern became British Rail Engineering Limited. Doncaster was one of the thirteen

works run by BREL and continued to build and repair stock for BR. A new remit, which had not hitherto been allowed by the Transport Act 1962, was to take contracts for projects unrelated to BR. The work received subsequently did depart from railway vehicles, such as fabricating girder

The finishing touches are applied to London Transport battery locomotive No L44, which was one of ten built between 1973 and 1974.

Class 56 No 56004 required more than four months of attention to repair this collision damage in early 1984.

sections for bridges and later farming equipment, but as the workshops' main strength was the construction of locomotives and wagons these were primarily built to ...order. In 1969 the Hunslet Engine Co subcontracted Doncaster to build diesel-electric locomotives for Northern Ireland Railways and in the early 1970s battery locomotives were erected for London Transport.

In the second half of the 1970s Doncaster was spurred into action after BR received thirty 3,250-horsepower Class 56 diesel locomotives from Electropute, Romania.

These required much modification to meet the necessary standard for operation in Britain, and subsequently the 'Plant' was given orders for a further eighty-five class members. The workmanship of these was so good that Doncaster was authorised to build the new Class 58s, and this required some changes to the New Erecting Shop. A modular construction technique was used whereby the locomotive was built-up from several sections, which reduced costs and increased interchangeability. The first (No 58001) was finished before the end of 1982 and a

New Build and Paint Shop staff celebrate the construction of the first Class 58 diesel locomotive on 11 April 1983.

Class 91 electric No 91017 is suspended by Matterson jacks in 2-bay of the Crimpsall Repair Shop. *Neil Daykin*

total of fifty would be erected up to 1986.

The workshops continued to be a major centre for locomotive maintenance and received several class types, from the 08 Class shunters to the powerful Class 55 'Deltic' express engines. Reconstruction duties were also undertaken on Class 84 and 85 electric locomotives, in addition to fifty of the Class 50 type from the Western Region. These had the ventilation improved, electrics simplified, new brake systems fitted and some external modifications to keep the class working into the late 1980s and early 1990s, when all were withdrawn; a large number have found their way into preservation.

As part of the break-up of British Rail in the late 1980s and early 1990s, BREL was split and sold off to private investors. Doncaster's Crimpsall Repair Shop (where some 750 people were employed) remained part of BR in the newly formed British Rail Maintenance Limited, which saw the works retain much of the maintenance remit that had been enjoyed for a number of years previously. However, the Government was fully determined to privatise all of BR and in 1995 Doncaster was purchased by Asea Brown Boveri, which soon afterwards merged with Daimler-Benz to form Adtranz; later in the early 21st century the concern was sold to Bombardier. During this period the 'Plant' continued with diesel maintenance and the works were also engaged with repairs for the Class 91 high-speed electric locomotives and carriage sets. A new task brought over from the old West Carriage Shop and North

Carriage Shed was repair work for DMUs.

While the Crimpsall was under the ownership of BRML/ABB/Adtranz, much of the early works site was taken over by RFS Industries, a new venture that acquired Thomas Hill Ltd of Rotherham. The latter was a well-known manufacturer of diesel shunting locomotives for industry and some of this work was undertaken at Doncaster, comprising narrow-gauge engines for the Channel Tunnel project. In the mid-1990s all operations were concentrated at Doncaster and this brought maintenance of the Class 08 shunters from Thomas Hill's Kilnhurst Works site. New construction and maintenance of locomotives and repairs to wagons were the primary duties, and this continued under Wabtec Rail after a takeover in 1998. The works also shared repair work for DMUs with the Crimpsall site.

During the late 1980s a National Supply Centre, later known as Railpart, was formed in several of the buildings at Doncaster, including the Iron Foundry, Boiler Shop, Stores, West Carriage Shop and North Carriage Shed. The role of the NSC was to centralise all necessary materials, both new and refurbished, for repairs to rolling stock and infrastructure.

Sadly, the Crimpsall Repair Shop closed in the mid-2000s and the extensive buildings were cleared quietly in 2008. Thankfully the main site is still in use by Wabtec and Railpart, now known as Unipart Rail, keeping Doncaster's strong railway connections firmly intact.

Above The Carriage Shop turned over to wagon maintenance.

Below The Crimpsall Repair Shop is demolished during late April 2008. *Derek Porter*

4

Gateshead

The Newcastle & Darlington Junction Railway (N&DJR) was formed in June 1842 after the original company – the Great North of England Railway, authorised to build a railway line from York to Newcastle – had run out of steam at Darlington. Both George Hudson and Robert Stephenson were heavily involved in the new scheme, which saw powers granted for running rights over existing lines and short sections of line installed to fill the gaps on the way to the terminus. The latter was located at Greenesfield, Gateshead, on the south bank of the Tyne, and the public opening took place on 19 June 1844. The station contained a single platform, covered by a roof of two spans, and the frontage was classical in the Ionic tradition; a small hotel was also provided.

With this project completed, Hudson moved forward with the next stage of his plan to connect York and Edinburgh. The Newcastle & Berwick Railway was formed to join the North British Railway at the latter point, although there was initial uncertainty as to where to cross the Tyne. Subsequently, the decision was made to bridge the river just to the north-east of Greenesfield station, and Robert Stephenson carried out the design work. A new station was also deemed desirable on the northern side of the Tyne and this also allowed the Newcastle & Carlisle Railway to access the facility for a free exchange of custom. Newcastle-upon-Tyne Central station was opened on 30 August 1850, and at the same time Greenesfield station was closed. By this time several amalgamations had occurred and the operating company was the York, Newcastle & Berwick Railway (YN&BR).

As the relatively new Greenesfield station was left standing, the company did not entertain the idea of demolishing the buildings and selling the land, but instead put them to a new use. Interestingly, this turned out to be

A map of Gateshead Works at the peak of the shops' importance, c1900.

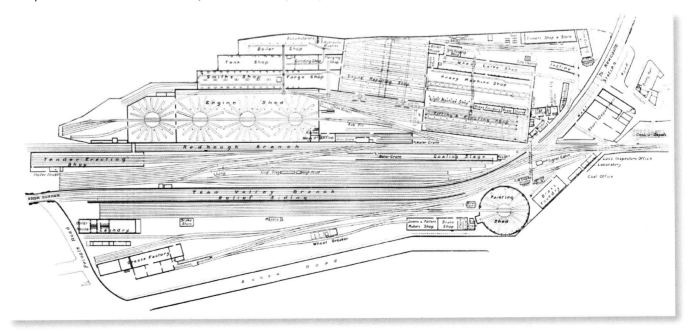

the YN&BR locomotive repair shops. The conversion started towards the end of 1851 with Richard Cail contracted to undertake masonry works, Hawks, Crawshay & Co engaged to alter the roof, and Robert Stephenson & Co to supply some of the machinery. Only a small amount of modifications were necessary for the transformation, and the original platform area became an Engine Repair Shop, a Tender Shop and a Machine Shop. Offices were established in the former hotel, although there was apparently a period when the shops were in use at the same time as the latter. *The Engineer* of 18 December 1896 commented that there were men employed at the works who could remember whisky being passed through to keep the cold out in the winter months – as well as the heat in the summer! Soon after Gateshead was operational a Boiler Shop was commissioned and later erected on land a short distance to the north-east of the main workshops, and by the mid-1850s a large roundhouse had been built nearby.

Gateshead Works became operational around the time that the North Eastern Railway (NER) was formed, and the Locomotive Department was headed by Edward Fletcher, who had been apprenticed to George Stephenson before taking the Locomotive Superintendent's position with the N&DJR and its successors. The stock of the NER at the time consisted of nearly 400 locomotives, with the majority, passenger types, belonging to the YN&BR. The companies each had their own workshops, which were evidently running smoothly, as there was no interference from Fletcher for a time following amalgamation. At Gateshead he was busy keeping the main-line stock in working order and up to date, yet before long he had the shops erecting a new locomotive for freight traffic – No 13 – in June 1857. This formed the basis of a type subsequently built regularly by the workshops. A 2-2-2 passenger engine was built before the end of the decade and soon afterwards 2-4-0s were being erected for the expresses,

supplemented by locomotives of similar design purchased from the trade. There were some minor alterations to the works site at the end of the 1850s and during the 1860s when a large stores was added, a Paint Shop established in an old running shed, and an extension made to the northern side of the main workshops.

The motive power of the 1860s and early 1870s was characterised by the construction of 2-4-0s for both express and secondary passenger trains. Many of these were built at Gateshead and augmented by examples built by firms such as Beyer, Peacock & Co and Neilson & Co, but the locomotives were not of one class and were mainly specialised for the duties intended. The two firms were also contracted to erect Fletcher's 'BTP' Class 0-4-4T for local services, and Gateshead was employed on this duty before the end of the decade. The works was again marginally involved in the production of 0-6-0 goods locomotives until the mid-1870s, as the majority of the engines for this role were produced elsewhere.

Towards the end of Fletcher's superintendence Gateshead took a more prominent role in construction duties for all types and was supported by Darlington Works. For example, between 1872 and 1876 more than 150 of the '708' Class were built by outside firms before Gateshead erected a similar number up to the mid-1880s. These engines had 17-inch by 24-inch cylinders, 4ft 3in-diameter boilers working at 140lb per sq in, and 5-foot-diameter coupled wheels. This also applied to the '901' Class for express passenger trains, as the first two locomotives were built at Gateshead in 1872 before twenty were completed by Beyer, Peacock & Co and Neilson & Co; thereafter the remaining thirty-three built to the specifications were completed at Gateshead. The class had 17-inch by 24-inch cylinders, a 4ft 3in-diameter boiler working at 140lb per sq in, and 7-foot-diameter coupled wheels in a 2-4-0 formation. Over the same period a

Fletcher 'BTP' Class 0-4-4T No 1000 was built at Gateshead in June 1880.

This section of the Machine Shop at Gateshead, looking east, was part of the original station, and some of the remaining ornate ironwork can be seen on the left.

The Boiler Shop in the 1880s.

version of the '901' Class with smaller 6-foot-diameter wheels was constructed in the shops, numbering fifteen and designated the '1440' Class.

To meet the added strain on the workshops at Gateshead a programme of reorganisation was begun at the start of the 1880s. Two roundhouses in use for stabling locomotives were taken out of use and transferred to the works to be refitted as a Smiths' Shop and Tank Shop, while land at the rear became the new Boiler Shop and space underneath was provided to accommodate

further smiths. The land between the Erecting Shop and the remaining roundhouses, which had partially been occupied by the old Boiler Shop, was claimed to build a large Repair Shop split into two sections and arranged with stalls running along the eastern and western sides. The locomotives gained access to these via two central roads (one for each section) and turntables were housed under cover at the southern end of the building.

After Fletcher's retirement, Alexander McDonnell was appointed and his first design went into production at Darlington. Gateshead was subsequently engaged to erect the new express passenger design, which departed

No 180 was the third of McDonnell's 4-4-0s to be built at Gateshead in 1884.

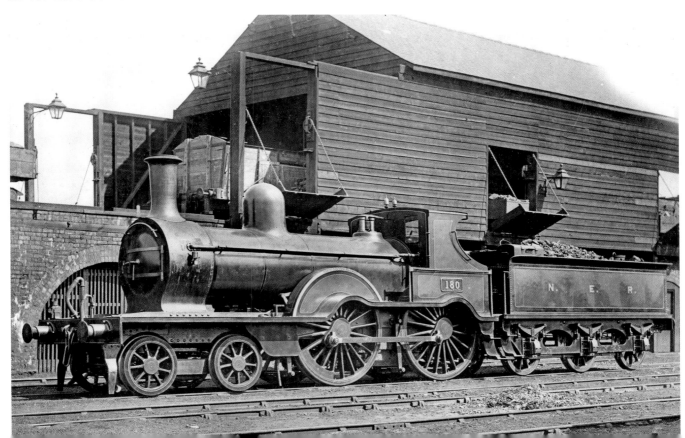

Worsdell Class 'A' 2-4-2T No 674 on the turntable at Whitby.

from previous NER practice by using a front bogie with swing-link suspension, and had left-hand drive. A total of eight were turned out from February to September 1884 with 17-inch by 24-inch cylinders, a 4ft 3in-diameter boiler working at 140lb per sq in, and 6ft 7in-diameter coupled wheels. A second batch of the same number was built before the end of the year, but by this time the drivers had built up a fierce opposition to the class, backed up by

poor performances in traffic. The negativity surrounding McDonnell forced his resignation in late 1884.

A committee was formed under General Manager Henry Tennant to design new express locomotives to replace the McDonnell 4-4-0s. While the first of these '1463' Class 2-4-0s were built at Darlington, ten were built at Gateshead in mid-1885. With regard to the 4-4-0s, material had been amassed for the construction of further examples, and

Class 'C' 0-6-0 No 619 was constructed at Gateshead May 1889 and was converted from compound working in December 1907. The engine survived to December 1949.

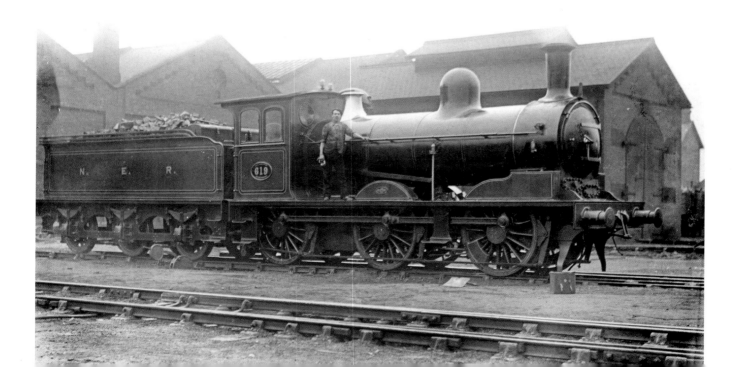

when these were cancelled thoughts turned to how to use this up. The result was a small number of eight Class '8' 0-6-0Ts built at Gateshead in the latter part of 1885 for shunting duties.

T. W. Worsdell took up the top position in September 1885 and during the five years that he was employed Gateshead and Darlington solely carried out the NER's locomotive construction. The first design to appear was the Class 'A' 2-4-2T in March 1886, which had 18-inch by 24-inch cylinders, a 4ft 3in-diameter boiler with pressure set at 160lb per sq in, and 5ft 7in-diameter coupled wheels. A total of sixty were completed in a number of batches up to 1892. Perhaps due to his indifferent experience with compounding express locomotives on the GER and the recent tribulations of McDonnell with engines for this work, Worsdell chose to trial the system on a goods design. This was the Class 'C' 0-6-0, with a high-pressure cylinder of 18-inch diameter and a low-pressure cylinder at 26 inches, both having a stroke of 24 inches, while the boiler was 4ft 3in in diameter, with a heating surface of 1,026sq ft and a 17.2sq ft grate. Joy's valve gear was fitted with slide valves in place of the usual Stephenson motion. Another notable feature was the cab, which was enclosed, offering the enginemen plenty of protection from the elements, a novelty at the time. While the first 'C' Class engine was in traffic undergoing trials, ten normal engines were built for comparative purposes, classified 'C1'. In the event the compound engine proved to be a success and 140 more were built at Gateshead to 1892.

The 'C' Class compounds provided the basis for the 2-4-0 express passenger type built in 1886, although an update was a larger boiler with the pressure increased to 175lb per sq in. No 1324 was the first of two locomotives built at Gateshead as Class 'D', and the second of the pair was fitted with experimental piston valves. After the pioneer engine had run in traffic for a time, the power created by the cylinders when running at speed was found to cause an unsteadying effect and the leading pony truck was replaced by a bogie for the production series. The first of these ten was built in 1887 and designated Class 'F'; ten simple expansion variants were built at the same time as Class 'F1'. A final batch of fifteen were built at the end of Worsdell's tenure.

An 0-6-0T design had the honour of being the second largest class produced during Worsdell's time in office, but the construction of the 120 class members fell on Darlington's shoulders. The remainder of Gateshead's output during this time consisted of a small number of locomotives of several classes, including the 'H' Class 0-4-0Ts, 'H1' 0-6-0Ts, 'I' and 'J' 4-2-2s, and 'K' 0-4-0Ts. The twenty 'singles' (split evenly between the two classes), constructed between 1888 and 1890, were all compounds, the former being for secondary passenger services while the latter took on the main-line expresses. The 'I' Class engines were similar to the 'F' Class compounds and had 7ft 1¼in drivers. For the 'J' Class the cylinders were slightly altered, the high-pressure one being 20 inches by 24 inches and the low pressure one 28 inches by 24 inches; the driving wheels were 7ft 7¼in in diameter.

Wilson Worsdell had been employed with the NER from 1883 as Assistant Locomotive Superintendent, and when his brother retired he rose to the Locomotive

W. M. Smith's experimental three-cylinder compound 4-4-0 No 1619 is pictured at York c1900. The engine has a cross-tube firebox that originally had no access points, but these were subsequently added as depicted.

Superintendent's role. Worsdell's first class consisted of just ten 0-6-0Ts for banking duties on the inclines around Newcastle, and were built at Gateshead between 1891 and 1892. The cylinders were 19 inches diameter by 24 inches stroke, a 4ft 3in-diameter boiler was fitted with 1,093sq ft of heating surface, and the working pressure was 160lb per sq in; the diameter of the driving wheels was 4ft 7¼in, which, in addition to the boiler, became standard for several classes subsequently.

Wilson Worsdell did not share his brother's favour for compound working and only built one of the type early in the 1890s. This was Class 'M' 4-4-0 No 1619, which was similar to the earlier 'F' Class compounds, but had larger-diameter driving wheels and boiler. Worsdell also had twenty simple locomotives constructed at Gateshead at the same time, classified 'M1'; these were generally similar to the 'M' Class but with 19-inch by 26-inch cylinders and valves operated by Stephenson's motion. Although there was said to be a small saving in fuel by the compound engine, this was not enough to offset the non-standard cylinder arrangement, and Worsdell and the Board were happy to end this experiment, in addition to beginning the conversion of the older compound locomotives to simple expansion.

At the end of 1894 the first of fifty 'P' Class 0-6-0s emerged from Gateshead for use on mineral traffic. The boiler was the standard 4ft 3in type used on other classes at this time and the cylinders were 18 inches diameter by 24 inches stroke. Construction continued up to early 1897 when slight modifications were made to the design, and the 'P1' Class was built at the works from 1898 to 1902. Later, the 'P2' Class was produced when the NER increased the loads moved by freight trains, and for this to be achieved a 5ft 6in boiler was fitted; twenty were built in 1905.

The Engineer of 18 December 1896 recorded that at the time there were around 1,500 at work in the various shops at Gateshead, which was managed by Robert Stirling, the eldest son of GNR Locomotive Superintendent Patrick Stirling. Also given was a description of the site. On the eastern side was the Erecting Shop (349 feet long by 88 feet wide), which was served by two 25-ton overhead cranes supplied by Craven Brothers, and flanking on either side was a large number of benches fitted with vices for various tasks to be carried out. Adjoining in the northern half of the building were the Machine and Fitting Shops. One of the tasks carried out in this section was the cutting out and machining of locomotive frame plates, which was done with a punching machine. Previously a cutter was used, but led to deformation of the metal; as a result a quarter-inch margin was given at the edges of the plate so this would not occur. Eight plates were cut at once and slotting and drilling of various holes was performed at the same time. A slotting machine built by Fairburn, Naylor & McPherson of Leeds was used to finish the frames to a high degree of accuracy and to cut out the gaps for the horns; the drilling machine was from another firm in the city, Buckton & Co.

A large-face lathe had recently been employed to machine the sliding blocks used as part of the Joy valve gear. This task had formerly been done individually on a milling machine, taking a great deal of time, but the new method saw up to thirty blocks prepared at one time. Two special steel chucks were said to be in use at Gateshead, proving suitable for several drilling tasks, and not to be seen in use at any other workshop in the country. All the cutters and drills were made on site. One corner of the Machine Shop was given over to the training of apprentices, where the youngsters made studs and bolts.

No 1897 was one of eight W. Worsdell 'P' Class 0-6-0s built at Gateshead in December 1897. The engine was one of the last of this group to be withdrawn in May 1951.

Gateshead Works' Forge is seen together with one of the hammers and a number of buffers that have been produced.

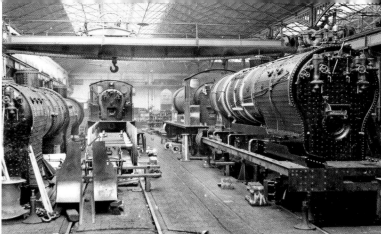

Locomotives under construction in the Erecting Shop.

A large number of the hearths used in the Smiths' Shop are visible in this view.

'M1' (later 'M') Class 4-4-0 No 1627 in Gateshead Works.

A compound steam engine built at Gateshead provided power for all the tools in the shop and six locomotive boilers supplied the steam. Both the Erecting Shop and Machine Shop were well lit and this was aided by the bright colours in which the machinery was painted – even being lined out with swirl decorations.

Many of the components fitted to the NER's locomotives were designed with interchangeability in mind – namely the exchange of parts between engines of the same class, although multiple classes were involved in some instances. In the production of these parts in the works (only a small number were bought in from contractors, such as gauges, injectors and asbestos), standard gauges were used and copies were on hand for drilling purposes. All items went under the close scrutiny of the Gauger, who made sure the specifications were upheld before the part was attached to the locomotive.

In the northern extension to the original station building was the Wheel Shop, and this contained some of the original jib cranes that had been installed to move goods. Some of the machines in use included a double-headed

This shot of the Wheel Shop gives an indication of the lack of space at the works.

wheel lathe, a quartering machine for boring the holes to accommodate crank pins, a key-way cutter and a crank axle lathe. Crank webs were of the circular kind, replacing the oblong built-up type previously used, as these were easier to machine and stronger. Two pieces of hydraulic apparatus were used to force wheels on to their axles: one was new, while the other was quite old, operated by a hand pump and said to resemble 'a huge siege mortar turned on its side than anything else'. Wheel centres were made of cast steel, rather than being milled from the solid, which was the former method of construction.

The Repair Shop – measuring 280 feet by 185 feet – had the use of six cranes driven by a vertical steam engine mounted on the wall. Repair tools were driven by pulleys connected to shafting. A portable boring machine for cylinders had recently been purchased and this impressively reduced the time taken to perform this task from two weeks to no more than two days; the cost had also plummeted from 20 to just 14 shillings. Another interesting tool was the two-faced grinder; this was permanently mounted on a bogie and slid between the frames to re-face the horns, each head acting on those parallel to each other, which made it virtually impossible to cut them out of square.

In the Boiler Shop the mild steel barrel plates were formed and had the rivet holes punched out before being annealed in gas ovens to remove any stresses in the metal. The sections were riveted together by Tweddell's hydraulic apparatus, while the tubeplates were produced under hydraulic presses. This process also applied to the steam dome, which had special matrixes produced, that were hinged together. The metal for the dome was rolled into a cylinder and strapped along the seam, then heated in a furnace before being moved over to the press where the

cylinder was enclosed by the matrixes and a die pressed the metal twice. A shop was established elsewhere on the site for cleaning and sorting used boiler tubes. These were weighed and checked against the specified weight; if the discrepancy was small they would be reused, but if it was too much the tubes were scrapped. For reused tubes new ends were attached using male and female taper cutters to allow a union, which was then heated by gas and soldered to make the match permanent. The tube was then made neat with a hammer and chisel before being hydraulically tested. The cost of the process was given as 2s 9d per dozen, and this work was carried out by youngsters. Underneath the Boiler Shop was a small Smiths' Shop where light work was carried out; one of the main tasks was the testing of springs.

Close to the running sheds was the main Smiths' Shop, also being next door to the Forge. There were a large number of hammers in both and these, which were no more than 4 tons capacity; they were placed at intervals throughout the building but not opposite each other. The hammers were powered by steam, the supply of which was carried underground. As the majority of the casting was done at Darlington and transported to Gateshead, the Brass Foundry was only small and carried out white metal casting. This shop was located across the two branch lines for Redhaugh and the Team Valley and the extensive sidings of the running shed. Nearby was the Paint Shop, which had recently been established in an old roundhouse built in the early 1860s. The Tender Shop – between the two branch lines – underwent the opposite transformation, being turned into a shed after the First World War.

Three relatively large classes appeared from Gateshead before the end of the century. The first was the 'Q' 4-4-0

Class 'R' No 1147 rushes over Wiske Moor water troughs with an express passenger train.

A pair of 4-6-0s are pictured in the Erecting Shop.

– together with two 'Q1s' that had larger driving wheels – and a total of thirty were erected for express duties. Drawing inspiration from the 'M' Class, the design had enlarged cylinders of 19½ inches diameter by 26 inches stroke, but a smaller boiler with a heating surface of 1,212sq ft. Another 4-4-0 class followed as the traffic on the main line had increased to such a level that the two aforementioned classes were struggling badly. The 'R' Class had cylinders 19 inches by 26 inches, 8¾-inch-diameter piston valves, a boiler with a heating surface increased to 1,527sq ft, and pressure raised to 200lb per sq in. No 2011 was the first out of the shops in August 1899, and O. S. Nock in *Locomotives of the North Eastern Railway* notes that the engine was used nearly every day for two years on the Newcastle to Edinburgh and Newcastle to Leeds routes – including return journeys – amassing a mileage of nearly 300,000 before the first general overhaul took place. Although the other nine engines of the first batch did not reach this height, they were not discredited by averaging more than 160,000 miles before returning to Gateshead for attention. A further fifty 'R' Class locomotives would be built at the works up to 1907. However, Worsdell was not content to let the 'R' Class bear the burden of the East Coast expresses and for this task he produced the 'S' Class 4-6-0s, which were the first in the country to use that wheel arrangement. The

dimensions were increased a small amount from the 4-4-0s, with 20-inch-diameter cylinders and a longer boiler giving a greater heating surface, while the number of tubes was reduced, and the coupled wheels were 6ft 1in in diameter. A certain amount of trouble was experienced with the first ten, which entered traffic between 1899 and 1900, leading to a gap of six years before another ten were erected, followed by a further twenty in 1908/09.

The new century saw the 'S1' Class 4-6-0 built as an immediate attempt to deliver the performance expected from the 'S' Class. A few modifications were made, including an increased wheel diameter to 6ft 8¼in and a longer boiler. Only five of the class were sent to work in 1900/01 and, while better performances were recorded, the Running Department was still not satisfied and no more were ordered. Gateshead moved on to fulfilling a need for heavy freight engines with ten 'T' Class 0-8-0s erected in 1901, followed by forty more up to 1904. The locomotives were similar to the 'S1' Class and had 4ft 7¼in-diameter wheels.

With the disappointment of the 4-6-0 designs and following a recent trip to America, where the 4-4-2 'Atlantic' wheel arrangement was in favour, Worsdell chose the latter for the next development of NER express passenger locomotive. No 532 was completed in November 1903 with a 5ft 6in-diameter boiler providing 2,455sq ft of

Worsdell Class 'V' 'Atlantic' No 742.

heating surface at 200lb per sq in pressure (later lowered to 180lb per sq in), a grate area of 27sq ft and cylinders of 20 inches diameter by 28 inches stroke with 8¾-inch piston valves. The remaining nine 'V' Class 'Atlantics' were built in 1904 and were successful in their roles but would prove to be the last express class built at Gateshead.

A special project at this time was the electrification of the short but problematic section of line between Quayside and Trafalgar goods yards – gradients were steep and there were a number of tunnels. The NER decided on electrification after the successful application of the method to the suburban services in the Newcastle area a few years earlier. Two electric locomotives were ordered to work the branch and these were assembled at Gateshead with electrical parts supplied by British Thomson-Houston. Electricity was taken from both overhead cables and third rail in the tunnels, the voltage being 600V DC. Four motors were fitted and produced 640 horsepower; the power was transmitted by eight 3-foot-diameter wheels arranged in two four-wheel bogies.

Before the end of the 19th century the 'M' Class compound 4-4-0s had been rebuilt with a three-cylinder compound arrangement that had been produced by NER Chief Draughtsman Walter Smith. This went against contemporary thinking by having the cylinders roughly the same volume, whereas normally the high-pressure cylinder was much smaller than the low-pressure one. The inside cylinder on 'M' Class locomotive No 1619 was for high-pressure steam, measuring 19 inches by 26 inches, and the two low-pressure cylinders outside the frames were 20 inches by 24 inches. A new boiler was fitted at the same time, and this had an unusual firebox with water tubes running through it to improve heat transfer; this was also designed by Smith. In traffic the engine gave excellent service, but was not perpetuated, although the

compound system would go on to be adopted by the Midland Railway and the London Midland & Scottish Railway. Worsdell allowed Smith to develop his compound system to four cylinders and apply the arrangement to a larger locomotive, which, by the time the plans were ready, was the 'V' Class 'Atlantic'. The two high-pressure cylinders – on the outside – were 14¼ inches in diameter by 26 inches stroke, and the two low-pressure cylinders were larger in this instance at 22 inches diameter by 26 inches stroke. Piston valves were used (of 7½-inch and 10-inch diameter respectively), and only two sets of motion were necessary to operate all four valves. For the first locomotive – No 730 – this was of the Stephenson type, whereas the second – No 731 – employed the new Walschaerts valve gear. The diameter of the boiler was reduced from the standard dimension of the 'V' Class to 5 feet and was also shorter, but the pressure was raised to 225lb per sq in and the grate area was increased to 29sq ft, offsetting this to a degree. An unusual feature for the NER was the adoption of the Belpaire-type firebox for the two engines. Performance in service was very good and dynamometer car tests highlighted the class as being superior to the 'V' Class, leading to plans for the production of ten more compounds. Unfortunately, Smith died shortly after the locomotives entered service and the project came to naught.

As the first decade of the 20th century drew to a close the final designs from Worsdell were produced, and these were for tank engines for local passenger and shunting work. The first of them was the 'W' Class 4-6-0T for the North East coastal routes where the terrain was adverse; a total of ten were constructed in 1907. The same number comprised the 'X' Class of 4-8-0Ts completed in 1909/10, and these were employed in the NER marshalling yards. The boiler was compact at 4ft 9in in diameter and 11 feet

The first of the NER's four-cylinder compounds, No 730.

long between the tubeplates, but this was enough for the work that needed to be done. To aid the engine three cylinders were provided, and these were 18 inches by 26 inches, also being constructed as one casting, which was an unusual practice at the time. No 1359 of the class was the last engine to be built at Gateshead, during April 1910, as the site was just too cramped to erect new locomotives in addition to carrying out repairs, and the latter were seen as the most practical option.

Gateshead was to prove useful for the War Office after the outbreak of the First World War as a number of items were manufactured. One of the first saw 9.2-inch guns made by Armstrong Whitworth mounted on 54-ton trolley wagons for use in defending the coastline. Breech blocks supplied by the company also had the various finishing processes carried out. Gateshead machined 250 6-inch howitzers, and Works Manager H. G. Bell was able to contribute an improvement to the design where a forging was able to replace two parts that were not secure and quite weak in comparison to the new component. A number of cradles and carriages were manufactured for a variety of artillery pieces and the works even turned to making bow defenders for trawlers. Shildon and Gateshead worked together on making 6,000 track links for tanks, and these were said to be some of the most sturdy ever received.

From the Grouping the remit for Gateshead Works continued to be for the repair and maintenance of locomotives operating in the area. As time wore on to the end of the 1920s the impact of the General Strike, then the global financial crisis, dealt a severe blow to the prosperity of the LNER, as its main source of revenue was the heavy industry of Yorkshire and the North East. The steel and coal mining businesses were badly affected by the depression as demand for the commodities dried up, resulting in unemployment and little need for the transport of the materials. Some 28 million tons of

merchandise was moved in 1924, the peak year, and more than 100 million tons of coal was handled by the LNER in the first year after the Grouping. But in the worst years of the depression (1931/32) these figures had fallen to around 20 million tons and 75 million tons respectively. Naturally, such drops dramatically reduced the revenue earned by the company, not helped by a similar decline in passenger receipts. There was an attempt to raise the rates, but as these were set by Parliament there was little political will to do so and this played into the hands of the ever-growing road transport industry.

The LNER found itself in a position where costs needed to be reduced in order to keep the company afloat. In the late 1920s all the staff working for the railway agreed to take a 2½% wage cut, while the number of employees was steadily allowed to dwindle from more than 200,000 in 1923 to just over 166,000 in 1933. Some locomotives, carriages and wagons were allowed to be taken out of service to save running and maintenance costs, also partly as a result of the drop in traffic requiring less motive power. The reduction in passenger traffic was most keenly felt on local branch lines and, despite several attempts to run services more economically, the LNER could not support these at the time, and closures and withdrawals of service occurred; the main lines also saw several intermediate stations shut.

Unfortunately the biggest casualty of the period was Gateshead Works. The fall in traffic and the need to cut costs saw the repair work transferred to Darlington and the shops were closed. More than 1,000 men and boys were affected by the decision, but LNER Chairman William Whitelaw insisted at the time that a great effort would be made to keep as many of the workers employed as possible by moving them to Darlington; much of the machine tooling was also sent south.

During the Second World War Darlington was overwhelmed by the amount of repairs needed by the

Above Despite being closed before the start of 1960, the Erecting Shop continued to be used by Gateshead shed for running repairs to be carried out. *Courtesy of J. W. Armstrong Trust*

Below Peppercorn 'A2' 'Pacific' No 60539 Bronzino of Heaton shed receives attention on 10 October 1954. *F. W. Hampson, courtesy of J. W. Armstrong Trust*

The Erecting Shop after abandonment. *K. Hudspith, courtesy of J. W. Armstrong Trust*

motive power allocated there for attention, in addition to the war work being undertaken. As a result Edward Thompson authorised the reopening of Gateshead as a repair centre and this was successful in improving the mileages some engines in the area were achieving between general repairs, being in some instances as much as an average of 20,000 miles. The shops were allowed to continue in this role through to nationalisation and during the 1950s until the second – and this time permanent – closure occurred in 1959. The original Greenesfield station was the first to be demolished in about 1970, and much of the site has subsequently undergone the same fate, with only a few of the stone walls and the shell of the old Boiler Shop surviving. Some of the land has been reused for apartment blocks while other parts await redevelopment.

In this view towards Gateshead shed on 7 June 1969, the area in the foreground and running to the archway would once have been covered with tracks leading to the Forge and Smiths' Shop in the distance and the Engine Repair Shop on the left. *K. Taylor collection, courtesy of J. W. Armstrong Trust*

5

Gorton and Dukinfield

Prominent citizens of Sheffield had been eager to form a connection with Manchester by means of a railway line from the early 19th century. Several schemes were put forward but collapsed, due to either poor support or lack of funds to construct the difficult route. With the success of other railways in the early 1830s greater enthusiasm was mustered for the Sheffield, Ashton-under-Lyne & Manchester Railway (SA&MR), which was founded in 1835 and received authorisation from Parliament in 1837. Charles Vignoles and Joseph Locke were the engineers for the line and they had the hard task of penetrating the Pennines at Dunford Bridge with a tunnel 3 miles 22 yards long to reach Woodhead on the other side.

While this was slowly being carried out the first section of the line was ready in late 1841, running from Manchester to Godley, reaching Woodhead in 1842. The company's first workshops were established in a number of wooden shacks at Newton (near the end of the first section) and were under the direction of Richard Peacock. He had a varied background in engineering, but was still quite young at 21, and was appointed in 1841. The first locomotives used by the company were 0-4-2T types bought from Kirtley & Co of Warrington, which turned out to be quite poor, requiring new engines to be ordered, and a number were rented to fill the gap.

As the traffic grew new engines were bought from Sharp Brothers & Co and Robert Stephenson. By 1846, when the SA&MR amalgamated with the Great Grimsby & Sheffield Junction Railway (GG&SJR) to form the Manchester, Sheffield & Lincolnshire Railway (MS&LR), there were approximately fifty locomotives at work and a further twenty were in the stock of the GG&SJR. Such a number, in addition to carriages and wagons – which were of the general standard of the time – made the facilities at Newton completely inadequate and Peacock was given the task of overseeing the establishment of new workshops. Twenty acres of land were purchased between Openshaw and Gorton in 1846, being a suitable distance from Manchester to avoid the heavy expense of the area

and the constraints of expansion that a city would impose. The site was on the north side of the main line, just to the west of the Manchester & Ashton-under-Lyne Canal. Construction took place swiftly and ended in 1848; the buildings alone cost nearly £27,000.

On the western side was a long rectangular building (320 feet by 70 feet) containing the Carriage and Wagon departments, which were strangely arranged on two floors. The former was on top, with vehicles hoisted up to the shop, where there was space for thirty-eight carriages; there was also a Trimming Shop. Immediately east was a broad square structure split into four sections. One was for the repair of eighteen locomotives, another was a Boiler Shop, the third a Fitting and Tool Shop, and the last a Smiths' Shop. To the south of the Erecting Shop was a Paint Shop, which bordered on the main line and measured 160 feet by 40 feet. A large roundhouse shed was installed on the eastern half of the plot and this could stable seventeen locomotives. Houses and a school were also provided for the employees and their children.

For at least five years Gorton Works concentrated on repairs to the rolling stock before the Board considered erecting any vehicles there. The first foray concerned carriages; six passenger brake vans were erected during 1854. This was also the year that Peacock left the MS&LR to found a new locomotive-building company with Charles Beyer. A site was chosen just across the main line on the south side, and the Gorton Foundry was soon building locomotives for the Great Western Railway. W. G. Craig became Locomotive Superintendent and in 1855 oversaw the spending of £8,000, raised through the sale of unwanted locomotives, to improve Gorton Works, including new shops, tools and the installation of a gas producing plant, as well as grease production facilities and a store. Some rebuilding work was carried out on some of the older locomotives, which became tank types, shorn of their tenders.

In early 1857 the decision was taken to erect two new locomotives to replace the same number that were deemed to be life-expired. The first was No 6 *Archimedes* and the other was No 7 *Phlegon*, both 0-6-0s with 5-foot-diameter wheels and 17-inch by 24-inch cylinders. A clamour for new stock did not follow, but a trickle of new locomotives and carriages left Gorton up to the start of the 1860s. Two composite carriages (consisting of three classes with a capacity of seventy-six – squeezed into the standard 18-foot long body) started off proceedings, and these were followed by twelve 1st and 2nd Class coaches for the King's Cross services. A large number of wagons were bought from a firm in Grimsby in the early 1860s and these were rented until the value of the stock had been reached.

Craig's reign was only brief as he was in the twilight of his career at his appointment. Charles Sacré succeeded in 1859 and for the first few years of his tenure continued the policy of buying locomotives from the trade and such firms as Kitson and Fairbairn & Sons. Two goods locomotives were built at Gorton in 1862 – Nos 28 and 29 – and these were similar to the '23' Class locomotives, although the wheels were reduced in diameter from 5ft 3in to 5 feet and the cylinders similarly treated – 16½in by 24in to 16in by 24in. There was some diversification at Gorton during this period as £10,000 worth of equipment was installed for the production of rails (at a rate of approximately 4,000 tons per annum), and a large quantity of bricks were made.

The *Sheffield Daily News* of 10 December 1859 announced that the MS&LR was forming a volunteer corps for the British Army under the general scheme that was begun following the Crimean War. Gorton Works was just one of the many railway establishments that became involved and this was done under the guidance of the Deputy Chairman of the company, J. Chapman, who contributed £150 towards the expenses. One hundred men joined the corps at the first meeting.

By 1863 Gorton was responsible for 143 locomotives, 311 carriages and 4,266 wagons, but this did not stop construction figures rising from single to double digits per year as the 1860s progressed. This period began with two prototypes for passenger classes. The first of these was the '1B' 2-4-0 for light passenger trains; these engines had 15-inch by 20-inch cylinders and 5-foot-diameter wheels. Through to 1869 a further eight locomotives of this class would be constructed at the company's workshops. The Class '24' type was for expresses and again had a 2-4-0 arrangement, while the coupled wheels were slightly enlarged with 6-foot-diameter drivers and 16-inch by 22-inch cylinders. A total of thirty were built at Gorton up to November 1868.

The construction of these two classes marked a turning point in MS&LR policy as Gorton became the sole supplier of engines from 1868 to 1887 – although a small number of second-hand 0-4-0STs and 0-6-0STs were bought during this time and several nominal rebuilds were carried out at Sheffield Neepsend depot. In the early 1870s production was concentrated on the '18' Class 0-6-0s, which had 5-foot-diameter wheels and 17-inch by 24-inch

Sacré Class '24' 2-4-0 No 57 was built in September 1867 and withdrawn in October 1903.

cylinders, and the saddle tank variation with smaller 4ft 9in wheels. The culmination of Sacré's 0-6-0s was the '6A' Class built from 1880 to 1885 (comprising a total of sixty-two); these had 4ft 5in-diameter boilers with 1,229sq ft of heating surface, 17½-inch by 26-inch cylinders and 4ft 9½in coupled wheels.

The Ashton Reporter carried the following notice on the front page on Saturday 4 November 1871:

'We, the workmen employed at the Gorton Works of the Manchester, Sheffield, and Lincolnshire Railway Company, beg to return our sincere THANKS to the Chairman and to the Board of Directors for having voluntarily, and without any solicitation on our part, granted the nine hours per day, to commence on January 1st, 1872; and also to THANK Charles Sacre, Esq, Stanhope Perkins, Esq, and Thomas Parker, Esq, for their many acts of kindness to us on various occasions.'

From the mid-1870s to the 1880s further express designs were completed. Sacré introduced a larger 2-4-0, but a short time after he joined the 4-4-0 wheel arrangement was generally adopted, and twenty-seven were in traffic by the end of the decade. The '6B' Class had a 4ft 6in-diameter boiler with 1,016sq ft of heating surface working at 140lb per sq in, 17-inch by 26-inch cylinders and 6ft 3½in driving wheels; a more substantial cab was provided for the enginemen than those in use previously.

At the end of the 1870s crank axle failures were becoming a problem, with several occurring in traffic. The components had been forged by specialist firms up to this time and they had supplied a number of improved types to stop these instances. Proving ineffective, Gorton turned to forging the crank axles at the works and considerably improved the quality and durability.

The MS&LR coaching stock during Sacré's period of office was adequate for the time and 1st and 2nd Class coaches were said to be comfortable. However, 3rd Class vehicles had just five compartments to seat sixty – twelve in each. Improvements were not helped by the fact that Sacré preferred to employ four wheels instead of six and was quite reluctant to adopt bogies when they were popular in the 1870s. However, four were built in 1878 and another two in 1879 and 1880 (with two lavatories), and Gorton even turned out a Royal Saloon for the Prince of Wales (later King Edward VII) in 1883 with two six-wheel bogies for the South Eastern & Chatham Railway.

Gorton was required to step in and provide wagons to fill the void between the operational stock and the necessary stock to handle the traffic in the early 1870s, and 565 vehicles were built, followed soon afterwards by a further 500. The Board appears to have followed a policy of obtaining wagons from the most suitable source when the need arose. By the mid-1880s the most numerous type in operation was the open goods wagon, followed by the coal and timber wagon. There were small numbers of covered, cattle and brake wagons.

As early as 1865 Sacré had told the Board that there was inadequate space in the Carriage and Wagon Shops at Gorton and had pressed for improved stabling facilities across the system to reduce the maintenance burden due to weathering of the stock. This exacerbated the perpetual backlog of wagon repairs as the shops were often 300 in arrears, forcing work to be taken in hand at yards across the system. New sheds for the stock – mainly the carriages – were not provided until the 1880s. A new locomotive shed was opened at Gorton early in the decade and the old roundhouse on the works site was converted into

Sacré Class '6B' 4-4-0 No 440 is seen at Manchester Central station c1900. The engine was erected at Gorton in June 1878.

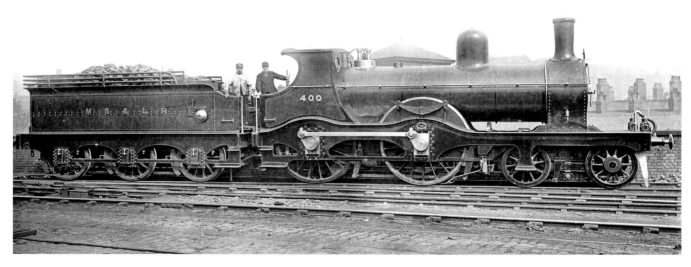

Parker Class '6DB' No 400 was built at Gorton in October 1888.

a new Smithy. Around the same time a Carriage Repair Shop and Wagon Repair Shop were erected along the western perimeter of the site accommodating the engine shed. Not until 1887 was the first locomotive weighing machine installed, this having been specially built for the International Exhibition of Navigation, Commerce & Industry held in Liverpool during 1886. At this time there were thoughts that the whole workshops might be transferred to a new site on account of space restrictions. In the event the cheaper option was taken and during the 1890s several developments took place, such as the new Machine Shop, Stores and Offices, which cost more than £100,000.

By the time Thomas Parker became Locomotive, Carriage & Wagon Superintendent in 1886, the stock

of each had more than doubled. His first changes were to adopt single frames and discard the double frames favoured by Sacré, in addition to making Joy's valve gear standard for all new construction. Some deviation from this did occur initially: the three 4-4-0 engines of the '6DB' Class built in 1888 conformed more to his predecessor's principles, while the Class '2' 4-4-0s erected at Gorton and by Kitson & Co from 1890 to 1894 had single frames but Stephenson valve gear.

There was a pressing need for locomotives capable of handling the suburban traffic at the end of the 1880s and the Class '3' 2-4-2T was introduced to fill this gap, bringing a new wheel arrangement to the railway. The first nine were built at Gorton, followed by another three, and the remaining twenty-seven were the product of Neilson & Co.

Parker Class '2' 4-4-0 No 705 is pictured at York.

Constructed at the same time was the '9A' Class 0-6-2T for shunting duties, and a certain number of details were shared with the aforementioned. Both had 4ft 4in-diameter boilers with 1,063sq ft of heating surface and pressure set at 160lb per sq in, Joy valve gear and slide valves. The cylinders only slightly differed in the stroke, being 24 inches for the former and 26 inches for the latter, but the 18-inch diameter was shared. The coupled wheels were 5ft 7in and 5ft 1in respectively. Gorton and Neilson & Co again shared the task of construction, six to forty-nine.

Parker was soon developing the '9A' design to be fitted with a Belpaire firebox, and when '9C' Class No 7 was sent into traffic from Gorton in September 1891 it became the first British locomotive to be built with that type to run on a home railway – Beyer, Peacock & Co had in fact been fitting Belpaire fireboxes for a number of foreign orders for at least twenty years. After a number of months on trial, two more were erected at Gorton before the above firm took orders for forty-two, perhaps as a consequence of their experience. In total 129 were built to 1901, fifty of which were from the MS&LR's shops.

Carriage construction continued in the same vein under Parker, particularly as he had previously been the Carriage & Wagon Superintendent. The 1st Class carriages were particularly luxurious even though six wheels were still being employed. Large orders for wagons were placed with contractors.

By the mid-1890s the works, which were bounded by Bessemer Street and Princess Street and with Wellington Street cutting through their centre, covered 50 acres. The main workshops were on the eastern side of the last-mentioned street, while the engine shed and Carriage and Wagon Shops occupied the western half. Taking up more than 27,000 square feet was the Boiler Shop, and this contained all the necessary equipment for the manufacture and manipulation of the boiler plates, together with tools for drilling and producing the copper stays; a 15-ton overhead crane served the entire shop. A building next door housed the Tube Shop, which was also where the boilers were tested before entering the Erecting Shop. Occupying a similar area to the boiler-making facility was the Tender Shop, where both repairs and new construction took place. At almost 50,000 square feet, the Machine and Turning Shop dealt with the axles, crank axles, cylinders, coupling rods and other items, both new and old, before they were fitted to a locomotive. An area had been claimed in the roof space for the manufacture of nuts, bolts and studs. The shop was served by several cranes from 5 to 15 tons capacity and these were rope-hauled by a wall-mounted steam engine.

The Erecting Shop was split into five bays, each 50 feet wide and 480 feet long with three tracks for the accommodation of locomotives; all had use of two 30-ton travelling cranes. A portion was given over to fitters, and power for the various tools used was obtained from wall-mounted steam engines. The Foundry had three cupolas and made not only all the castings necessary for the rolling stock, but also the smaller items necessary for the permanent way – the manufacture of rails was discontinued and the plant offered for sale in the mid-1880s.

H. Pollitt became Locomotive Superintendent after Parker's retirement in 1894, having previously been Works Manager at Gorton. Even though both men were in office for the same period – seven years – Parker's

Pollitt '11A' Class 4-4-0 No 860 was completed in November 1898.

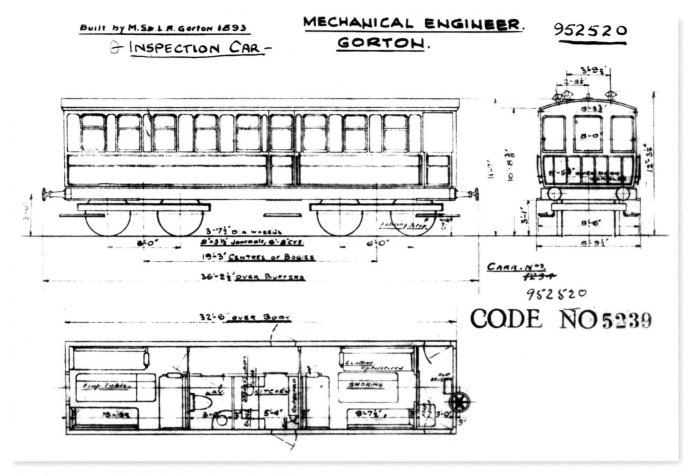

Plans for an Inspection Car built at Gorton in 1893.

tenure saw 237 locomotives erected compared with Pollitt's seventy-three. This was despite the opening of the London Extension in 1899 and the consequent increase in traffic. His first design actually only appeared in 1897, the preceding types being based on Parker locomotives and slightly modified. The most numerous design was the '11A' Class 4-4-0 for express trains; thirteen were built at Gorton and a further twenty at Beyer, Peacock & Co up to 1899. The boiler was 4ft 4in in diameter with 1,101sq ft of heating surface and pressure of 160lb per sq in, while the cylinders were 18½ inches in diameter with a 26-inch stroke with Stephenson motion operating piston valves. Pollitt also produced a 4-2-2 design to work with the '11A' Class, but only six were built as the type was soon seen as being behind the requirements.

For the new traffic to the capital, Gorton constructed a number of dining vehicles and kitchen carriages that were given clerestory roofs and twelve-wheel bogies. The standard of decor continued to be high for 1st Class, with liberal use of polished woods and mouldings, while 3rd Class accommodation was comfortable. A new feature was the addition of buffet cars to the set for those not wishing to take advantage of the fine dining available in the restaurant carriages. Compartment stock formed the remainder of the new trains and these had elliptical roofs and four-wheel bogies. Gorton also had a hand in the

wagon stock, producing 1,000 coal wagons in 1895, and was generally helped by the erection of more than 2,500 each from Cravens and Ashburys Carriage & Iron Co for other traffics.

At the turn of the century the Great Central Railway – the rebranding had occurred in 1897 – was facing a motive power shortage and the new Locomotive Superintendent (later restyled Chief Mechanical Engineer) J. G. Robinson agreed with the Board to order 2-6-0 engines from the Baldwin Works in the USA. When these arrived in Britain they were assembled at Gorton. As freight was the primary traffic on the system, Robinson pushed for new locomotives, leading to his first design. This was the '9J' Class 0-6-0, which had a 5-foot-diameter boiler with 1,452sq ft of heating surface, working at 180lb per sq in, with two 18½-inch by 26-inch cylinders operated by Stephenson valve gear and slide valves, and 5ft 2in-diameter wheels. The first order was for forty-nine engines and this was placed with Neilson, Reid & Co, all appearing between 1901 and 1902. Gorton did not add to the class until 1903/04, but only built twelve. This would prove to be indicative of much of the early part of Robinson's reign, as the capacity of the Gorton workshops, which also had to maintain the locomotives in traffic – as well as rebuilding some of the older designs – was not enough to meet requirements. A total of 183 engines were built

Robinson '9K' Class 4-4-2T No 47 is at the head of a London suburban service.

up to the start of 1910, compared to 281 locomotives ordered from contractors.

Even though there was nothing approaching the rigorous health and safety precautions of today during the early 1900s, serious accidents do not appear to have been as frequent as one might expect. However, there were some reported at this time, such as in late October 1900 when Thomas Cowley (57, wagon builder) was working in a gang of four to lift the body of a wagon on

to jacks. After this was done he went under the body to place a bolt in the headstock but a moment later the body fell down on top of him and he died the same day of his injuries; he had been employed at Gorton for twenty-eight years. The following year William Morris, furnaceman, was killed when the boiler supplying steam to the 3-ton hammer exploded. The Board of Trade enquiry into the accident failed to determine an exact cause for this and found the GCR at no fault in its practices with regard to

3rd Class corridor carriage No 1287.

boiler inspections. The *Manchester Courier and Lancashire General Advertiser* carried news of another fatality in 1904 when Herbert Francis Evans (14) had his head caught by one of the metal-forming machines at Gorton. In this instance the jury at the inquest said that some sort of apparatus for safety could be installed to the equipment to prevent any subsequent accidents.

Following on from the '9Js' were types for express passenger ('11B'), heavy freight ('8A') and mixed traffic (Class '8') duties, the majority of these being bought from outside firms, although Gorton built some '8A' 0-8-0s later in the decade. The first Robinson design to emerge from Gorton was the '9K' 4-4-2T in 1903; eight were built during the year and a further twenty were completed to 1905, with twelve from Vulcan Foundry making up the class total. Beyer, Peacock & Co was tasked with introducing 4-4-2 and 4-6-0 designs to the railway, but Gorton was given the interesting assignment of building four compound 'Atlantics' in 1905 and 1906. These had three cylinders and worked on the system of W. M. Smith, whose son J. W. Smith coincidentally became Chief Draughtsman and Gorton Works Manager in 1906, replacing William Thorneley, holder of the same position from 1894. Despite finding some success, the compound type was not perpetuated.

Another fashion was taken up at Gorton in the mid-1900s as the workshops turned out three railcars for local services around Hull and Wrexham. These were powered by a vertical boiler, outside cylinders and Walschaerts valve gear. Seating was for twelve in 1st Class and forty-four in 3rd Class in a 61ft 6in body. Other coaching stock built at Gorton at this time included more restaurant carriages for the London trains and vans for parcels traffic. However, much of the new construction was taken in hand by outside firms as were the wagon orders, which resembled that of the locomotives in being two to one against Gorton.

As the London Extension was now fully completed the Board was free to concentrate on improving the workshops at Gorton. The only solution to free space for each department was the removal of the Carriage and Wagon Departments to a new site east of Guide Bridge station. Thirty acres were purchased at Dukinfield for £11,000 in 1903 and, surprisingly, Craven Bros and Markham & Co were asked to provide plans for the new shops, which were accepted and estimated to cost £165,000, although in the event this figure reached nearly £200,000. The main building measured 700 feet by 539 feet with ten bays split into sections for the various requirements, such as two 120-foot-wide bays for wagon repairs. In addition the block contained a Sawmill, Forge, Smithy, Underframe Shop and Brake Shop. Electricity was supplied from a power station on the works site, which contained four large boilers feeding steam to a vertical engine driving two 400kW and two 200kW generators. The building also contained hydraulic equipment and air compressors for the variety of tools employed at the shops. Other buildings in use included Offices, Mess, and Timber Shed.

A six-wheel carriage is lifted at Dukinfield.

A view inside the Carriage Repair Shop at Dukinfield around the time of opening.

A permanent platform has been installed in this stage of the Repair Shop to facilitate access to the exterior panels.

Robinson '8K' Class 2-8-0 No 966 was built at Gorton in September 1911 and was in traffic until November 1959.

When the workshops opened in 1910 orders were placed for seventy-two new carriages for services travelling across country, in addition to those running to London and the city's suburbs. The stock was either 56 feet by 8ft 6in or 60 feet by 9 feet with steel underframes carried on two bogies with 10ft 6in wheelbases. Exterior panelling was in teak matchboard with brass lettering for the company's initials and the carriage's running number. The main-line stock generally used saloons to accommodate the passengers, while the suburban stock had compartments; seating for 1st Class was four and 3rd Class six. Interestingly, the GCR did not build any wagons in the new shops during the year in order for the carriages to have priority; additions to the wagon stock were made by Cravens.

The new suburban stock entered traffic with new locomotives at its head. These were 4-6-2T engines – classified '9N' – with a 5-foot-diameter boiler with 1,379sq ft of heating surface, in addition to 145sq ft from the 18-element Schmidt superheater, and the boiler pressure was 180lb per sq in. Two 20-inch by 26-inch cylinders were fitted, alongside 10-inch-diameter piston valves operated by Stephenson motion, and the coupled wheels were 5ft 7in in diameter. Robinson had previously equipped a '9J' 0-6-0 with a superheater, and when this met with success the '9Ns' were the first GCR class to be fitted with the apparatus. Robinson would later develop his own superheater, which eliminated the need for joints and other areas that could leak. These would be subsequently fitted to the '9Ns', other GCR locomotives and many engines at work around the world.

Also built at Gorton in the early years of the new decade was a new freight type, the '8K' Class, with a 2-8-0 wheel arrangement. This was a development of the earlier 0-8-0s and had a leading pony truck added to improve riding

and support the increased weight of the locomotive at the front end. A superheated 5-foot-diameter boiler was fitted, together with 19-inch by 26-inch cylinders, 10-inch piston valves and Stephenson valve gear. No 966 was the first from Gorton in September 1911, followed by a further fifty-eight to 1914, with another twenty coming from Kitson & Co and fifty from the North British Locomotive Co (NBLC) in 1912/13. The design had the honour of being chosen for construction as the Railway Operating Division's standard freight locomotive during the First World War, and many were subsequently purchased by the LNER after the Grouping.

Robinson continued to produce new designs and the next out of Gorton was a large 4-6-0 for express trains. No 423 *Sir Sam Fay* was the first of six Class '1' engines and was a departure from previous products in having a 5ft 6in-diameter boiler, which was fitted new with a Robinson superheater, and big inside cylinders of 21½-inch diameter by 26-inch stroke. Unfortunately, several problems arose in service and Gorton had to fit two different types of boiler in an attempt to overcome these, but the class never performed as well as intended, spending most of their existence on light passenger trains. Surprisingly, Robinson perpetuated the design a year later for the '1A' Class of mixed-traffic engines, with 5ft 7in-diameter wheels compared to the 6ft 9in of the originals, and eleven were erected at Gorton.

With the 4-6-0s proving a disappointment, the CME reverted to the 4-4-0 and ten '11E' Class locomotives were built at Gorton in 1913. A 5ft 3in-diameter boiler was used (with superheater) and the heating surface was 1,963sq ft, working at 180lb per sq in; the two inside cylinders were 20 inches by 26 inches, using 10-inch piston valves and Stephenson motion. The first into traffic

No 430 *Purdon Viccars* was the second member of the '11E' 'Director' Class to be built at Gorton in September 1913.

was No 429 *Sir Alexander Henderson* and all were named after Directors of the company.

The last new locomotive design to appear before the war interrupted matters was the '1B' Class 2-6-4T, the first instance of this wheel arrangement being used in Britain. Finding employment on freight trains, the locomotives had 5ft 3in-diameter boilers with 1,752sq ft of heating surface, 21-inch by 26-inch cylinders and 5ft 1in-diameter coupled wheels. The first two were constructed at Gorton in 1914 and a further eighteen would appear in successive years before the end of the First World War.

Both Gorton and Dukinfield were heavily involved in the effort to supply munitions and other items for the armed forces. The latter was called into action first as two ambulance trains were requested soon after the outbreak and were ready by the end of September. A similar set of carriages was erected early the following year and two sets were assembled for the Americans after they engaged Germany and Austria-Hungary.

Between 1914 and 1918 the shops converted nearly 3,000 10-ton wagons for use at the front, and also made 330 general-service wagons, thirty water carts, 2,150 stretchers, 2,000 picketing posts and 20,000 picketing pegs. A number of metal items were forged, such as 5,000 nose caps, 5,600 breech bolts and 9,500 water indicators for the Admiralty. Gorton was mainly tasked with producing munitions, and 76,909 high-explosive shells were machined, banded, internally varnished and painted ready for filling, in addition to making nose pieces and base plate stampings from the rough forging; more than 30,000 nose pieces were also supplied to other munitions factories. A total of 5,513,790 18-pounder cases were refurbished, 28,315 primers for cartridges repaired, and for packing fuses 76,300 new tin cases were made. Other work included air reservoirs for submarines; motor lorry parts; pressing bullet-proof shield plates; casting and machining bronze range dial cases for 4-inch guns; travelling carriages for

Express passenger Class '9P' 4-6-0 No 1169 *Lord Faringdon* in works grey livery.

No 1165 *Valour* was in service until December 1947 and the nameplate was subsequently retained, now residing in the National Railway Museum.

naval 6-inch guns; saddles and trunnion brackets for 4.5-inch howitzers; and pedestals for 3-inch anti-aircraft guns. The GCR also lent a number of locomotives for use by railways at home and overseas.

Robinson returned to the 4-6-0 wheel arrangement in 1917 with the '9P' Class. But instead of two large cylinders he provided four that were 16 inches by 26 inches with 8-inch piston valves and Stephenson motion; the drive was divided. No 1169 *Lord Faringdon* emerged from Gorton Works at the end of the year and was the sole representative until 1920, when five were constructed; No 1165 was named *Valour* to honour the GCR staff who had fought in the war. Another 4-6-0 class was built in 1918,

No 1165 *Valour* was in service until December 1947 and the nameplate was subsequently retained, now residing in the National Railway Museum.

but these were based on improvements made to the '8K' Class 2-8-0s and, unlike the other 4-6-0s, were considered strong engines. However, only three were built – Nos 406, 52 and 53 – the first in 1918 and the other two in 1921, all at Gorton.

The final new design built for the GCR at the company's workshops was the '9Q' Class 4-6-0, which was a mixed-traffic version of the '9P' Class, having 5ft 8in-diameter wheels, but the same boiler and cylinders. Nos 72, 73 and 78 began life in May, June and July 1921 respectively and were followed by a further ten from Vulcan Foundry before the end of the year. In 1922 Gorton built another ten and Beyer, Peacock & Co five, and all were frequently used on the GCR's fitted freights heading all over the system, as well as several short-distance passenger trains.

Robinson celebrated his 65th birthday in 1921 and, although this was the retirement age at the time, he continued through to the Grouping of 1923, when he was offered the position of CME of the newly formed LNER. As he felt that he was not the man to take the company forward, he declined the position and recommended Gresley, who was appointed. R. A. Thom – Robinson's assistant since 1913 – then became District Superintendent for the GC Section of the company before taking the same job for the Scottish area.

An order for ten more '9Q' Class locomotives was put in hand at Gorton in 1923 and these differed from their predecessors in having modifications to reduce the overall height so that travelling into new areas would not be problematic. The GCR's loading gauge was quite generous and approximately 5 inches were removed from the 4-6-0s, which were classified 'B7' by the LNER. Another modification applied to a few members of this batch was a steam chest that improved the passage of steam from the boiler to the cylinders. Another class added to at this time was the '9N' (LNER 'A5') 4-6-2T, and ten were

Robinson 'A5' Class No 5003 entered traffic in January 1923 and was condemned in November 1960, being scrapped at Darlington Works.

completed at Gorton, allowing a number to be released from their duties on the GC Section and redeployed to the West Riding. The new locomotives were not altered to the LNER loading gauge, but a batch of thirteen built at Hawthorn, Leslie & Co in 1925 were, and this was one of several improvements made before the engines entered service in the NE Area.

The carriage shops were also busy, with a number of 1st, 3rd, 3rd Brake and Bogie Brake carriages under construction at Dukinfield during 1923 and 1924. The first LNER vehicles emerged in 1924 and these were 1st and 3rd Class compartment stock to Diagrams 46 and 58 respectively; the latter were similar to those in use on the GC Section, being 56ft 0½in long, and squeezed 108 passengers into nine compartments. Although the

workshops lacked the importance of Doncaster or York, orders continued to be placed throughout the 1920s and Open 3rds (Diagram 27), 3rds (Diagram 56), 3rd Brakes (Diagram 61), Composite Brakes (Diagram 52) and 1st Class carriages (Diagram 48) were completed. Amid this work, Dukinfield continued to maintain the stock running in the GC Section.

Also retaining responsibility for the wagons, the workshops were called upon to contribute many of the various types required by the LNER after the Grouping. The first designs produced were the Diagram 9 coal wagons (770), Diagram 10 type (1,000 between 1924 and 1926) and 500 six-plank open wagons. In the following year 500 double bolster wagons and 40 refrigerator vans were turned out, as well as 145 Diagram 34 20-ton brake

Composite Brake carriage No 495 was one of two built at Dukinfield in 1932 to Diagram 134.

A 20-ton glass well wagon constructed at Dukinfield to Diagram 36 in 1927.

vans. From 1925 Dukinfield's role became slightly more focused as smaller numbers were completed and the designs became more specialised. During the year fifty 20-ton tube wagons, five gunpowder vans, two 15-ton glass wagons, one pulley wagon and one 50-ton trolley wagon left the works, and in 1926 fifty-seven ballast, rail and sleeper wagons, which were mounted on bogies, were built for several of the LNER's Permanent Way Departments. Two more glass wagons and sixteen brake vans appeared in 1927, while 1928 proved a productive year with twenty four-wheel plate wagons, 120 quintuple bolster wagons, four trestle type to Diagram 62, and 260 underframes for brake vans, which were subsequently taken to Doncaster for final assembly. Only two types were built in the final years of the decade; these were

40-ton ballast, rail sleeper wagons and thirty double bolster wagons.

The *Journal of the Institute of Mechanical Engineers* carried a short description of the Dukinfield site and the shops during 1929. Comprising a total of 30 acres, 12 of these were covered and, in addition to the large main building, there was a shop on the east side of the site for paint and stripping purposes, measuring 625 feet by 120 feet; connecting both was a traverser. A total of 1,500 people were employed at the works, the majority in the main building where the ten bays were divided into several areas for specific tasks to be carried out. At the southern end of the shop were the wheelwrights and electrical department, and adjoining was the area for construction of new frames and repairs of used sets.

An all-steel soda ash wagon built at Dukinfield in 1937.

Finishing was performed in the third bay, while the fourth, fifth and sixth bays were dedicated to new construction, which was arranged for the progressive system, and the sawmill. Next to this area were the repair bays and the Machine Shop and Wheel Shop. The latter possessed a 5-ton overhead crane and various lathes, presses and grinding machines. There was also a Forge containing a large number of steam hammers and hydraulic presses.

In 1932 R. A. Thom detailed the step-by-step processes of the progressive system at Dukinfield for the *LNER Magazine*. The first act was for the carriage to be classified according to the attention required at the shops. This was done in the sidings that were part of the site after a thorough examination had been carried out, and a lettering system was applied to the body to give quick identification. Running from A to F, the first two letters represented general overhauls for bogie and six-wheel stock, then C and D for light repairs. The letter E represented just light repairs for any vehicle, while F denoted special attention. After classification the carriages were shunted to the reception roads outside the lifting shop, which were also represented by the same letters as above. For repairs that required the body to be lifted off the underframe, the control office determined the order the vehicles entered the shop, and they went to either road 2 or 5 in the Repair Bay in groups of either two or five; other repairs were dealt with in sets of five.

In the Lifting Shop the bogies were removed, then the wheels taken out of the frames so that both could be fully examined and refurbished; this was done to the former after being dipped in caustic soda to remove dirt and grease. After the necessary work had been carried out the frames were submerged in a vat of paint before reassembly. Once the body had been returned to the bogies the carriage moved forward into the Repair Shop, which was split into six stages, each accommodating two vehicles, where specific tasks were carried out. Raised platforms running along the sides of the carriages were provided for ease of access. The first stage encompassed removals: stripping paint or varnish, and interior fixtures and fittings. In the next two the necessary repairs were carried out inside and outside. The fourth stage saw work move to the roof, and special platforms were arranged for the purpose. After this had been done the interior and outside panels were painted and varnished ready for the final stage when all the furniture, etc, was reinstalled. Lastly, the carriage was inspected before returning to traffic. Thom said that the increase in productivity from the introduction of the progressive system was 42% and the reduction in the average time vehicles spent out of traffic was 37%.

Another report filed by Thom in the *LNER Magazine* detailed the shops at Gorton Works that had the task of manufacturing permanent way items for the GC Section. Expansion had recently occurred and new buildings occupied on site to allow the manufacture of 1,000 points and crossings a year. The Machine and Fitting Shop was 261 feet long by 41 feet wide and possessed

Looking south-east to Dukinfield Carriage Works. *Courtesy of Brian Longbone*

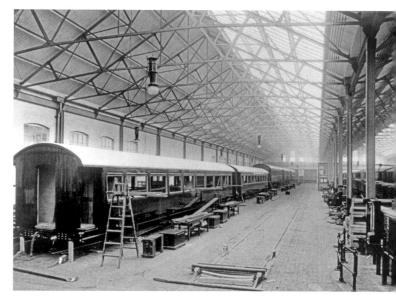

Carriages under construction in the Building Shop. *Courtesy of Brian Longbone*

Looking west towards Manchester, with the tracks for the traverser in the foreground. *Courtesy of Brian Longbone*

Frames laid out in the Underframe Shop. *Courtesy of Brian Longbone*

Wagons in the course of erection during GCR ownership. *Courtesy of Brian Longbone*

several tools specific to the work. One was a Loudon switch planing machine with a table 18 feet long by 4ft 6in wide, being electrically driven and having the use of an overhead crane. Another was used to plane point and splice rails, and this had a table 10 feet long by 4ft 6in wide. Four planing machines could be called upon to cut

rails at speeds ranging from 60 to 120 feet per minute and these were driven by 40-horsepower electric motors; the heads used 4½-horsepower motors. Two radial drilling machines were provided – both using a 7½-horsepower motor – and a cold saw was situated centrally in the shop. A hydraulic press was in use and this was upgraded to

A plan of Dukinfield shops with a diagram of the route taken by vehicles under repair.

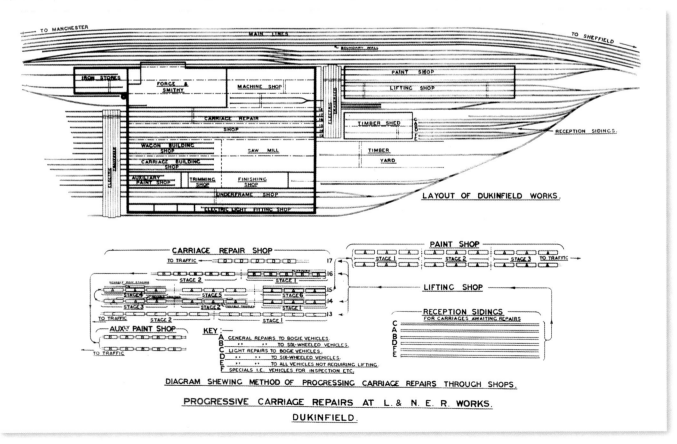

A Diagram 129 special tank wagon for Imperial Chemical Industries. The vessels could be removed to road vehicles for transport to the final destination.

produce a force of 300 tons; the metal was usually cold. A 100-ton hydraulic press was present for the fabrication of buffer-stops, these being formed in conjunction with a smiths' hearth. All of the machines were arranged on the eastern side, and the western section was dedicated to making the track sections. A 5-ton overhead crane was used in the workshop, and there was also one in the storage yard nearby.

Gorton Works continued to construct locomotives for the LNER but this at a much reduced capacity – up to 1928 only forty were built. These were of the 'N7' Class (GER Hill 'L77') of 0-6-2Ts, and the first order for ten was received after the Grouping, being completed in 1925. Taking numbers at irregular intervals between 409 and 475, the locomotives were slightly altered from the original design to conform to the new loading gauge, in addition to having two Ross 'pop' safety valves, injectors instead of top feed, and a left-hand drive. The ten engines were sent new to King's Cross. Coming shortly after this work was the task of completing a further twenty, between January 1926 and February 1927, and again these took an irregular sequence of numbers between 826 and 873. All of these belonged to class part one, whereas the last

ten that were built in 1927-28 (Nos 2632 to 2641) were class part two. In this instance the modifications included new valve gear to improve the valve events, which also saw the cut-off increased to 75% from 70%, a new rear pony truck with smaller wheels, and high-sided bunkers. After the completion of this batch there were no more orders for locomotives for a decade.

Repairs were the main occupation for Gorton Works after the amalgamation and, in the main, for the first few years these remained the ex-GC types. Among the first 'foreign' locomotives to visit the shops were the 'A1' Class 'Pacifics', as some were run in from Gorton shed after being constructed at Doncaster in 1924. At least No 2548 *Galtee More* and No 2550 *Blink Bonny* are recorded as receiving light attention at the works during October and December respectively. Although not an unfamiliar design, the ROD 2-8-0s bought from the Government between 1923 and 1927 were sent to Gorton for overhaul (apart from some shipped to Darlington) before entering service for the LNER. One of the main tasks was the fitting of copper fireboxes in place of those made from steel during the shortages of the war years. In some instances there was a backlog of engines awaiting replacements from the Boiler Shop and these ran in traffic for a number of months before receiving the standard type. In 1927/28 a number of new 'J39' Class 0-6-0s were allocated to Gorton shed and later other depots in the area acquired the type. This left the works responsible for the maintenance of the newcomers for much of their service life. Despite being constructed for the GE Section, the 'B17' Class was considered a suitable replacement for the '11E' and '11F' 4-4-0s (LNER 'D10' and 'D11' 'Director' Class), which were working the principal expresses on the GC main line in the early 1930s. As a result Gorton was made responsible for the engines based on the section and even some of the GE Section locomotives, as Stratford was not always able to fit those in need of attention in the works. The 'B17s' were later allocated to Darlington for repairs during the war years before transferring back to Gorton and Stratford, while this cycle was repeated after nationalisation. Taking over from the 'B17s' in the late 1930s were the 'V2' Class 2-6-2s, though only a few members of the class ever visited Gorton for light attention.

In the early 1930s the LNER began trials with welding techniques in the construction of wagon underframes. Gresley's assistant O. V. S. Bulleid was a keen believer in this practice and was perhaps instrumental in encouraging the CME to test the merits for and against. Dukinfield was chosen to be first of the company's works to produce a welded underframe for the standard 12-ton high-sided wagon. When completed in 1933 the process was said to have reduced the number of rivets used from 800 to 170, thereby saving a good deal of weight and labour, as well as money. After testing, the wagon was said to stand up to the rigours of shunting quite well.

After a slow start to the 1930s, with regard to construction of new wagons – which only saw 150 container flats sent into traffic, together with thirty-five underframes being sent to Faverdale for new refrigerator vans – Dukinfield was quite busy through the middle and latter part of the decade. The resurgence started in 1933 with a change of management as D. R. Edge took responsibility of Dukinfield alongside the Carriage and Wagon Shops at Doncaster (at the same time F. W. Carr became the Gorton Works Manager). During 1934 there were 500 sets of welded underframes produced for the Diagram 25 covered goods

van with pressed steel ends, in addition to 100 container flats. The order for welded underframes more than doubled in 1935, with 1,200 sent to Faverdale to have the bodies attached, and this work was supplemented by fifty pipe wagons and more ballast, rail and sleeper wagons. The height of Dukinfield's wagon construction came in 1937 when 756 examples were completed. Several types formed this number, including: 300 container flats; 100 pipe wagons; 250 single bolster; fifteen seven-bolster wagons with a capacity of 40 tons; sixty-one plate wagons; six 50-ton and four 55-ton trestle wagons; one well trolley; and nine 40-ton flat wagons to work with the new Morris tracklayer. In the following year a similar number of the heavy type of wagons was built, which was a result of the rearmament programme proceeding apace. Gorton Works assisted in this task by building five 20-ton machine wagons for approximately £2,000.

Throughout the early 1930s the Carriage Shops constructed a number of Composite and 3rd Brake vehicles before being given the large task of building new stock for the GE and GC Section suburban services in the London and Nottingham areas. The first were produced in 1935 to Diagrams 202-205 for trains to Ilford and these consisted – in pairs – of Brake 3rd, 2nd, 3rd and Composite (built by the Gloucester Railway Carriage & Wagon Co Ltd), with 54ft 1½in bodies and ten compartments seating twelve each. In 1936 work began on the coaches for the GC Section and these comprised Diagrams 210, 213 and 214 articulated twins, which were Brake 3rds and Composites with 55ft 6¼in bodies. The compartment arrangements were, respective to the diagrams above: six seating ten each and two 1st and five 3rds accommodating seven and ten; five/ten, three 1st taking seven and four 3rds seating ten; the Brake 3rd was the same as Diagram 210, while there were four 1sts with space for seven and three 3rd Class for nine passengers each. The final types of articulated stock to be built at Dukinfield in 1938 and 1939 were the Diagram 242 1st and 3rd Class carriages and Diagrams 272-274, consisting of 1st/3rd Brake, 3rd Brake/3rd and 1st/Composite.

Even with the valuable contribution Dukinfield had made to both the carriage and wagon stocks of the LNER, the company gave 'financial considerations' as the reason

A Diagram 47 septuplet bolster wagon built in 1937.

'B3' Class 4-6-0 No 6166 *Earl Haig* fitted with Caprotti valve gear. The structure over the cylinders housing the cam boxes was subsequently removed.

for removing the responsibility of new carriage and wagon construction and carriage repairs from the works in 1939. These tasks were delegated to Doncaster and York, to which a third of the workforce was expected to relocate; around 200 people lost their jobs. The MP for Gorton, William Wedgwood Benn, appealed to the Minister of Labour in August for Government work to be put in hand at the shops in order to stop the men from uprooting their families, but this was to no avail. Even after war broke out no carriage or wagon construction was given to the works, although armament jobs were received. While full wagon repairs remained part of the remit, only light carriage repairs were given and this remained the case right through to the BR period; each of the other LNER workshops had between 2,500 and 3,500 (approximately) carriages allocated.

After the last engines were built at Gorton in 1928, Gresley instructed the shops to convert two of the '9P' (LNER 'B3') Class 4-6-0s as part of his poppet valve experiments. In December and September 1929 respectively Nos 6166 *Earl Haig* and 6168 *Lord Stuart of Wortley* had Caprotti poppet valves and rotary cam valve gear fitted in an attempt to reduce their coal consumption, which had been a problem for several of Robinson's 4-6-0 classes. The Caprotti arrangement consisted of four valves per cylinder, one for inlet steam and one for exhaust at each end, and these were operated by a similar rotary cam design to that fitted to the 'D49/2s'. The distinguishing feature between the two applications was that the cut-off positions for the Caprotti valves were infinitely variable, giving much greater control in the operation of the locomotive. In service the coal consumption of the Caprotti 'B3s' was reduced by approximately 16% in relation to the average of the piston-valve 'B3s'. After overcoming a small number of setbacks,

the application was extended to No 6167 in June 1938 and No 6164 *Earl Beatty* in June 1939. The operation of the valves on the latter was slightly changed so that they were re-seated using steam instead of springs. These four 'B3' Class engines were the only examples of Caprotti valves being used on the LNER and the locomotives retained the equipment until withdrawal, which occurred between September 1946 and December 1947.

Gorton provided the valuable service of producing cylinders for many of the LNER's locomotive classes. A noteworthy event for the works was the casting of the cylinders and valves for Gresley's new 'P2' Class 2-8-2 locomotive No 2001 *Cock o' the North* in 1934 to form a 'monobloc' cylinder unit. The production of this was

Casting cylinders at Gorton, c1930.

The cylinder block made at Gorton for 'P2' Class 2-8-2 No 2001 *Cock o' the North*.

partially the responsibility of R. A. Thom, Mechanical Engineer, Doncaster, and the piece was probably one of the most complicated castings of the type to be produced at the time because of the greater number of valves used in the poppet valve system. Twelve valves were provided in this instance, with four serving each cylinder – two for steam inlet and two for exhaust – and space also had to be provided for the passageways and ports. The steam valves were 8 inches in diameter and the exhaust valves had a diameter of 9 inches, with large ports provided to allow free steam flow. With a width of 8ft 11¾in, the unit had the outside cylinders centred at 6ft 8½in and inclined at 1 in 30, while the inside cylinder was inclined at 1 in 7.713 to allow for clearance over the leading coupled axle and to drive on to the second coupled axle as per Gresley's preference. The monobloc casting was attached to the frames by flanges 1³/₈ inches thick and 4ft 3¾ inches apart, the cylinder walls were 1¹/₂ inches thick, steam inlet valve walls were 1⁷/₈ inch deep and the exhaust walls were ⁷/₈ inch thick. The monobloc weighed approximately 7 tons.

Before the Second World War Gorton built fourteen 'J50' Class 0-6-0T locomotives, the design for which had originated on the GNR by Gresley in 1914 and subsequently made a Group Standard type. The new engines, which were built between November 1938 and August 1939 and taking numbers between 599 and 615 (first series) and 584 and 598, were notable for using welding in the fabrication of the side tanks, and they had hopper-style coal bunkers. The locomotives were widely dispersed throughout the Southern Area of the LNER after entering service.

Around this time *The Engineer* reported that a new acetylene generating plant was to be installed at Gorton to keep up with the demand. Approximately 158,000 cubic feet was being consumed annually for welding and cutting procedures and had been purchased or produced by portable machines.

During the conflict the *LNER Magazine* noted that women had been taken into Gorton Works to help with a number of tasks:

'When women were first introduced at Gorton it was felt that the Boiler Department "could not possibly make use

Shells being made at Dukinfield during the Second World War.

'B3' No 6166 as rebuilt with Thompson 'B1' appointments. The engine is pictured at Neasden shed during July 1947.

of them." But time marches on, and we decided to try. The first two – hefty Lancashire lassies – remained at their post exactly ten minutes. "Ee, we conna stand thet neise," they reported. But stand it they did after a little persuasion, and to-day, in spite of the noise, in spite of the inevitable dirt, in spite of the gloom of black-out workshops, we have women crane drivers, pneumatic drillers, planers, shapers, machine drillers, tube welders, storekeepers, tractor drivers, boilermakers' helpers, rivet girls and labourers, all putting up with it and sometimes enjoying it. Special mention should be avoided, but two of our crane drivers certainly merit a pat on the back. The ticklish job of slinging a boiler exactly where it is wanted is managed very efficiently by these two women who were, I think, "Nippies" [waitresses] in peace-time. Even in a department as "heavy" as this, women are capable of performing a great deal of the work, and it is possible to find employment for them in the proportion of one woman or girl to every ten men.'

After Thompson's appointment in 1941, Gorton was told to implement some of his rebuilding plans, which concerned the 'J11' Class (GCR '9J') 0-6-0s and the 'B3s'. The former were to receive new cylinders of the same type as used by the 'J39s', having a diameter of 18½ inches, and piston valves, with slight modifications necessary for these to be fitted. No 6009 was the first in July 1942 and was followed by a further twenty-three up to nationalisation, then seven under BR until 1953, when the project was discontinued. No 6166 *Earl Haig* was used as a prototype for Thompson's two-cylinder 4-6-0 conversions and during 1943 the locomotive was dismantled and much of the original scrapped. The majority of the new parts belonged to Thompson's 'B1' Class, including front

frame sections, cylinders, bogie, boiler and valve gear. After re-entering traffic, the locomotive's performance was not good enough to warrant the modification of the remainder of the class and all were scrapped in 1946/47, being followed in April 1949 by No 6166 as BR No 61497. A more widespread conversion scheme was that of the 'O4' (GCR '8K') Class 2-8-0s to 'O1' Class specifications, which again took their lead from the Thompson 'B1'. This included the boiler, cylinders and motion, but the original frames, pony truck and tender were retained. No 6595 was the first alteration in February 1944 and was followed by a further fifteen up to the end of the year, and thirty-five to nationalisation. Only five more received the changes under BR and the last was No 6617 in October 1949. The class were maintained at Gorton from 1944 until 1962.

In 1948 Gorton Works covered just over 30 acres, 15 of which were under cover, and employment was found for more than 2,500 people. Dukinfield had the same number of acres but those under cover were slightly less at 13, while the workforce had fallen to less than 550. The role of both places in British Railways was little altered from that defined by the LNER before the war. One of the last jobs entrusted to Gorton before the demise of the latter was the fabrication of thirty boilers for the 'B1' Class locomotives being built by the NBLC in 1947, and this was followed by an order for ten members of the class from Gorton, which was placed in December of that year. The locomotives were built from November 1948 to July 1949 and took numbers 61340 to 61349 – the last-mentioned being the final steam locomotive to be built at Gorton. Around 1,000 had been erected in almost 100 years, although the exact number was not a certainty as works numbers were never issued.

Thompson Class O1 2-8-0 No 63678 in Gorton Works yard, during 1948.

The Manchester to Sheffield electrification scheme was interrupted by the war and recommenced in the late 1940s. The motive power for the traffic on the line was based on the prototype built at Doncaster to Gresley's design in 1941 and a start was made on constructing these locomotives in 1949. For this there was a certain amount of reorganisation at Gorton so that the bogies, frames and bodies could be assembled, and space was made at Dukinfield for the installation of the electrical equipment.

Components for the electric locomotives ready for assembly.

This was supplied by Metropolitan Vickers and consisted of four motors with a continuous rating of 1,360hp at 56mph, and at the 1-hour rating of 1,868hp at 45mph, with a maximum starting tractive effort of 45,000lb; the maximum speed was 65mph. No 26001 was the first to be completed in October 1950 and was subsequently followed into service by a further fifty-six members of the class, which was designated 'EM1' initially, later becoming Class 76 under the TOPS scheme. Also constructed during this period was a six-wheel (Co-Co) bogie version with six motors that had a continuous rating of 2,298hp at 46mph, and the 1-hour rating was 2,490hp at 44.3mph. The maximum starting tractive effort was the same as the 'EM1s', but the maximum speed was 90mph. Only seven of these were built between 1953 and 1954, being numbered 27000-27006, as, unfortunately, the 1,500DC system soon proved undesirable and the remaining twenty ordered were cancelled. The 'EM2s' were later sold to the railway of the Netherlands.

There was little evidence of the BR Standard classes at Gorton as none were allocated there for repairs. Some 9F 2-10-0s did receive general repairs there as Doncaster was weaned away from steam and concentrated on the maintenance of diesel locomotives. By the early 1960s both Gorton and Dukinfield were seeing a considerable reduction in their capacities and the decision was taken in 1962 that both should be closed and all tasks distributed elsewhere; the electric locomotives went to Crewe and steam locomotives to Darlington. Gorton closed in 1963 with the loss of nearly 1,500 jobs.

Above 'EM2' No 27003 and an unidentified 'EM1', c1955.

Below 'D9' Class 4-4-0 No 62302 stands alongside the Boiler Shop on 29 April 1950 after being condemned in March. The bridge over the main line from Manchester is seen in the background. *K. H. Cockerill, courtesy of J. W. Armstrong* Trust

6

Inverurie

Many railways had been proposed and constructed across the country before serious consideration was given to a railway line serving the northern city of Aberdeen. In mid-1844 a Great North of Scotland Railway company applied to Parliament to build a line, but this was rejected. Subsequently, two rival parties decided to join forces for a line to the south, linking with the Arbroath & Forfar at Guthrie. The Aberdeen Railway succeeded in gaining an Act of Parliament in 1845, and was completed in 1848.

Also founded in 1845 was a second Great North of Scotland Railway (GNSR), which promoted a line from Aberdeen to Inverness. This enterprise generated a good deal of support as the prospective traffic was said to be worth more than £170,000 and the share dividend some 7%. Royal Assent was given to the Act for the route in 1846, although by this time the 'Railway Mania' had subsided and the funds and will to build the line disappeared overnight. Three years passed before action was taken to start the project moving again, but further delays with regard to the

A map showing Kittybrewster Works, Aberdeen, at the start of the 20th century.

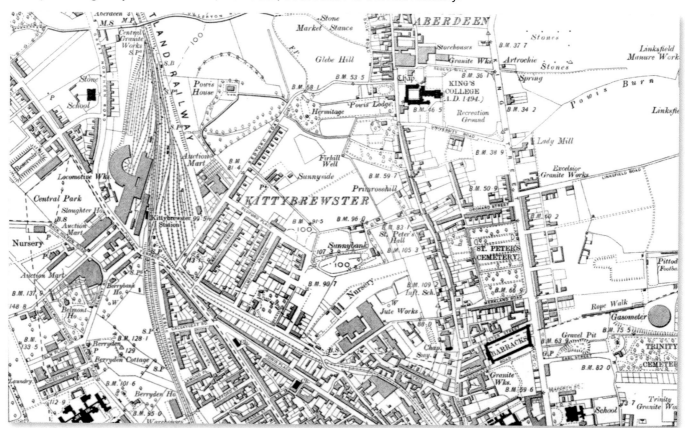

Clark Class '1' 2-4-0 No 4 was built by William Fairbairn & Sons in 1854.

finances crippled progress until late 1852, when the first sod was cut for a short section from Kittybrewster to Huntly. After several more setbacks this section of just under 40 miles was ready for opening on 19 September 1854.

The GNSR's bad luck soon spread to the motive power and rolling stock, as only half of the twelve locomotives bought were delivered on time, and this was also the case for the carriages and wagons. The passenger engines were 2-4-0s bought from William Fairbairn & Sons, Manchester, and designated Class '1'. Cylinders of 15 inches diameter by 20 inches stroke were provided, the boiler worked at 130lb per sq in, the total heating surface was 749sq ft and the driving wheels were of 5ft 6in diameter. Five of the twelve locomotives were for goods services and these were sent north in 1855, being generally similar to the passenger type but with 5-foot-diameter wheels. Both were designed by the company's Locomotive Superintendent, D. K. Clark, who was quite unorthodox in wanting to fulfil his role from London through a representative in Aberdeen. The Board quickly pressed him to take his responsibility more seriously, yet Clark's response was to resign, and he was replaced by J. F. Ruthven. He had been Clark's assistant and Works Manager of the small shops located at Kittybrewster on the west side of the station near the engine shed. Ruthven oversaw the purchase of two 0-4-0WT and four 2-4-0 engines in 1856 and 1857 before departing south and being succeeded by William Cowan. The carriages used during this period were four-wheel vehicles for both 1st and 3rd Classes, and were generally quite basic.

Progress was made to Inverness when the Inverness & Aberdeen Junction Railway took the initiative of building a line to meet the GNSR at Keith, which was the second section built by the latter company. The two cities were subsequently joined by rail in 1858, but the lines were worked by the respective companies as no formal running rights were granted. The GNSR subsequently sought to lease and amalgamate several smaller lines during the 1860s, accumulating more than 200 miles to its network by the mid-point in the decade. This brought several classes of locomotives into the fold, many of which would continue in service on their respective lines for many years afterwards. Cowan had also been introducing his own designs, and these were 2-4-0s built by Robert Stephenson & Co, followed by 4-4-0 versions in 1862, that wheel arrangement being quite unusual at the time. The success of the type allowed further 4-4-0s to be ordered from Neilson & Co in 1866, and these had slightly enlarged dimensions from their predecessors with 16-inch by 24-inch cylinders, a 4ft 0$\frac{1}{8}$ in-diameter boiler with a heating surface of 1,049sq ft and working at a pressure of 120lb per sq in, and 5ft 6½in-diameter driving wheels.

The GNSR's fortunes declined in the late 1860s, and throughout the first half of the 1870s financial austerity was very much in effect. Towards the end of the decade, when the situation improved, much of the system was overhauled, including the repair shops and locomotive shed at Kittybrewster, which were reorganised and expanded to the limit of the site. The main block of buildings consisted of a Boiler Shop at the east end, an Erecting Shop in the middle, and a Smiths' Shop on the west end, with a Finishing Shop connected to the Erecting Shop's south face. There were also facilities for constructing and maintaining the

No 35 was one of Cowan's Class '28' 4-4-0s and was erected by Robert Stephenson & Co in 1864; it was later rebuilt in 1882.

carriages and wagons. At the time the latter had wooden underframes, a 9-foot wheelbase and 3ft 7in-diameter wheels. The main traffic was in cattle and fish. and much of the stock catered for this.

No new additions were made to the locomotive stock until the mid-1870s, when further engines from Neilson & Co with the same wheel arrangement were introduced, numbering twelve up to 1879. Cowan retired from the company in 1883 and took a position as a representative for Krupp. In the early 1860s the GNSR had experimented with that firm's design of seamless steel tyres and had found them to be much more durable than the cast-iron type previously employed. Cowan was succeeded by James Manson, who introduced his first design in mid-1884, an 0-6-0T for good and shunting duties. These engines were received from Kitson & Co, as were several 4-4-0s and a different design of 0-6-0T in ensuing years.

Kittybrewster would be called upon to build two locomotives in 1887, which is surprising given that part of the workshops had been destroyed by a fire on 25 October 1886. The blaze was discovered in the Boiler and Finishing Shops during the early hours of the morning by Foreman Engine Cleaner Hugh Campbell, who quickly summoned help from the shed and the fire brigade, which was soon

Class '49' No 49 was constructed by Neilson & Co in March 1876 and was subsequently rebuilt during August 1898. It was placed on the duplicate list in October 1920, then carrying an 'A' suffix, before withdrawal four years later.

Manson Class 'N' No 5 *Kinmundy* has become LNER No 6805 of Class 'D46' and stripped of its name.

at work trying to stop the flames from spreading. While this was successful the destruction of the two shops and the machinery contained therein was said to have cost the company £2,000, not to mention disruption to the repair and maintenance of the company's stock. In spite of this event, Kittybrewster was able to complete 4-4-0 No 5 *Kinmundy* in February 1887 and No 6 *Thomas Adam* later in the year, these being of Manson's 'N' Class design, which only consisted of the two locomotives. They had 4ft 4in-diameter boilers with 1,186.7sq ft of heating surface and 140lb per sq in pressure, with 17½-inch by 26-inch cylinders and 5ft 7in-diameter drivers. The expected saving of £300-400 in constructing the locomotives at Kittybrewster either did not materialise or the space – only four engines could be taken into the Erecting Shop – and manpower taken up by the task was too great, as these two 4-4-0s were the only locomotives to be erected there.

The GNSR prospered during the late 1880s and early 1890s, meaning that the locomotive, carriage and wagon stock was generally hard at work and had an increased need for attention in the workshops. At the turn of the decade the expense of repairing the locomotives had fallen slightly, but that for the carriages and wagons had risen by nearly £500. The latter came about because of a lack of space at Kittybrewster, causing an ever-growing backlog. The Board was contemplating extensions to several shops on site when a proposal was formulated to relocate the workshops entirely. A committee was then formed to oversee the project, which began with the group visiting several building centres across Britain and consulting a number of prominent figures in locomotive engineering regarding a possible layout.

Meanwhile, Manson retired in 1890 and his role passed to James Johnson, who only produced two

classes during his four years with the GNSR. These were the Class 'R' 0-4-4Ts and 'S' Class 4-4-0s, both being generally similar in their main features to preceding designs. William Pickersgill moved from the GER in 1894 to become Locomotive Superintendent and he continued the 4-4-0 tradition with three classes built at Neilson & Co between 1895 and 1899. The boilers were 4ft 6in in diameter with 1,207sq ft of heating surface, a pressure of 165lb per sq in and an 18.24sq ft grate, the cylinders were 18 inches by 26 inches, and the coupled wheels 6ft 1in in diameter. Pickersgill also introduced the compartment carriage to the railway in 1896 when 1st Class, 1st/3rd Composites and 3rd Class vehicles were built. These had four, two/three and five compartments respectively and two toilets at one end, while six-wheel underframes were provided. However, only two years later the GNSR's first bogie carriages were introduced from Kittybrewster for the express to Inverness; these were 1st/3rd Composites with two and four compartments provided for each.

By the end of the 19th century the GNSR had bought 24 acres at Inverurie, 15 miles north-west of Kittybrewster, on the western site of the main line, for the erection of complete workshops for locomotives, carriages and wagons. Land was also purchased for the erection of houses a short distance away, as many hundreds of workers and their families had to relocate. The Carriage & Wagon Department was the first to make the move in 1901, as several of the locomotive shops were still some time from being ready. Much of the exterior was finished, with Pringle & Slessor of Aberdeen using blocks of granite from Tyrebagger quarry. The Carriage & Wagon Shop was at the northern end of the site and was 360 feet long by 150 feet wide. Flooring

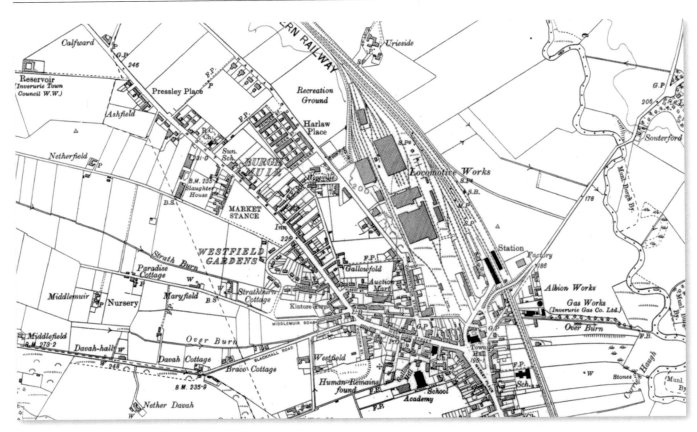

A map of Inverurie and the Works, c1930.

was of Norwegian pine, and some 15 tons of nails were used to fix the planks in position. John Buchanan was contracted for the task, while the roof's iron beams were supplied by Alex Findlay & Co of Motherwell and the slates were affixed by George Davidson of Aberdeen. Seven tracks passed through the building and machinery was arranged along the western side. Power was obtained from an engine supplied by Belliss & Morcom of Birmingham, and a dynamo by Thomas Parker Ltd. Electric lights, numbering more than 400, were used

in addition to the large number of windows running along the eastern and western sides of the building; electricity was also produced at the works for the homes of the employees. Occupying the south-west corner were the pattern-makers and underneath them was the shop's stores.

Adjacent to the Carriage & Wagon Shop's west side was the Paint Shop, slightly smaller than the former at 250 feet by 100 feet and with only five tracks entering. Ample lighting was provided throughout the shop, using both natural light admitted from the large number of windows on all sides and more than 200 electric lamps. Flooring was of concrete and in the south-east corner was a workroom for trimmers and electricians, and stores. Near the Paint Shop was a bowling green, tennis court and park, while across Harlaw Road was the house built for the Works Manager; to the north of this were the seven groups of houses erected for the employees. Some had four rooms, while others contained three; the former had two bedrooms, a kitchen and parlour, which were all furnished.

A short distance to the south of the Carriage and Wagon Shops was a building containing the Forge, Tinsmiths' Shop, Brass Foundry, Tyre Shop, Coppersmiths' Shop and Smithy. The latter contained a furnace, steam hammers, nut and bolt machine and grinding machines. In the Tyre Shop there were several blowers and in the Tinsmiths next door all the lamps used by the railway were made and repaired. With several fires being experienced at Kittybrewster over the years a fire station was built at the rear of the Smithy, housing a hose cart and apparatus by

The electricity generating equipment at Inverurie Works.

Hammering a component in the Forge.

Driving wheels and a travelling crane are proudly displayed in the Wheel Shop.

Mason & Co., which was capable of delivering 300 gallons of water per minute. At several places around the shops there were standpipes placed in case of an emergency, in addition to a number of hose reels. Water for the various fire-fighting equipment was drawn from the company's supply at Polinar – some 20 miles south – a second supply came from the same source for general use and a third was drawn from the Inverurie supply, which could be drunk. The main pipes were 4in diameter and branches 3in diameter.

A large block on the southern end of the site contained the Machine and Fitting Shop in the northern section and the Erecting Shop and Boiler Shops in the southern half. The Machine Shop was 266 feet long by 98 feet wide with two bays, but part of the space was dedicated to a variety of functions other than the primary one. The machine tools were arranged in the northern bay and were served by a 5-ton overhead crane. In the southern section there was an office, several stores, an accumulator for hydraulic equipment, and plant supplying power to the workshops. This took up more than 1,500sq ft and consisted of compound engines by Beliss & Morcom and dynamos from Siemens and Parker. A large steam engine was also present and this had two 12-inch by 24-inch cylinders fed by four locomotive boilers. The apparatus was fitted to a wall 31 feet thick.

The structure containing the Erecting Shop and Boiler Shop measured 289 feet by 270 feet and each had an area of 24,500sq ft. The former had fifteen pits to receive locomotives, spaced at 50-foot centres and served by an 80-ton electrically driven crane. Two of the bays were given over to cylinder boring, and special machinery was installed there for the work. A large amount of dedicated plant for boiler manufacture was housed in the Boiler Shop including plate benders, shearing and punching apparatus and cutters. Electricity was supplied by a 20-horsepower motor, while compressed air was used for the drills, rivet hammers and furnaces. A fireproof pattern store was located near the Paint Shop, and facing Harlaw

The cylinders of a locomotive receive attention in the Erecting Shop.

Above Pickersgill Class 'V' No 28, seen here as LNER 'D40' No 6828, was erected at Inverurie in March 1913.

Below Heywood Class 'F' No 45 *George Davidson* carried the number 6845 for the LNER and 62273 for BR from May 1925 and July 1948 respectively, managing to keep its name throughout.

Road were the main offices. This building was also made from granite and contained the rooms of the Locomotive Superintendent, Drawing Office and Stores Department; in the attic the works photographer had a dark room.

Perhaps the first vehicles to be built at the works were three-plank wagons of 8-ton capacity, later being followed by new carriages in the middle of the first decade of the 20th century. Pickersgill's final new passenger carriages were slightly old-fashioned in continuing to use six wheels when erected in 1906.

The first locomotive was not turned out of Inverurie until 1909 when No 27 of a second batch of 'V' Class 4-4-0 engines was built. Seven locomotives of this type followed steadily from the workshops up to March 1915. After Pickersgill left for the Caledonian Railway, Thomas Heywood took his position and produced similar 4-4-0s to the Class 'F' design; the final two of this eight-strong group – Nos 45 *George Davidson* and 46 *Benachie* – were from Inverurie, while the other six were bought from the North British Locomotive Company.

Aberdeen was an important location for the Navy during the First World War and as a result the GNSR stock was worked hard, and Inverurie was on hand to keep the vehicles in service. The shops also managed to produce materials for the war effort including wagons, picketing posts and pegs, stretchers, snow ploughs, fuse adaptors, mortars and ambulance trains.

At the Grouping Inverurie employed approximately 500 men, and nearly the same number of wagons were on the building programme for the year. Being a relatively small operation in the newly formed LNER, there was naturally some nervousness as to whether the shops would continue under the new regime. *The Aberdeen Daily Journal* voiced such a concern in an article of 5 August 1922 and noted the impact that this would have on the local economy as a quarter of the community were employees at Inverurie. The uncertainty lasted until 1924 when the LNER Board gave the works full backing for the repair and maintenance of the stock in the area for the coming years after visiting the site in 1923 and being suitably impressed with the arrangement and the machinery employed. T. Heywood left his position in 1924 and became Mechanical Engineer, Gorton, but later oversaw the workshops again as part of his role as Mechanical Engineer, Scotland, from 1927 until his retirement in 1942.

As the 1920s wore on the hopes that Inverurie could take on more work, which had been indicated by the Board in 1924, were dashed as the period of financial difficulties began. The works was hit in 1928 when the staff were put on short time and were not required to work on Saturdays. This lasted for around a year before the Locomotive and Carriage Departments – consisting of around 400 men – were given notice of their hours being reduced to just 4 per day. The time was subsequently restored, but a 5½-day week was not restored until March 1938, when the shops readied the stock for the summer traffic.

During early July 1937 the works shut down for the annual ten-day break and during this time the electrical

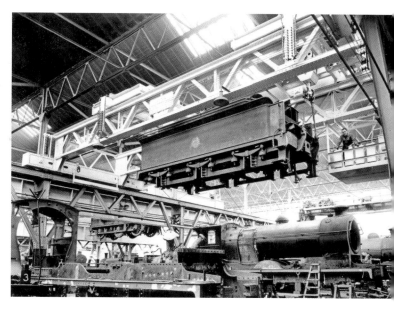

A new 40-ton crane lifting a tender in 1955.

supply apparatus was completely replaced and old steam engines dispensed with. This allowed the current to be taken from the Grampian Electricity Supply Company, which had recently arrived in the district. As the works used DC current and the Grampian Co AC, mercury arc rectifiers converted the 440 volts received to 220 volts. The electricity was not only distributed to the tools in the shops but also to 120 houses nearby for the men.

In 1946 the *LNER Magazine* told the story of William Burns Junior – a fitter at Inverurie – who had answered the call to arms early in the Second World War and was at Singapore when the city fell to the Japanese. He was taken prisoner and was forced to work on the Burma Railway before being moved to Japan. On his way there the ship he was on sank after being torpedoed, and he spent 12 hours on a raft, then 26 on a lifeboat before

A new 50-ton crane has hold of 'J37' Class 0-6-0 No 64569.

Above McIntosh 0-6-0 No 57612 outside Inverurie Works in the early 1960s. *Bill Reed*

Below 'J37' No 64572 is resplendent after a visit to the shops. *Bill Reed*

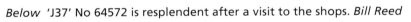

being rescued by a Japanese vessel, spending the rest of the war in a POW Camp. After his release in September 1945 he returned to Inverurie via Manila and America.

The Paint Shop was fortunate to be left standing in 1947 as a fire broke out towards the end of the year. Luckily, the blaze was spotted from one of the houses nearby and only a large amount of paint was lost before the fire brigade was able to intervene.

At nationalisation there were around 650 people employed at Inverurie and more than 100 general repairs were carried out annually, in addition to just under eighty light repairs. The Carriage Department undertook more than 750 light and 250 heavy repairs, while the Wagon Shops saw 853 general repairs take place and in excess of 6,000 vehicles underwent light attention. Many of the GNSR classes were gradually retired throughout the LNER period and replaced with standard LNER classes such as the 'B1s' and 'J39s', while, amongst others, 'B12' Class 4-6-0s also worked in the area. Naturally, these classes visited Inverurie to receive repairs, while 'V2' Class 2-6-2s sometimes arrived for light attention, and in their

final years 'A4' Class locomotives were taken in and patched up to save some from otherwise heading to the scrapyard. After the BR Standard classes were introduced some made their way to the works for various tasks to be carried out.

The arrival of diesel locomotives in the area during the late 1950s and early 1960s initially allowed Inverurie to be reorganised to carry out repairs to both these and steam engines as the latter were run down. Type 1 and Type 2 designs entered the workshops, together with the new diesel multiple units. Inverurie survived the first round of closures in 1962, as the location of the shops was more convenient than sending rolling stock south to St Rollox. Unfortunately, BR was hard-hit by poor returns at the end of the 1960s and needed to reduce expenditure. Inverurie was one of three works scheduled for closure by the end of the decade. The shops fell silent at the end of 1969 and subsequently much has been demolished including the Erecting Shop, Machine and Fitting Shop and Paint Shop. Surviving are the Smiths' Shops and Carriage and Wagon Shops.

Class 'F' No 49 *Gordon Highlander* was repainted at Inverurie after withdrawal in June 1958 and was based there for a short time to run excursions. *Bill Reed*

7

Shildon and Faverdale

John Dixon, who was an assistant to George and Robert Stephenson when they surveyed the route for the Stockton & Darlington Railway (S&DR), once proclaimed that 'Shildon is the nursery of the locomotive'. But the inhabitants of the village would have been incredulous to such a statement before the arrival of the railway in 1825, as there was nothing there. *The Engineer* of 29 September 1876 explained: '…part of Old Shildon was in being, whilst an inn, Dan Adamson's, was the nearest house to the site of New Shildon, which was wet,

The first locomotive built at Shildon Works was Hackworth's *Royal George*.

swampy fields – a likely place to find a snipe or a flock of peewits.'

Shortly after the line's opening a number of buildings began to spring up around the station, which was a short distance from the village. Two of these were a blacksmith and a joiner, both finding jobs with the new concern, and there was an engine shed capable of stabling two of the three locomotives at work. Repairs – frequently required at this stage – were carried out here and were performed using very basic equipment. Ropes and pulleys lifted objects, screw jacks raised boilers, and hand lathes were used on the various components. Dedicated workshops soon had to be established as the locomotive stock grew, and these were placed west of the station, latterly on the south side of the Haggerleases branch. Shildon Works was opened during 1826 under Locomotive Superintendent Timothy Hackworth. He had been employed previously at Robert Stephenson & Co and had overseen the construction of the S&DR's first locomotive *Locomotion* before being employed by the company.

The first locomotive was built at Shildon in 1827 to Hackworth's design and was a considerable improvement on the small number that had been bought previously. The *Royal George* was a six-coupled locomotive with a coal cart at one end and a water supply at the other, all weighing 15 tons. The boiler was 4 feet in diameter and 13 feet long, and the cylinders were 11 inches in diameter by a 20-inch stroke. The most important feature of the engine was the use of a blastpipe to improve the draught on the fire, while a novelty was a pre-heater for the water fed into the boiler.

The workshops continued to build locomotives sporadically throughout the 1830s – the output has been said to be no more than three of four per year – and also repaired the company's motive power. In 1947 the *LNER Magazine* produced an article on the works and recorded that Hackworth entered into an unusual arrangement with the Board. He became a leaseholder of the works in 1833 and paid the S&DR 5% on the value of the buildings and content, while receiving four-tenths of a penny of the revenue earned by the locomotives for every mile travelled per ton of merchandise. At this time Hackworth also founded Soho Works at Shildon, north-east of the station between the junction of the Haggerleases branch and the line to Bishop Auckland. This was done in partnership with his brother, who ran the shops, and Nicholas Downing. Hackworth's arrangement with the S&DR lasted until 1840, when he resigned and left the company to run the Soho Works himself.

William Bouch assumed control at Shildon under a similar arrangement and he followed the lead of his predecessor, initially building engines in the same vein as the *Royal George*. Works No 1 was constructed early in his tenure; this was No 7 *Prince*, which was used on mineral trains and had 15-inch by 20-inch cylinders. Several older engines were rebuilt to resemble this locomotive, the task being performed at the nearby Soho Works, and further examples were erected at Shildon throughout the 1840s. Bouch broke away from Hackworth practice in the latter

Men from the Soho Works pose for the camera.

half of the decade with three 0-6-0s, the first of which was No 35 *Commerce*. These had cylinders of 16 inches by 24 inches mounted horizontally, and had fireboxes designed to burn coke. The motion was unusual in having the connecting rod attached to the crank pin inside the connecting rod. This required a large circular section to stop the crank pin for the connecting rod on the leading pair of wheels from being fouled. At the same time two new passenger engines were completed with a 2-4-0 wheel arrangement and 14½-inch by 24-inch cylinders; all the aforementioned were provided with six-wheel tenders to carry both coal and water.

There was little unorthodoxy in the locomotive stock during the ensuing years and many engines were built by outside firms such as W. & A. Kitching, Gilkes, Wilson & Co, Robert Stephenson & Co, and R. & W. Hawthorn & Co. The second-mentioned was called upon to build the first of Bouch's long-boilered 0-6-0s, which became stalwarts of the line for many decades subsequently. One of the more unusual types were the two 4-4-0s built in 1860 by Robert Stephenson & Co, which for the day also possessed a very generous cab. In 1850 Hackworth died and the Soho Works was subsequently abandoned until 1855 when the S&DR began to use the buildings for the maintenance of its own stock.

The *LNER Magazine* of 1947 also recorded some of the features of working at Shildon in the 1840s. Men were originally contracted for a month's employment, but this was later altered to two weeks. Working hours were 6.00am to 6.00pm, and at 8.00am there was 30 minutes for breakfast, while dinner was consumed at 12.00 midday; a bell was rung to call or dismiss them from the shops. These long hours were periodically shortened for the men to take afternoon tea with their families and for entertainments to occur. During the early 1840s the men were put on 'short time' rather than being dismissed, and there was a reduction in the wages. The latter was rescinded in the mid-point of the decade, but only for some of the workers. Smoking was banned in the workshops and a fine of 3d was imposed on any guilty parties; this was presumably to

The Erecting Shop at Shildon, with metal hoppers under construction.

keep productivity high and the men free from distraction, rather than concern for health. However, steps were taken to address the latter issue as the company engaged a Dr Clarke and his assistant Dr Henderson to attend to all workmen and their families after the sum of 2d per week had been paid. There were several outbreaks of cholera during the 1840s and 1850s, causing the company to take action by providing disinfecting fluid without charge to those who wished to take precautions. Free schooling was introduced around 1870; before this, those who wished to send their children to school had to pay either 3d or 2d per week, but if the child had a good attendance record and the fees had been delivered promptly there was a discount to just 1d per week.

Men in the Timber Yard at Shildon.

Even though the Soho Works had been absorbed by the S&DR there was still a shortage of space in the shops at Shildon. This led to Bouch being given the task of setting up new workshops at Darlington, and these were opened in 1863. As a result, Shildon was no longer expected to produce new locomotives, which was a remit that ceased entirely in the late 1860s and was followed by a reduction in locomotive repairs, but the shops were subsequently used for wagon repairs and new construction. *The Engineer* of 29 September 1876 proclaimed that Shildon had recently performed 100,000 repairs on locomotives, wagons and trucks during one year, and had also built 500 new trucks.

From the beginning of the company's existence the wagon stock had been bought on an 'as required' basis from several firms. These consisted of chaldron wagons (in the main made from wood, but also iron) and low-sided wagons, numbering fewer than 100 by 1840. During the 1850s high-sided wagons with a 10-ton capacity and 15-foot underframes were introduced and built in numbers subsequently. The chaldron wagons were predecessors of the modern hopper wagons and were designed to provide a funnel for the coal to be discharged through doors in the floor. Brake vans were in use by the 1840s, although they did not become generally widespread until some twenty years later.

As with the locomotive works at Darlington, Shildon continued to serve the S&DR system for a number of years after the takeover. When the S&DR finally relinquished control to the North Eastern Railway (NER), Fletcher soon put work in hand to expand the Soho Works to provide more area for repairs to take place. This was only a temporary measure as the decision was taken in the mid-1880s to expand Shildon Works and close Soho Works. A new Repair Shop was erected, in addition to a Forge and Smiths' Shop, at a cost of approximately £7,000. Before

The Store House, Shildon.

the end of the decade the NER had completely remodelled the site into a modern wagon building and repair centre, spending some £35,000.

Generally, the wagon stock was built using oak frames supported by metal fittings and had wheels with eight open spokes. Standard buffers were used, as were coupling hooks and three-link chains to secure the wagons together, while in some cases screw couplings were employed; automatic couplers were trialled for a brief period. Grease was used in cast-iron axleboxes until the turn of the 20th century, when oil became the favoured option. Morton brakes, with levers on both sides of the wagons, were introduced in 1897 and wagons used on expresses were equipped for both vacuum and Westinghouse brakes as there was a chance the wagon would encounter a railway that spurned the chance to utilise the latter.

The most numerous designs from the start of the 20th century to the Grouping were low-sided goods wagons of 8-ton capacity, later of 10- and 11-ton capacity with modifications being made to the journals and oil being introduced as a lubricant. High-sided open wagons were of four-plank construction and limited to 8 tons, but some were later upgraded to 10 tons. Subsequently, the NER introduced 12-ton six-plank wagons, and more than 20,000 of these were constructed. The single bolster type was also prevalent, and double bolster wagons were formed from permanently coupling two of them together. Coal wagons had capacities varying between 10 and 12 tons and had sides formed from five planks of wood. At

the turn of the century Shildon was building high-capacity coal wagons of 15 tons with bottom discharge and oil lubrication and a 20-ton version of similar design. An interesting development in the design of coal wagons was the 32-ton all-steel variety, which was mounted on two four-wheel bogies, the larger 40-ton type, and a 23-ton coal wagon mounted on four wheels; the first two

A photograph showing the various stages in the manufacture of a wagon coupling hook.

The Smiths' Shop, Shildon.

were built by contractors while the latter appeared from Shildon. All of these were inspired following a trip by NER officials to America where the type was in widespread use, as the steel offered cheap and quick construction, together with durability.

Shildon built a number of wagons for the transportation of coal for locomotive purposes, and these were similar to five-plank open wagons rather than hoppers as there was no need for a bottom discharge; access to the coal could be gained from either the top or a side door. Coke wagons used the 10-ton hopper wagon as a base but had extensions to the tops to increase the load. Ten-ton brake vans were the standard at the turn of the century, although there were some 20-ton examples constructed around the middle of the first decade. Shildon erected a number of long-wheelbase brake vans for the permanent way department in about 1910.

Before the start of the First World War, the NER had felt the strain of having only Shildon as a main workshop, despite support from several smaller repair centres. The company was operating nearly 120,000 wagons annually (of which nearly 60,000 were for coal), and the renewal programme was reaching numbers around 5,000. To meet the renewal requirement without placing orders with the trade – which was deemed undesirable – the NER set about planning new wagon construction facilities at Darlington on land acquired near Stooperdale. The Faverdale Hall estate was bought at the end of 1913 for more than £25,000 and consisted of approximately 240

acres. However, the war soon stopped the plans moving forward, and work did not recommence until the start of the 1920s, when the Minister for War Transport Sir Eric Geddes approved the scheme. The cost for the new works was £750,000 and the 'final touches' were being given to the shops when the LNER came into existence in 1923.

Located to the north-west of Darlington Works' Stooperdale Boiler Shop and the Paint Shop, and on the opposite side of the Barnard Castle line, Faverdale covered 60 acres. The site consisted of a Wagon Erecting Shop with twelve roads, Paint Shop, Sawmill, Machine Shop, Wheel Shop, Wood Drying Shed, Stores and Offices. Full use was made of electricity and mechanisation where possible. The estimated output was said to be 10,000

A 30-ton steel hopper, built in 1906.

The Sawmill, Faverdale. *K. Taylor collection, courtesy of J. W. Armstrong Trust*

wagons a year and the first of these was sent into traffic during August 1923. Employment was found for nearly 500 men and boys.

Wood arrived on site as logs (approximately 200 trees per week), and these then taken into the Saw Mill and put on a table for cutting by two 10-inch vertical band saws; metal grippers turned the log as necessary. The timber then moved on to other machines depending on the requirements. Waste was meticulously collected by suction apparatus to be used for several items, such as keys for the permanent way, treenails and fuel for the boilers. In the Wood Drying Shed, 520 feet long by 120 feet wide, there was enough space to keep material sufficient for a year of wagon building at maximum capacity. The wood was allowed to lose moisture naturally and the sides of the building were louvered to this end. All of the most modern tools were installed in the Machine Shop and the timber passed through on a conveyor system before entering the final stage. In the Erecting Shop (300 feet by 240 feet) the frames and bodies were built up before being lifted by overhead cranes on to the wheels and suspension, which was assembled alongside. The completed wagon then moved into the Paint Shop. A heating and ventilation system was installed here, the latter allowing for the refreshment of the atmosphere three times every hour. After being painted, the wagons were moved by electric capstan and weighed at the end of the shop, and were then sent into traffic.

Two noteworthy machines were the vertical and horizontal boring machines, made by Messrs Wilkins & Mitchell of Walsall. These had seventy spindles and reduced the previous time taken to mark and bore these individually from 35 minutes to just 1 minute. Bits up to 3¼ inches could be fitted and penetrated all the woods used in wagon construction; the drills were all perfectly in line, which eliminated the chance of error. Two 40-horsepower

Cutting logs at Shildon.

One of the saws in action at Faverdale c1930. *K. Taylor collection, courtesy of J. W. Armstrong Trust*

12-ton open wagon No 66682 was the first to be erected at Faverdale in 1923.

One of the large saw blades used at Faverdale, c1930. K. Taylor collection, courtesy of J. W. Armstrong Trust

motors were employed to drive spiral gearing and the two tables had five rollers to aid movement of the timber. The horizontal borer had five 10-horsepower motors and was used to drill through 12 inches of wood. To achieve this successfully – again in 1 minute – bits were used on both sides to take out half the distance, and this also eliminated the chance of the holes distorting.

This 17-ton-capacity coal hopper was built in 1926.

Faverdale was ready to head the LNER's new construction programme in 1924 and was supported by Shildon, which produced all the metal items used on wagons. Generally, the Railway Clearing House standards were adopted as the specifications for the mass-produced types, such as the coal wagons and goods vans. The former were mounted on wooden underframes measuring 16ft 6in with a 9-foot wheelbase, and the latter had underframes 1 foot longer and the same wheelbase; both had a capacity of 12 tons. Axleboxes were made of cast iron, lubrication was by oil and standard buffers were fitted, while spoked wheels were used until the mid-1930s when they were replaced by cast disc wheels. Manual brakes were applied on the right-hand side and vacuum brakes were favoured over the Westinghouse system preferred by some of the LNER's constituents; only a small percentage of the 300,000 wagons inherited by the LNER were equipped with any type of automatic brakes in 1923.

Even though there had been an attempt by the absorbed companies to make up for the lack of replacements during the war years, there was still a large number of old and worn-out vehicles. The LNER tried to turn the situation around in 1924 when nearly 12,000 wagons were ordered from the company's shops, in addition to 300 brake vans from contractors; the total cost was approximately £2,400,000. Faverdale was tasked with producing a number of six-plank high-sided wagons (construction continued through to 1926, when more than 4,000 had been completed), 750 coal wagons, 300 perishable goods vans (of 10-ton capacity and similar to the NER type, but updated to standard specifications in the following year when another 250 were erected), 255 cattle wagons, and seventy-five 10-ton brake vans – these were from an NER order.

This work kept the shops busy until 1926, when the building programme comprised 7,400 wagons, estimated to cost £1,250,000. Both Faverdale and Shildon were occupied building more six-plank open wagons and eight-plank hopper wagons of 20-ton capacity. However, part of this figure for the year was given to the trade, and work was no doubt disrupted by the General Strike of

Constructed in 1926, this 12-ton goods van possessed many Railway Clearing House features.

A 12-ton fruit van built in 1928 to Diagram 43.

This 20-ton capacity locomotive coal wagon was built in 1928 to Diagram 44.

1926. During 1927 the shops were again fully employed with open wagons featuring prominently; this continued into the following year, a variation being the fitting of automatic vacuum brakes. A further 250 coal wagons were erected to Diagram 10 specifications. A number of detail alterations were made to the latter (Diagram 63) and a large fleet had emerged from Faverdale by 1930. Two types of locomotive coal wagons were produced during

this period. The first was to Diagram 44 with a 20-ton capacity, a 21ft 6in underframe and 12-foot wheelbase, eight-plank sides and steel underframe. A total of 325 were built at Shildon and Faverdale, followed by 250 to Diagram 77; with these, the fitting of bottom and end doors was discontinued, with only side doors provided. The standard 12-ton goods van was also completed in both unfitted (Diagram 14) and automatic vacuum brake-equipped (Diagram 16) varieties, beginning in 1927 and ceasing in 1932, when a good proportion of the total number had been erected at the shops.

Faverdale experienced a record-breaking year in 1928 when 6,763 wagons were completed. This number included 400 fruit vans to Diagram 43 and 200 double bolster wagons of 12-ton capacity. Shildon built six gas transporters to collect the fuel from outside sources for use in the LNER's kitchen carriages, as much of the constituents' plant had been closed by this time. Conveyance of foodstuffs was covered in 1929 when 660 covered goods vans adapted for fish traffic were constructed alongside 300 banana vans to Diagram 52. Furthermore, a convertible bulk grain wagon design was produced to move the commodity inland from the East Coast ports. The traffic was thought to be too intermittent to require a dedicated vehicle, so the floor could be moved from an angled position, where the grain was directed to an opening in the centre, to a flat position so that other items could be carried. A total of twenty-five were built for approximately £13,650, and found sufficient employment that twenty fixed-position bulk grain hopper wagons were built in 1931. Cattle wagons became increasingly obsolete as the 1920s wore on, and 1929 saw the last batch for several years built at Faverdale, numbering 200 examples. One industry experiencing an upturn was that supplying electricity, and in 1929 the LNER saw fit to supply two new special wagons to move transformers for power stations. These were 62ft 6in long with two four-wheel bogies at either end to support the load, which was carried centrally.

In 1929 the *LNER Magazine* gave details of Shildon's role at the time. The site covered 32 acres and there was roofed floor space of 7 acres. As many as 1,400 men were engaged on producing forgings and metalwork – not just for wagons, but also for locomotives and carriages. In the main, repairs concerned mineral wagons operating in the central division of the NE Area and amounted to approximately 25,000 wagons per annum. Wheels, axles and some castings were bought, though the remainder of the metal fittings were made at Shildon. The output was said to be 150 sets for the standard types each week; this set consisted of 2,350 individual items, each being treated before fitting to guard against corrosion, and weighing 30cwt. Mechanisation had been employed where possible to keep parts to standard dimensions. The processes used to forge axleguards and buffers had recently been rationalised so that the metal required to be heated only once. The axleguard required a series of steps that took 4 minutes, beginning with heating the

Standard 10-ton fish van No 159918 was built at Faverdale in 1930.

A specially designed bulk alumina wagon built in 1931.

'Transformer-A' wagon No 158253 (left) was completed during the summer of 1929. A second example, No 158356, which is presumably the wagon on the right, was built in the following year.

metal for shaping in a hydraulic press before moving over to another press where the final inverted 'U' shape was achieved, then having holes punched and excess metal sheared off. For the buffer, half of a rolled steel bar was heated to allow the formation of the head by several

Type BD container No 1461 (built in 1939) and 'Conflat' No 204548 (constructed at Dukinfield in 1939) are posed outside Faverdale Works.

tools in a forging machine and at the steam hammer. This task took 3 minutes and, to economise on time, a new steel bar was placed in the furnace as one was taken out. Other parts were roughly made by the steam hammer before being finished by the drop hammer. Oil-fired furnaces were employed at the shops and the boilers were also equipped to receive heat from waste gases. From the Forge the components passed through to the Machine Shop where holes were drilled where necessary using an assortment of jigs.

The LNER continued to cater for industry in 1930 with the construction of 100 four-wheel steel-plate wagons, capable of taking 12 tons; they were 27ft 1½in long with a 15-foot wheelbase. While the order was originally for 500, the financial crash of the previous year was starting to have an affect and would continue to do so throughout 1932 and 1933, when construction levels declined. Small numbers of brake vans were built in 1930 and 1931 and in the latter year sixty-five 10-ton meat vans were erected. Some of the larger orders comprised 350 container flats and 500 fruit vans in 1932, with fifty fish vans also constructed. During the year the decision was finally made to abandon Westinghouse brake equipment for the wagon stock, and this was subsequently removed.

At the height of the economic downturn Shildon and Faverdale turned their attentions to producing containers and container flat wagons for the new form of goods transport, recently adopted by the LNER. Thirty insulated containers were produced for the movement of meat, and thirty-five with ventilation were constructed; both could accommodate 3 tons. The sixty-five container flats had the standard frames and wheelbase, were only compatible with these containers, and were fitted with steam pipes to allow them to run in passenger formations.

A major change in 1934 was the adoption of a 10-foot wheelbase for many wagons of new and existing designs, as the old arrangement was found to be unstable at high speeds, which were becoming more prevalent. One thousand six-plank high-sided wagons were ordered during the year with this feature, together with 1,250 that were fitted with vacuum brakes; these were followed by a further 1,000 from Faverdale and Shildon in 1935. Other designs from 1934 included 667 12-ton vans (also with automatic brakes and the 10-foot wheelbase) and 500 vans with steel underframes and pressed-steel ends. These were a joint enterprise between Dukinfield, which produced the metal items, and Shildon, where the bodies and frames were put together; this continued through to 1936 and comprised a further 1,200 examples. Shildon and Faverdale also collaborated on 700 steel-plate wagons between 1934 and 1936; the former fabricated the all-steel body and the latter added the wooden floors. Diagram 64 brake vans with steel underframes saw numbers increase by 262 between 1934 and 1935.

Shildon was the last LNER workshop to build locomotive coal wagons to Diagram 77 as part of the 1935 building programme, consisting of 400 vehicles; the subsequent 1,655 were all erected by contractors. Additionally, 500 wooden-underframe fruit vans were the final examples before steel was adopted for future construction. More than 600 vans to the new steel-end design appeared from the works during 1936, differing slightly from the earlier type by having ventilators installed as there was a tendency for condensation to form on the inside. A new addition to the diagram book was the 12-ton low-sided wagon, taking No 109. This had the 10-foot wheelbase but still had wooden underframes; 1,378 were built between 1936 and 1938 before the programme was discontinued. Many more vehicles for container traffic were made, including 300 Type A containers (Diagram 24), 100 Type H with a 2¼-ton capacity to be transported in the standard open wagon, and 730 container flats. These embraced all the modern features previously mentioned as well as being adjustable to carry any of the containers then being produced by the LNER. The last of the Diagram 27 double bolster wagons were built at Shildon in 1935 before enough details were altered to require Diagram 96 to be adopted, and 400 of these were constructed at the works in the following year. This period also saw the erection of 295 20-ton brake vans; a further 550 would be completed up to 1939.

The LNER embarked on a major construction spree from 1936 when large numbers of 12-ton open wagons were ordered over successive building programmes, totalling 7,200 from Shildon and Faverdale. As the majority of these were completed in 1937, Faverdale was able to hold a new record of 9,082 for output during a year. Other designs produced at this time included more than 1,000 sleeper wagons and 400 eight-plank hopper wagons. Shildon was busy erecting 2,000 goods vans to Diagram 116, which had reduced dimensions, 336 fruit vans with steel underframes, and twenty-four bulk alumina wagons. These were specially made for the traffic between Burntisland and Fort William; the previous

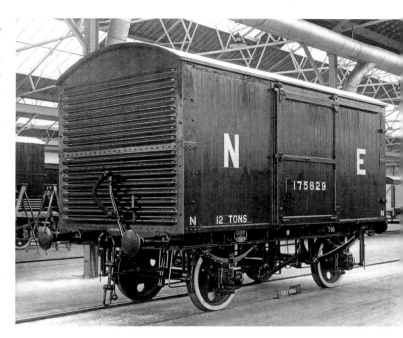

This Diagram 25 12-ton goods van with split metal ends, vacuum brake and screw coupling was built in 1934.

A vacuum-brake-fitted 12-ton open wagon constructed in 1934.

method of movement – the powder was placed in bags – had not proved suitable, so new steel hopper wagons were erected, 20 feet long with space for 738 cubic feet of alumina. The ore was delivered from hoppers at the terminal into the wagon by six openings in the roof, and was released at the other end by four 6-inch Saunders valves operated from the side of the wagon.

Open wagons were still being ordered in 1938, when 1,500 six-plank and 500 five-plank examples were completed with vacuum brakes, together with 500 eight-plank hopper wagons, but these were unfitted. Eight hundred fish vans with a slightly longer wheelbase were also erected at Faverdale alongside 200 brake vans. Shildon was tasked with building 100 steel hopper wagons with side discharge and a 20-ton capacity as an experiment due to trouble experienced with the usual bottom release.

A 12-ton coal hopper wagon erected to Diagram 137 in 1938.

All-metal bulk alumina wagon No 229080 was built at Shildon in 1938 using newly introduced welding techniques.

Outside Faverdale shops is this Diagram 141 flat wagon, built in 1938.

Unfortunately there were several problems and no further examples were built. Another special endeavour was a 100-ton flat wagon mounted on four bogies.

In the early 1930s the reliability of the Railway Clearing House (RCH) standard axlebox became so poor that a type based on the former GN pattern was introduced. Further thought on this matter, led by Shildon Works Manager T. H. Cruddas, resulted in the production of a steel version that proved to be much superior to both predecessors in all areas. By the end of the decade new machinery had been installed at Shildon so the processes of manufacture could be carried out on a large scale. This included forging the metal sheets and shaping them with the hammer before the sides were welded together and other items were attached by the same method. The workshops were said to be able to fabricate 40,000 axleboxes per year.

After the outbreak of war there was a number of large orders placed at Shildon and Faverdale by the LNER to meet the needs of the war effort. There comprised many general service wagons, such as open wagons, coal hoppers, single and double bolsters, plate wagons and vans (numbering in all some 5,000 vehicles, including non-fitted stock). As time progressed the supply of wood traditionally used in construction became unavailable and substitutes had to be found. However, this did not slow down production as thousands more – many being of the type listed above – were built through to the end of the conflict. There was some cooperation between the railway companies as there was in locomotive construction; for example, Ashford Works built 775 five-plank open wagons in 1943. W. Wells-Hood retired as Faverdale Works Manager at the start of the war and was replaced by S. L. Baister, who arrived from Stratford. The latter joined the forces in 1943 and B. Holroyde, formerly Assistant Locomotive Works Manager, Doncaster, filled the gap in his absence.

The LNER had been gradually moving towards all-steel construction from the start of the 1930s, and by the end of the war this practice was fully embraced. Shildon Works was chosen to receive the special machinery for this, and a

Specialised Type AX container No 942, for the transportation of dry ice, was completed in 1938.

This 13-ton metal open wagon was constructed in 1940 to Diagram 91.

25-ton ironstone hopper wagons like this were built as the war drew to a close.

Extensions were undertaken at Shildon after the Second World War, allowing for the construction of all-metal wagons. *K. Taylor collection, courtesy of J. W. Armstrong Trust*

In Shildon's Building Shop are metal wagons and welding equipment on the left. *K. Taylor collection, courtesy of J. W. Armstrong Trust*

Apparatus for welding at Shildon. *K. Taylor collection, courtesy of J. W. Armstrong Trust*

A multi-head welding machine at Shildon. *K. Taylor collection, courtesy of J. W. Armstrong Trust*

number of alterations were made to the site. The first type to be completed was the open wagon, which had a 13-ton capacity with a 10-foot wheelbase and ¼-inch-thick sides; the floors remained wooden. Production began with 100 in 1945. The bodies were produced on an 'assembly line' system, moving along as various parts were fitted, with

This Type A container was built in 1947, and carries BR's 'E' prefix for ex-LNER stock.

This insulated fish van, with a capacity of 12 tons, was built at the close of 1949.

An LNER 20-ton brake van to Diagram 147, built in 1947.

A 12-ton van fitted with shock-absorbing apparatus.

welding widely employed. *The Engineer* of 7 November 1947 gave a description of the process from start to finish. The steel for the underframes arrived in sections that had to be cut to length and drilled before moving into the Frame Welding Shop. There were four assembly points contained therein and each had a jig that allowed the sections to be tacked together. Then the frames were moved on to stands for all the associated components to be attached and the wheels fitted. After a coat of primer the underframes were completed.

Steel plates started in a similar manner, being cut to size on a shearing machine, then moving over to a 1,200-ton press where one end and the two sides were formed. A jig was provided for the next step, which saw the end stanchions welded on to the body by a four-head welding machine, following which the ironwork was mounted. The body and underframe met at the end to be fixed together through riveting, as this was deemed easier to undo if either section required separating. Finally, painting was completed by the spray method. Introducing these techniques and systems was said to have pushed production up to eighty wagons per week. With this being successful for the open wagons (7,100 were built at Shildon up to 1948), the process spread to ironstone hopper wagons to carry 25 tons, and 330 were completed from 1946 to 1948.

The final two LNER building programmes consisted of large numbers of eight-plank hopper wagons (2,400), covered goods vans (3,250), all-steel locomotive coal wagons (1,200), containers, plate wagons, and brake vans. The company's wagon stock had fallen by around 30,000 vehicles from the time of the Grouping, but many modern types had been introduced and the general design, components and manufacturing processes were improved during the intervening years. Some 50,000 wagons were fitted with vacuum brakes in 1947 and, while perhaps not as many as would have been deemed desirable, was a sound base on which to build.

At nationalisation BR inherited more than 1,250,000 wagons from the 'Big Four' railway companies. All of these varied in age and condition, the latter being a concern at the time due to the backlog still being experienced after the war – some 70,000 were under or awaiting repair just before 1948. BR's wagon policy was to scrap the old vehicles and replace them with new and modern types on a large scale, using both the inherited workshops and private contractors. Initially, the standard features were steel underframes, oil lubrication and three-link couplings for unfitted wagons, and the Instanter type for those with vacuum brakes. Covered vans were of 12-ton capacity and mineral wagons could contain no less than 16 tons.

As the transition of the industry took place, BR allowed the designs of the 'Big Four' to be perpetuated until the standard designs were formulated. Many all-steel wagons were built at Shildon, including coal hoppers, ironstone hoppers, and single and double bolster wagons. An interesting project was the 12-ton shock-absorbing wagon, which was built between 1948 and 1949, drawing on a concept conceived by the LMS in the late 1930s. In this arrangement the body was allowed to move slightly by means of springs mounted on the underframe, while any unwanted forces were taken by the buffers. The container principle was also stretched to the transportation of alcoholic beverages, whereby tanks were secured to container flats, then removed to road vehicles at their destination. Faverdale constructed a number of brake vans, fish vans and fruit vans during this period.

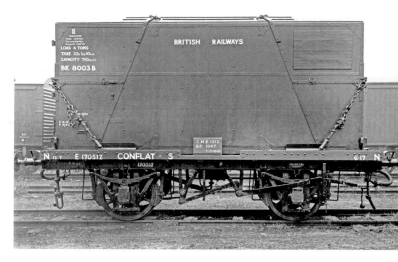

The BK Type container has British Railways identification, although the 'Conflat' still has LNER branded axlebox covers.

The first orders placed by BR at Shildon and Faverdale in 1950 were from a small group of types. These included standard 13-ton high-sided goods wagons, numbering 2,000, and 40-ton bogie plate wagons (seventy-five) – both from Shildon. In addition, 1,000 fruit vans were built, consisting of 250 to the LMS design and the remainder to the LNER specifications. The latter company's brake vans also provided the basis for the BR standard type when the

A machinist at work at Shildon, c1955.

Looking east towards Shildon Works in 1964. *Courtesy of J. W. Armstrong Trust*

first of the 2,855 were built at Faverdale during the year; 250 of the LNER brake vans were erected at the same time. Faverdale was the busier of the two shops in 1952 as several classes of vans – banana, ventilated and shock-absorbing – were scheduled from construction together with tube wagons and a number of containers. Requested from Shildon were 100 20-ton coke hoppers, 576 22-ton plate wagons and 300 20-ton sleeper and ballast wagons.

The Modernisation Plan did little to affect the output from the shops as the rate of construction and types were generally unchanged. A step forward was the application of vacuum brakes to all new stock, but in the event this was not fully enforced. The report did see the placing of the largest order for wagons, when one for 27,500 of 16-ton capacity for mineral traffic was given to Pressed Steel Ltd. In 1956 Shildon was the busier of the two works, having received an order for 3,000 single bolster wagons, in addition to 140 pig iron wagons, 300 match wagons and 270 33-ton ironstone hoppers with vacuum brakes. Faverdale constructed 700 vans fitted with shock absorbers, 150 banana vans and 550 meat containers. In all, 1956 would prove to be the peak of wagon construction for BR, as 61,479 vehicles were erected in the shops and by private firms. However, the optimism of the Modernisation Plan was not backed up by actual traffic requirements, with road transport siphoning off ever greater quantities of traffic as the decade wore on.

For the 1957 and 1958 programmes the standard types were again perpetuated. Shildon turned out mineral hopper wagons of various capacities while Faverdale made just under 2,000 vans. Despite new single bolster wagons being ruled out of future construction early in BR's

existence, a great number were ordered in 1957, totalling 4,000 in a few batches, and were a slight variation of the LNER type. Also during this period Shildon completed a number of flat wagons and trestle wagons (of 12- and 21-ton capacity respectively), which were types relatively uncommon to the works and only produced in small numbers. Further special designs, such as low machine, flat trolley and wheel wagons, were built in 1959.

One of the main advancements in wagon design was the use of roller bearings in the axleboxes, and this served to improve lubrication and greatly reduce wear. In 1959 both Shildon and Faverdale were using this type, the former on 1,500 plate wagons that were also vacuum fitted and the latter on 727 brake vans. A major trial was the introduction of disc brakes in 1960, when Ashford Works supplied a number of hoppers for power station traffic; these were followed by 24¼-ton hoppers from Shildon, numbering 250 up to 1962. There were hopes that the new type, although costing more money, would be longer-lasting that the cast-iron shoes in use at the time, and more reliable in operation.

While Shildon had the task of constructing and repairing wagons – approximately 40,000 were attended to in the early 1950s – there was a third role that saw the works scrapping redundant vehicles. The withdrawal rate rose and declined several times between nationalisation and the early 1960s, but the peak year was 1958 when 129,987 wagons were removed from traffic. *British Railways Eastern Region Magazine* featured the Break-Up Department at Shildon as part of the 'My Day's Work' series in 1948. Supervisor J. W. Handley described the various processes. The department was arranged so the wagons

The interior of Shildon Works in April 1984. *Ken Gregory, courtesy of J. W. Armstrong Trust*

moved through as various items were stripped by a gang of eight men, whose tools included hammers and chisels and, when necessary, an oxy-acetylene cutting torch. Up to 100 wagons were dealt with weekly and much of the material that was removed found further use on wagons admitted for repairs. Timber was salvaged, together with ironwork, bolts, axles and wheels. A dedicated shop had recently been installed for the reconditioning of the latter two items, while a shop already existed to deal with the second-mentioned. There the bolts were sorted to their respective diameters, cleaned by shot-blasting, sheared and re-threaded if of good length; if not, a new end was welded on and the threading process then performed. As much as 4½ tons was recovered each week, while the total material that was not required was 1,900 tons.

BR's poor financial performance through the late 1950s and the heavy expenditure incurred by the Modernisation Plan forced the politicians in Whitehall to reappraise the powers of the British Transport Commission. Broadly, this meant the body's dissolution and the formation of the British Railways Board, which was tasked with taking a hard look at every facet of the organisation. The subsequent creation of BR's Workshop Division saw a rationalisation of the tasks carried out at the various places and the facilities' role in the future was considered. Unfortunately for Faverdale and its employees, the shops were deemed surplus to requirements, given the phasing out of stock using wood as a construction material and the cost of putting the shops to another use, and closure occurred in mid-1963. In relation to the latter point, there was little need for new repair facilities as the stock continued to fall – by the end of 1968 there were just over 450,000 wagons in service, which was considerably down from around 950,000 at the start of the

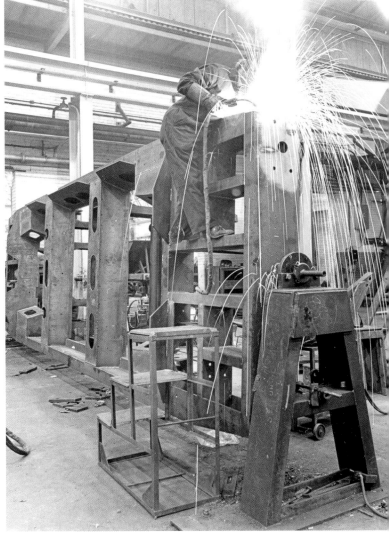

Welding a wagon frame at Shildon in November 1980.

169

A Shildon worker undertakes welding in April 1984. *Ken Gregory, courtesy of J. W. Armstrong Trust*

Dismantling a condemned hopper wagon in April 1984. *Ken Gregory, courtesy of J. W. Armstrong Trust*

decade – and the generally improved reliability of the more modern stock built under BR.

Shildon was in a stronger position due to the equipment being modern and in line with the future construction of all-steel wagons, in addition to the workforce being well-versed in the techniques necessary for their erection.

Nevertheless, BR spent £800,000 improving the works in the early 1960s to spearhead new projects and repairs for the wagons used by the many industries then still very much active in the area. As one of the largest works in

Maintenance checks being carried out on hopper wagons during November 1980.

This exterior view of Shildon Works was taken in April 1984, before closure. *Ken Gregory, courtesy of J. W. Armstrong Trust*

operation, this role continued to be filled through to the formation of BREL in 1970.

One of the main tasks undertaken by Shildon – and which had begun in the latter half of the 1960s – was the construction of 32-ton hopper wagons for use by power stations. The type formed a part of BR's new 'merry-go-round' services that moved coal loaded into the new hoppers from the collieries to power stations on a continuous basis. By the early 1980s Shildon had erected more than 11,000 of these wagons, in addition to hoppers for other uses, and maintained a large number, having a capacity of 800 in the shops. In between fulfilling orders for BR, Shildon found time to build items under contract; one of the first came from Malaysia, for 150 pallet wagons, and these were completed during the early 1970s.

Because the heavy industries in the area had declined during the 1970s and early 1980s, the official news of Shildon's vulnerability did not appear out of the blue in April 1982. BR gave the reasons behind the loss of 2,500 jobs as the lack of orders and other work to keep all the shops occupied – the number of wagons allocated for repairs had fallen from 45,000 in 1976 to 12,000 in 1982, and was projected to decline even more, therefore the economic viability of the works was considered nil. The workforce was not content to let the matter be cordially accepted, and there was a fight to keep them at work, but unfortunately this met with no success. In 1983 notice was given that the run-down of operations was to commence, with Doncaster taking over responsibility for new construction and repairs for the area. Shildon closed in 1984 after just short of 160 years of tireless

service. Much of the site and buildings have since been taken over by small businesses as part of an industrial estate. Thankfully, Shildon's association with the railways was revived in 2004 when the National Railway Museum opened the Locomotion Museum to the south of the station, on the west side of the line, for the exhibition of items that were unable to be housed at York.

All tracks have been removed from the Shildon Repair Shop and yard after closure in May 1985. *R. Goad, courtesy of J. W. Armstrong Trust*

8

Stratford Works and Temple Mills

Throughout the 1820s many people explored the possibility of laying down a route from London to East Anglia. The first serious scheme was not formulated until 1834, after the surveyor's original plan to run a line from London to Edinburgh via Cambridge was replaced by a more manageable endeavour. Specifically, this was a route from London to Ipswich and Norwich via Colchester. The prospectus issued for the Grand Eastern Counties Railway (later losing the 'Grand') highlighted railways such as the Stockton & Darlington, with its rapid growth in passenger and freight traffic, as the benchmark for its aspirations, despite many people being in opposition due to the rural nature of the area.

These protestations – delivered vociferously to Parliament when the Bill was submitted in early 1836 – were overwhelmed by the benefits to the majority of the people and businesses that lay close to the route. Royal Assent was given on 4 July, and at the time this was the longest railway to receive authorisation. The construction was carried out in stages, the first to be ready being that from Mile End, London, to Romford. Opening took place on 30 June 1839 and a 5-foot gauge was used. This latter place hosted the company's first workshops – known as Romford Factory – although these were some distance away to the north-east of the station and settlement, and a row of houses had to be provided close by.

Financial difficulties soon set in and Colchester was not reached until 1843. Nevertheless, the ECR was able to merge with the Northern & Eastern Railway (N&ER) the following year, converting both lines to standard gauge and reaching Norwich in 1845. This outward appearance of progress did little to hide the turmoil within the company, and as a result the time was right for the 'Railway King' George Hudson to step in and take the reins. Some progress was made under his stewardship, including the formation of new workshops at Stratford.

In the first half of the 1840s a large amount of land had been purchased around the station area at Stratford, which itself was located close to the junction of the ECR's main line and the N&ER route to Cambridge. Construction of the repair shops began in 1845 and they were completed at the end of the following year. The land around the site – laying just north of the station between the two lines – was also built up at this time with 300 houses for the employees, a church and a pub, all becoming known as 'Hudson's Town' or 'New Town'. An official opening ceremony was performed by Hudson on 31 December 1846, with the 1,600 people in attendance treated to dinner and a dance afterwards; employees that had to work were given an extra day's pay for missing out. The original workshops comprised an Erecting and Fitting Shop, Tender Shop, Smithy, Boiler Shop, Iron Store, Paint Shop and Offices. The cost of the entire undertaking was £100,000.

The locomotive stock of the ECR up to this point had been purchased from a number of firms, such as Braithwaite, Milner & Co, Jones & Potts, and Stothert & Slaughter. These were generally of the 2-2-2, 2-4-0 and 0-6-0 wheel arrangements, with inside cylinders and boilers typical of the period. James Samuel was appointed Locomotive Engineer in 1846 and only produced a small number of designs during his brief tenure. One of these was an engine with a vertical boiler, which had a low coke consumption, and he was involved in the design of a railcar with W. B. Adams of a local engineering firm (which also produced the aforementioned). In 1848 he developed an idea for compound working with a fitter at the works named John Nicholson, and this was the first application of the method to be recorded.

J. V. Gooch (brother of the GWR's Daniel Gooch) succeeded Samuel in 1850 after having previously been employed by the London & South Western Railway (LSWR). His first design was for a class of 2-2-2T locomotives, which followed practices he had used on the LSWR: inside cylinders (11 inches by 22 inches), 110lb per sq in boiler pressure, double frames and 6ft 6in drivers. No 20 was the pioneer – also holding the distinction of being the first product of Stratford Works – and was followed by a further six in 1851.

With several amalgamations taking place up to the mid-1850s a wide array of stock was inherited for Stratford to maintain. Moreover, a number of Gooch's 2-2-2T designs were built before his resignation in 1856. Robert Sinclair was then appointed, leaving the Caledonian Railway, where he had spent almost ten years in charge of the locomotive stock. Unfortunately, he did not continue to build engines in numbers at Stratford and his largest class – the 'Y' 2-4-0s – came from several firms, including one in France. One positive feature of his appointment was that he attempted to bring standardisation to his designs and there were only detail differences between batches. A small class of 2-4-0T locomotives was built at Stratford and were used on North Woolwich services during the early 1860s. A momentous event in 1862 was the amalgamation of the ECR with the Norfolk, Eastern Union and Newmarket & East Anglian railways to form the Great Eastern Railway (GER).

While the new company was busy trying to expand into Great Northern Railway (GNR) territory, the locomotive stock was left to stagnate. Samuel Johnson replaced Sinclair in 1866 and immediately had to design passenger and freight engines. A mixed-traffic 2-4-0 design was quickly put in hand and fulfilled by Neilson, Reid & Co during 1867, with Stratford adding another three to stock in 1868. Ten similar engines – referred to as 'Little Sharpies' – were built at Stratford around the start of the 1870s, together with thirty erected at Sharp, Stewart & Co. There were also a small number of 2-2-2s and another 2-4-0 type. The largest class built at Stratford up to this point followed between 1871 and 1875 when fifteen 'T7s' were sent into traffic. These were 0-4-2T locomotives and were used on the London suburban trains. Johnson's final class was the 'C8' 4-4-0, but these engines did not appear until

1874 and took the numbers 301 and 302. They were the first in England to have that wheel arrangement coupled with inside cylinders; the drivers were of 6ft 6in diameter, the cylinders were 17 inches by 24 inches, and the boiler pressure was 140lb per sq in.

Johnson moved to the Midland Railway in 1873 and William Adams took his position upon parting company with the North London Railway. He continued with the 4-4-0 wheel arrangement and twenty such locomotives were completed by contractors, while Adams's most numerous class was an 0-4-4T for suburban work. Only one class was built at Stratford before his tenure ceased, and this was the 'K9' 0-4-2T for light passenger service.

Only eighty locomotives had been erected at Stratford by the time Massey Bromley was appointed Locomotive Superintendent in 1878, and he ensured that the locomotive building trade would only supplement the construction work performed in the main shops. His first major design was the 'E10' Class 0-4-4T for suburban and local passenger trains. A total of sixty were built from shortly after Bromley's arrival to 1883. On the building programme in 1881 were ten 0-6-0T shunters, then in 1882 ten of Sinclair's 2-4-0s were rebuilt as 4-4-0s. In the event three classes were built by contractors, totalling forty engines, and one of them – the '245' Class – comprised the largest engines to yet run on the GER, having 7ft 6in drivers in a 4-2-2 wheel arrangement.

An important development for workplace safety was made during Bromley's time in office when the St John Ambulance was formed, and one of the earliest railway workshops to be involved was Stratford. A large number of the employees were instructed by Dr Collingridge, Medical Officer for the Port of London, and later tested in 1880 by a Sergeant Major in the Grenadier Guards. Soon afterwards

No 251, one of Bromley's Class '245' 4-2-2s, was built at Dübs & Co in 1879 as part of a batch of ten; another ten were received from Kitson & Co.

T. W. Worsdell's Class 'G14' 2-4-0 No 645 was built at Stratford in 1883.

branches were formed at several places on the network, including Liverpool Street station and Ipswich, and the time in which help could be received was said to have been reduced to less than 10 minutes. By 1892 members of the Stratford and Liverpool Street Brigades were teaching other GER employees the intricacies of first aid, and a GER Ambulance Brigade Committee was formed from the heads of several departments. The body founded the GER Challenge Cup in the following year and the competition later spread to the other railway companies, with an inter-railway contest also instituted; the GER ambulance team at Peterborough took the first honour.

T. W. Worsdell was happy to follow Bromley's lead in locomotive matters and, of the 140 engines constructed during his three years in office, only nineteen were not completed at Stratford. Those built included a 2-4-0 with 18-inch by 24-inch cylinders, Joy valve gear, 140lb per sq in working pressure and 7-foot diameter coupled wheels, classified 'G14'; an 0-6-0 for goods work, which in just two years totalled fifty examples; and thirty 'M15' Class 2-4-2T locomotives. An unusual design produced in this period was a tram-type locomotive with an 0-4-0 wheel arrangement to work in Yarmouth where several lines running in the streets would have to be navigated. The Board of Trade stipulated that for this to be allowed a 'cowcatcher' and side skirting enclosing the motion would have to be fitted and the speed limited to less than 10mph. Five were built initially, followed by another five before the

Holden's 'C53' Class 0-6-0T steam tram locomotive was a descendant of the 'G15' Class introduced by Worsdell. Twelve were built, and No 138 was sent into traffic during 1908.

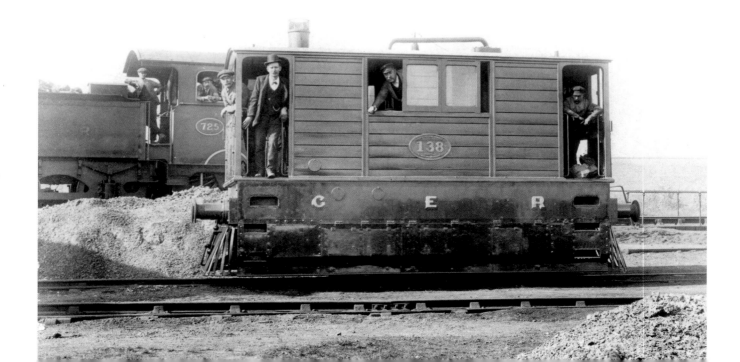

end of the century. The cylinders were 11 inches by 15 inches, the wheels 3 feet in diameter, the boiler pressure set at 120lb per sq in and the weight 21 tons. Worsdell also experimented with compounding, having developed a system with August von Borries. Eleven engines were completed, being based on his earlier 2-4-0s, but with a leading bogie, 160lb per sq in boiler pressure, a high-pressure cylinder of 18 inches by 24 inches, and a low pressure cylinder 26 inches by 24 inches.

In 1881 *The Engineer* ran a feature on Stratford Works and noted several details of the shops in its issue of 14 October. As many as 550 locomotives were maintained at Stratford, in addition to 2,000 carriages and 10,000 wagons. As these figures were somewhat in excess of the numbers the works were expected to handle in the mid-1840s, several alterations had been made by both Adams and Bromley to the original layout, which was planned by a Mr Hunter. These had achieved an output double that attained previously without costs being increased at all.

The Offices and Erecting Shop had borne the brunt of these reorganisations but were still largely in their original form. For example:

'The erecting shop is interesting for being one of the earliest examples of using permanent cast iron wall plates for placing pulleys and countershafts at any advantageous position without disturbing the masonry.'

The travelling cranes were formed from timber beams and movement was affected by cotton ropes 1 inch in diameter, moving at 1,800 feet per minute. The shops were served by a network of 18-inch-gauge tracks for the movement of parts and materials.

A wheel lathe, built by Smith, Beacock & Tannet, had recently been installed and weighed 34 tons. The face plates had a diameter of 8ft 9in and the loose headstock was driven by a wrought-iron shaft 6 inches in diameter. A tyre furnace was close by and the process of heating the item to the required temperature took just under 5 minutes. The Smiths' Shop contained the tools necessary for wheel manufacture and a horizontal steam hammer was used to fashion the rims in a method developed by studying American practice.

Almost all boiler riveting was performed by hydraulic plant supplied by R. H. Tweddell. The testing of springs was carried out by one man, as this reduced the instances of breakages. Large patterns were made in cast iron while the smaller types used steel. Whitney of Winchendon, Massachusetts, had supplied a special woodworking machine that took a very small amount of material off the face of a panel, leaving a very smooth surface that required no finishing, thereby saving a good deal of labour. Stratford had also designed a revolving cutter, which saved time and effort. The Wagon Repair Shop was said to be of 'cheap construction' using galvanised metal sheets covered in board; it could accommodate 100 wagons at once. An attempt was made to complete the repairs in unison so that the vehicles could move forward together.

The Smiths' Shop at Stratford, pictured near to the turn of the 19th century.

A view of the Boiler Shop.

The GER was able to benefit from some consistency in the locomotive department after having appointed five locomotive engineers in thirty years between 1856 and 1885. James Holden was given the task of moving the stock forward in the latter year, having served an apprenticeship with the NER and become Assistant to W. Dean on the GWR. Holden would hold his position as Locomotive Engineer until 1907, and during that time he produced several notable classes, modernised a number of older ones, and oversaw the expansion of Stratford to be on a par with any other workshops in the country.

Holden produced four types in his first year and these refreshed the stock operating the different services offered by the company. All of the classes turned out to be very satisfactory and were built in large numbers at Stratford throughout Holden's tenure. They comprised: 'T19' 2-4-0 (110); 'Y14' 0-6-0 (200); 'T18' 0-6-0T (50); and 'M15' 2-4-

The entrance to the Erecting Shop at Stratford is occupied by Holden 'T19' Class 2-4-0 No 714, the last of the first ten examples to be built between 1886 and 1887. The engine is perhaps decorated to celebrate Queen Victoria's Golden Jubilee.

2T (130). The 'T19' Class was quite similar to Worsdell's 2-4-0 but enlarged, as were the 'Y14' and 'M15' Classes, while the 'T18s' had 16½-inch by 22-inch cylinders, 4-foot-diameter coupled wheels, a 12.4sq ft grate area, 967.24sq ft of heating surface, and a boiler pressure of 140lb per sq in. Holden also followed his predecessor by designing a solitary compound 0-6-0 built in 1888; however, it did not prove a success and was rebuilt subsequently, with no more compounds being constructed.

C. J. Allen, in *The Great Eastern Railway*, records that the invention of steam sanding and a subsequent test carried out with a 2-4-0 that had the wheels uncoupled resulted in the construction of further 2-2-2s by Holden in 1888. The twenty-one locomotives, which were built over a five-year period, shared specifications with the 'T19s' and found employment on expresses being worked on the GN&GE

Joint line. Another experiment concerned 'T18' No 294. The engine was put at the head of a suburban service to determine how well the wheel arrangement coped with the load against the 0-4-4Ts and 2-4-2Ts then being used. Positive results were achieved and the wheel arrangement was used for the new suburban class that appeared from Stratford in 1890. The two classes were virtually identical and only differed on minor points such as frame length and wheel spacing. In eleven years 140 engines had been erected, the majority being used for suburban services, though some found employment on shunting duties.

In 1891 Stratford Works was making headlines around the world after the men built 'Y14' Class 0-6-0 No 930 in a world record time. There had recently been a number of similar feats in this area by other companies, such as the London & North Western Railway at Crewe in 1888

'T19' No 743 was one of fifty not to be rebuilt as a 4-4-0, but was part of a group of twenty-nine that were fitted with boilers possessing Belpaire fireboxes. Pictured at Ipswich with a train for London, the locomotive was the first of the rebuilds condemned in 1913.

'C32' Class 2-4-2T No 1099 was the last engine to be completed as part of the first batch in 1893, and almost survived into BR ownership, being withdrawn in December 1947.

when an engine was completed in just over 25 hours. In the same year the Pennsylvania Railroad built a 4-4-0 at Altoona Works in just 16 hours, although the frames were already assembled, saving a fair amount of time. The decision was made to attempt the record at Stratford because of the rate of production at the time, which was two locomotives every five days, and tenders could be fabricated in 18 working hours.

The task was begun at 9.00am on 10 December, with the Erecting Shop's three chargemen and 137 men and boys split into two groups of eighty-five (engine) and fifty-two (tender). The delegation of tasks to various sections within these was carefully planned and clearly defined to avoid wasting time. Each individual fitting was brought into the Erecting Shop beforehand and arranged in a sequence for assembly. There was only a very small amount of work carried out beforehand, such as the mating of the horn blocks and spring brackets to the frames, fitting of boiler details and machining of the cylinders, which would have already been performed in the course of normal construction. The smokebox was fixed to the boiler during the build with seventy-eight rivets, countersunk, and the cab and chimney were also installed at this time. The holes to secure several features had been drilled but required reaming and this took some time. An hour was taken for luncheon and the day ended at 5.30pm with the majority of the work completed.

Everyone returned at 6.00am the following day, and at 7.15 the application of the works grey livery began. On the stroke of 7.40 the assembly of the tender was fully completed and 35 minutes later breakfast was taken for 45 minutes. At 9.10 the engine was finished and, after being coupled to the tender and the boiler filled, etc, steam was raised for the first time at 10.00am. The time

taken for the work to progress to this stage was 9 hours 47 minutes and, after weighing, the engine was sent on test to Broxbourne (30 miles away). After returning, No 930 was handed to the running department and used straight away on revenue-earning trains. The locomotive would continue in traffic for several months before returning to the works for the standard livery to be applied, and it would go on to have a service life of nearly 45 years. Although a special one-off, this feat demonstrated the high quality of workmanship at Stratford and the very efficient organisational skills of the staff.

A new class in 1893 was the 'T26' 2-4-0, although there was little variation from the 'T19'; the reduction of the coupled wheel diameter to 5ft 8in was the only change made. One hundred were built over the next eleven years alongside fifty 'C32' Class 2-4-2T engines, which

No 963 was the thirty-seventh 'N31' Class 0-6-0 to be built, appearing in 1896.

A scene captured in Stratford Works' Erecting Shop.

In the early 1900s there were some 4,000 people employed in the various shops at Stratford Works and more than 1,000 locomotives required maintenance. In 1903 *The Engineer* paid a visit to give an account of the site and the various tools and practices in use. The working hours from Monday to Friday were 6.00am to 5.30pm, with 45 minutes allowed for breakfast and 1 hour for luncheon. On Saturday work was performed between 6.00am and 12.00pm, and time was given for breakfast only. The shops only fell silent for the major holidays, in addition to all the staff taking one week's break in August.

The Erecting Shop was located in the centre of the southern half of the site and measured 850 feet long by 142 feet wide and 60 feet high. Up to fifty locomotives could be accommodated at one time and they were arranged in four bays running the entire length of the building. The two centre bays had six tracks and were reserved for erecting locomotives, while the outer bays were used for boiler work and machining. Some of these included boring, planing, milling, grinding and slotting machines, two hydraulic presses of 50 and 30 tons capacity, and a large quantity of pneumatic tools powered by Ingersoll Sergeant compressors. Two 30-ton-capacity travelling cranes were provided and smaller 3-ton cranes

shared many components with the aforementioned. A development of the 'Y14' design was made at this time to incorporate steam chests below the cylinders, as had been used on other locomotives. The first 'N31' 0-6-0s were built in 1893 and the class would boast eighty-one members by the end of the century.

The Drawing Office is seen at around the time of the First World War. *Courtesy of Kidderminster Railway Museum*

Men working with some of the lathes at Stratford. *Courtesy of Kidderminster Railway Museum*

were also on hand in all bays for lifting. Above the north bay another shop was established for the refurbishment of the Westinghouse brake equipment. A hoist was provided to raise the apparatus into the room, which was well-equipped with all the necessary tools. Once ready for traffic each locomotive was removed by hydraulic capstan and passed through an archway in the office block to a turntable that moved it on to the line for the weighbridge. This was located next to the main line – just north-east of the station – and had eight scales for the wheels to sit on. The Offices contained a Laboratory, Drawing Office (with around thirty Draughtsmen), Photographer's Department, a working model of valve motion to determine the events, and a library of nearly 20,000 drawings.

The Machine Shop (measuring 132 feet by 134 feet) was situated to the south-west of the Erecting Shop and possessed nearly 200 tools of various types driven by some 12,000 feet of leather belting. Just over a quarter of these were lathes, with a similar number for milling components such as the connecting rods and other motion details. Piston rings had recently stopped being made on the normal lathes and switched to two new small boring mills by George Richards & Co. In the former instance the rings had cost 4d each, and the new method, coupled with the reduction in staff required for the various operations, had reduced this to 1½d. A greater saving was made by moving the facing work for slide valves from a planing machine to a vertical lathe, effecting a reduction of 6½d. To make up

for the loss of manual work performed by the men, the company encouraged them to take on as many machines as they could productively operate and an increase in wages followed. Drills also featured prominently. Much of this work was performed using a template to promote

The Wheel Shop.

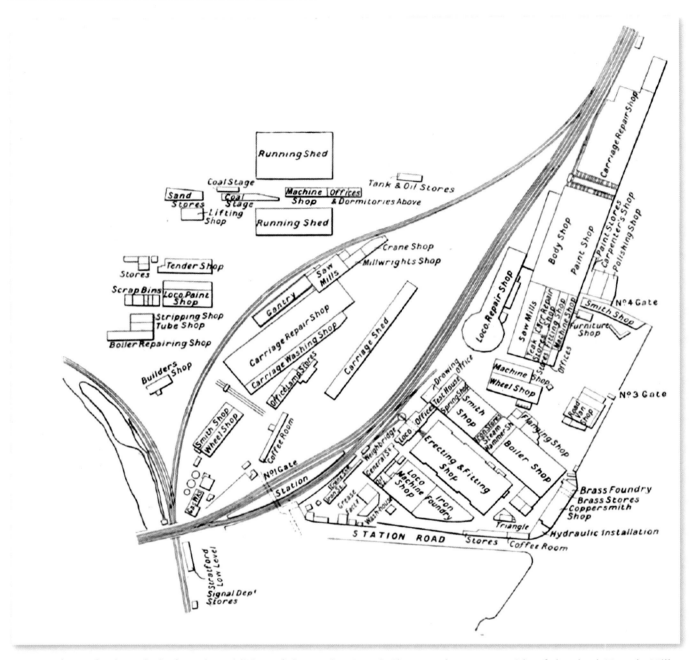

A map of Stratford Works before the addition of the Engine Repair Shop on the western side of the shed. Temple Mills was located a short distance away to the north-west.

conformity, and reduce time and costs. Many of the tools were made in the works' Tool Shop, which was located above the south bay of the Erecting Shop.

On the eastern side of the Machine Shop was the Iron Foundry, which had use of three cupolas – one of 2ft 9in diameter and two of 2 feet. The total capacity of these was 13 tons of metal per hour and air was supplied by Root duplicate blowers. A number of machines were used for producing the moulds to create standard parts, such as carriage and wagon axleboxes and brake blocks. A new method of forging coupling rods had recently been implemented. Originally the rods were made solid then the channels to create the I-section were milled out. The new method saw the mild steel go through the process

of hammering to form the rough shape and to have the ends stamped to shape as well as the hole for the crank pin punched, which was a departure from the method of boring previously employed. Then a pair of dies of the required shape were fitted to the hammer to form the reheated rod. The former were made from cast iron rather than steel as had first been tried, bringing about a significant saving in time and cost in itself. The price of producing two rods had fallen by £3 10s. The output from the Foundry, which employed around 250 people, was approximately 55 tons per week. The two travelling cranes in the shop were of 15 and 10 tons capacity and nine smaller cranes had limits of between 5 tons and 2½cwt.

Several shops were arranged along the south-eastern perimeter of the site. The southernmost was the Hydraulic Shop where the power was developed for all of the hydraulic tools at the works. This was done by two engines with 17-inch by 24-inch cylinders supplied by steam from three locomotive boilers and pumps with rams of a diameter of $3^{3}/_{16}$ inches. The working pressure was 1,680lb per sq in and the accumulator weighed 82 tons. Attached to the northern wall of this building was the Coppersmiths' Shop, which was 95 feet long by 50 feet wide. Inside were a number of pots for melting copper, using gas obtained from coal. The last shop in the block was the Brass Foundry. Measuring 50 feet by 50 feet, there were nine pot furnaces and one open-hearth furnace. The former could be loaded eight times a day while the latter had a capacity of 32cwt a day, or 8cwt at one time, and the output of all during a week was around 10 tons. All of the furnaces were powered by oil. Finishing the products of this building was performed in an adjacent shop, which had two levels: in the upper the small components were machined and boiler stays produced, while the lower level was a store for materials and equipment and was reached by means of a hoist. A capstan lathe had recently been placed in the shop and had achieved remarkable savings in time when machining a number of components. Westinghouse cocks were now completed in 50 minutes when the quickest time formerly was 2 hours; the same reduction was achieved for stuffing boxes used in relation to steam injectors. Financial savings were also made by employing new automatic pin and stud machines, three of which had been installed, and as much as £360 had been saved during the course of a year. Moreover, labour had been reduced through the responsibility of the three falling on one man, who had recently been given charge of a new machine that turned out firebox roof stay bolts. These were made from bars of bronze cut to length by a circular saw, then straightened. A cut was made in the blank to centre the item in the screw lathe and this was done by a youth. The screw lathe (from Craven Brothers) ran at 500 revolutions per minute and had the stay bolt completed in just over 1 minute 30 seconds.

A large building hemmed in the Erecting and Machine Shops and this contained several shops and offices. On the extreme western edge of the block was the Test House, where many of the various components used by the railway were checked for strength. A 50-ton Buckton machine was used in tandem with a Wicksteed recorder, which produced stress diagrams, to determine the strength of the metals used and produced at the works. As chains were made, testing apparatus that could produce 75 tons of load was present for the task. On the eastern side of this was the Spring Shop (132 feet by 40 feet) where all the springs used in locomotive, carriage and wagon construction and repair were produced.

The largest section of the western half was the Smiths' Shop. Measuring 132 feet by 136 feet, it contained sixty-eight forges and eight steam hammers. Furthermore, there were several automatic machines for making nuts and

Above Drop hammers in the Smiths' Shop.

Below The Laboratory performed an important role for the GER and LNER before being destroyed in the Second World War.

The flanging press in the Boiler Shop.

east corner was a space dedicated to hydraulic riveting, with two special appliances located there; five portable riveters were used elsewhere. The main shop contained large tools for edge planing, boring, straightening plates, punchers and cutters, plate rollers and a quantity of drills (seven million holes were made annually and the material removed amounted to 250 tons). The tender and locomotive frame plates were also cut there using dedicated equipment. A total of six overhead cranes were employed – one was of 5 tons lifting capacity whereas the others could handle 10 tons – and the number of portable lifting apparatus exceeded thirty examples. Pneumatic tools were supplied by an air compressor at 80lb per sq in. Another extension was located in the north-east corner and this was used for flanging metal plates. The hydraulic press was capable of working at 1,680lb per sq in, with a 20-inch-diameter ram forcing the metal against the die with a force of 230 tons. Several smaller presses supplemented this.

bolts, the rate for both being around 1,200 a day. An area on the right was partitioned off to store materials, then there was the Steam Hammer Shop, which possessed four hammers ranging from 3 tons to 15cwt. Eight furnaces – four fuelled by coal, the others by coal gas – supplied heat to six boilers that produced the steam required. Stamp forging was carried out for items such as safety valve seatings and spring hangers. Three machines were present for cutting and forming metal.

The Boiler Shop occupied all of the eastern side, and measured 215 feet by 139 feet. An addition in the south-

Roughly in the middle of the main site was the Wheel Shop, which was split into two sections, each possessing an overhead crane of 6 tons capacity. There were a total of sixteen wheel lathes (the largest had a 9-foot-diameter faceplate), and nine other lathes were used to machine crank pins, etc. The crank axles were of forged Bessemer or open-hearth steel and were turned before being machined in preparation for the hoops to be shrunk on. When in place the keyways were cut on the duplex milling machine and the cranks were then forced on the axles under hydraulic pressure approaching 120 tons. The holes for the crank pins were then bored and they were forced

Dating from 1904, this is one of the vehicles built for the GER in the Road Van Shop at Stratford.

in, again by a hydraulic ram. The tyre was then heated, mated with the wheel centre and secured by rivets after holes had been drilled through both and a retaining ring. The tyre was then turned on a lathe to the standard profile. Close by was the Road Van Shop, which maintained the 1,300 road vehicles used by the GER, also erecting new examples for goods and parcel duties.

To the west of this structure was the Locomotive Repair Shop. This had originally been built in two phases by the Northern & Eastern Railway. The first dated from 1840 when a polygonal building had been erected for the stabling of the company's engines, and the second was a rectangular extension (230 feet long by 62 feet wide) on the northern wall built in the mid-1860s; both were turned over for works use in 1887. In the southern half of the building the sixteen roads were equipped with shear legs of 25 tons capacity, and two other cranes of 30 tons capacity were also available to provide assistance. There were forty-two berths for locomotives. Situated a distance away to the west – between the spur connecting the North Woolwich branch with the Cambridge line and the North London Railway's network – were the Tender, Paint and Boiler Repair Shops. The former measured 170 feet by 44 feet and had three pits running the length of the building, capable of holding twenty-one tenders simultaneously. The Paint Shop was a similar size, had another track installed, and provided space for sixteen locomotives. On the northern side was an engine shed that housed the works' shunters. The Boiler Repair Shops were not of substantial construction, being only made from corrugated sheeting. A number of machines were provided to clean boiler tubes, cut the items to length and weld new ends to them.

The northern section of the main works site was taken up by the various departments dedicated to the GER's carriage stock (numbering around 5,000 vehicles at the time), and the numerous tasks kept 1,678 people busy. Interestingly, the carriage builders were required to provide their own tools and the chests in which they were kept – these were built during the workers' spare time. The Body Shop and Paint Shop were at the centre of the section; the former had an area capable of holding more than thirty-five six-wheel carriages, with space free for some repairs to take place. At the time the carriage frames were made from oak, and steel was used for the angles and channels. Teak was utilised for the exterior panels, in conjunction with walnut, oak and white deal internally. Adjoining the Paint Shop was the Paint Stores, where several tanks each of 400 gallons capacity contained the various varnishes, oil and turpentine. A mill was used to grind the paint pigments and the final mix was performed by dedicated apparatus. At the time two coats of varnish were applied to the carriages over a five-year period – the first lasted two years and the second three – after which the coach was painted brown due to the destructive effect of the atmosphere in the capital. The northernmost shop was used solely for repairs, entry and exit being gained by a steam traverser; this was also the case for the shops

Milling machines in the Machine Shop.

previously mentioned. The building measured 352 feet by 153 feet, and seventy carriages could be squeezed in.

At the south end of the Body Shop and Paint Shop were several smaller departments such as the Saw Mill, Wood Stores and Carriage Machine Shop. Located above the Fitting Shop was the Trimming Shop where all the cushions, window straps, etc, were made. Also on this level was the Hair Store, where a special machine was used to clean the old hair from reclaimed seats, while another sorted new hair ready for use. Upholstering was performed next to the Paint Stores and only women were employed in this section. This practice had been in force since 1894 and mainly applied to orphans of former servants of the GER. Up to sixty were at work sewing, polishing wooden panels, and machining certain items. Another role was painting the company's coat of arms on to the panels affixed to the sides of locomotives, as well as carriages and GER offices. Additionally, the women cleaned and made carriage blinds, with as many as 30,000 seen at the works annually.

Between the main line and the spur for the North

Stocks of wood and wooden wheels in the Saw Mill.

A van for the transportation of butter, built at Stratford in 1891.

Stratford erected this 10-ton egg van in 1900.

The GER made a tentative foray into the construction of all-steel wagons early in the 20th century. This example appeared in 1910 and was used to move 20 tons of coal for locomotive purposes.

A GER 8-ton refrigerator van built just before the start of the First World War.

turn two journals at the same time, and two general lathes. Rounding off the machinery were two boring tools, two hydraulic presses, balancing apparatus, a bolt machine and a furnace for tyre heating.

The final place of note at Stratford was the Gas Works. This fuel was obtained from oil – as opposed to coal, due to the higher power obtained for illumination – and was used for carriage lighting, being stored under the vehicle in a cylinder 20 inches in diameter and 6 feet long; this lit the whole coach for 36 hours. The gas was stored in holders at 12 atmospheres and was then pumped to carriage sidings or transported to stations in special wagons. A by-product of the process was tar, and this was initially allowed to run to waste into the Channelsea River. The local authority eventually had the company stop this practice and Holden devised several uses for the substance in the works. Oil fuel spread to the locomotives in 1886 when 'T19' No 760 was converted, being renamed *Petrolea* in the process. Only slight changes were needed and a base for the fire to take hold was made using chalk and bricks. In service the consumption of oil amounted to a third of that of an engine of the same type consuming coal. As a result other locomotives were altered, but as the carriage stock moved over to electricity the demand for gas fell away and the locomotives reverted to coal.

From 1896 wagon construction and repair took place at Temple Mills. This area was to the north-west of Stratford Works and on the western side of the Cambridge line, and all the departments were grouped together in a single block. More than 600 people were at work in the Saw Mill, Wagon Erecting Shop, Machine Shop, Underframe Erecting Shop, Smiths' Shop and Machine Shop. The capacity was 600 repairs a year, in addition to 550 new wagons being turned out. In the Erecting Shop, covering 35,100sq ft, there were ten roads for this work to be carried out.

The GER was late in developing dedicated construction

Woolwich branch further Carriage Repair Shops had been erected, used mainly for the company's suburban stock. Built along the eastern wall was a Carriage Washing facility, 450 feet by 37 feet, and this was arranged with two tiers of platforms running the length of the structure allowing access to all parts of the vehicle. A short distance to the south-west was the Carriage Wheel Shop, and this possessed six wheel lathes, two axle lathes, which could facilities for wagons, which did not occur until the early 1880s. Stratford Works originally hosted the task but as space soon diminished a move had to be undertaken. Holden was instrumental in this, and he was also an early pioneer in the use of metal underframes at a time when wood prevailed. Brakes were not deemed important and throughout very few vehicles were fitted with them by the company. The most prevalent designs were the 10-ton high-side open wagons with a 9-foot wheelbase, with variants having sides built from seven planks instead of five and a wheelbase 6 inches longer. A large number of goods vans were built between 1900 and 1923 – approximately 5,000 – and these were of three specifications, but all of 10-ton capacity. An interesting development in the early 20th century was the 20-ton all-steel wagon built for transporting locomotive coal, and just over 900 were erected before the Grouping.

Up to the late 1890s the coaching stock of the GER comprised four- and six-wheel vehicles. The first bogie carriage was added in 1897 and this was a Composite with two 1st and four 3rd Class compartments. Side corridors and clerestory roofs were adopted at the turn of the century for a similar coach, in which 3rd Class passengers were given access to a toilet. As the GER's inter-city trains did not travel as far as those of some other large companies, there was not a great rush to provide restaurant facilities and the first such carriage was not provided until 1891. Nearly fifteen years would elapse before connections were provided to other coaches in the formation to allow passengers to move freely between compartment and restaurant rather than book in advance. Steel underframes were tested intermittently through the late 19th century until officially adopted for all stock at the start of the 20th.

Suburban traffic was catered for by sets of several four-wheel carriages accommodating 1st, 2nd and 3rd Class passengers. The standard body length for a number of years was 27 feet and the object for the draughtsmen at Stratford was to fit as many people in as possible! With the ever-increasing volume of patrons using the suburban services out of Liverpool Street swamping the sets, an ingenious method of increasing the capacity of the older stock was devised. This saw the carriages split in half longitudinally and a 1ft 1in section inserted to increase the width from 7ft 6in, and thus the capacity, to be in line with new construction. More than 700 coaches received this modification at the modest cost of £30 each.

With the introduction of heavier main-line stock, Holden was obliged to supply a more powerful locomotive. The end product was a 4-4-0 with 7-foot-diameter drivers, a 4ft 9in-diameter boiler with a round-top firebox, a total of 1,624.38sq ft of heating surface and a 21.6sq ft grate area working at 180lb per sq in, and 19-inch by 26-inch cylinders with Stephenson motion and slide valves. The first was No 1900 *Claud Hamilton*, which was constructed at Stratford in March 1900; it was followed by a further forty up to 1903, and the engines were classified 'S46'. In the meantime a Class 'F48' 0-6-0 (similar to the former

This carriage has not fallen apart, but has been split in order to accommodate a new section to cheaply increase the capacity.

The carriage with the extra section added.

class) was fitted with a Belpaire firebox and was judged successful enough for the type to be adopted for future construction. Another seventy 4-4-0s were built with this firebox up to 1911, being designated the 'D56' Class.

The heavier suburban trains also contributed to a new design. However, in this case another contributory factor was the promotion of electrically powered railways for the London suburbs. A prominent argument supporting the scheme was that the locomotives would be cleaner and the trains much quicker than the present steam-powered examples. While the former was probably not doubted, the latter point was dismissed by the GER for London's travelling population. Holden set to planning a locomotive that would accelerate a train of 300 tons to 30mph in less than 30 seconds – the motive power of the day could not manage this with a third of the weight. To transmit the required power to the rails and distribute the weight,

Holden 'S46' Class 4-4-0 No 1897 was amongst the second order of 'Claud Hamiltons' to be constructed in 1900.

Holden chose the untried 0-10-0T wheel arrangement. The 'Decapod' had three cylinders of 18½-inch diameter by 24-inch stroke; the centre cylinder drove the leading coupled axle and the outside pair the third axle. Separate sets of Stephenson motion were provided for the valves. The boiler was 5ft 3in in diameter with 2,873.3sq ft of heating surface working at 200lb per sq in, and a wide firebox was provided. The weight in working order (with 2 tons of coal and 1,300 gallons of water) was 80 tons. 'A55' Class No 20 was sent into traffic during 1902 and tested in early 1903, easily beating the target with

eighteen carriages weighing 335 tons gross. In the event the locomotive did not enter service and was later rebuilt as a two-cylinder tender engine, being put to work on freight duties until scrapped in 1913. The promotion of electric railways was damaged as a result of the test and did not progress any further.

Holden retired in 1908 and was succeeded by his son Stephen Dewar Holden. There had been no new designs since twenty 'S56' 0-6-0Ts had been constructed at Stratford in 1904, but several classes had been in production during this period. S. D. Holden's first design

GER employees pose proudly with 'D56' Class 4-4-0 No 1819 at Liverpool Street station.

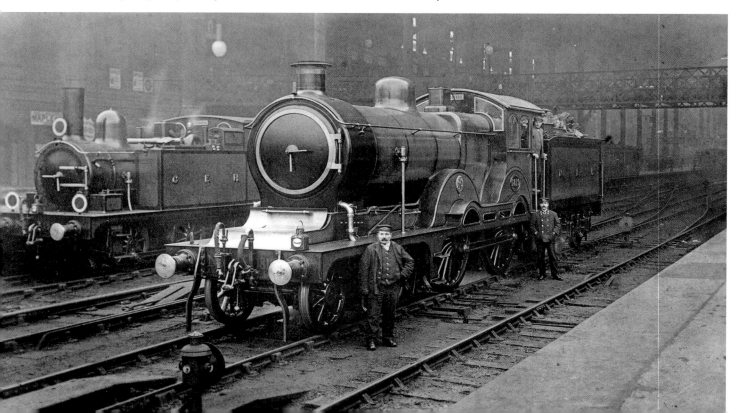

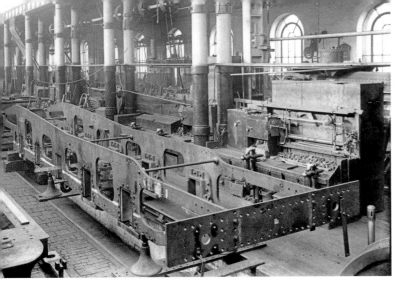

The frames for the 'Decapod' in the Erecting Shop.

The driving rods for the 'A55' 0-10-0T.

No 20's boiler and firebox before the installation of the inner firebox.

The five sets of wheels and axleboxes. The leading axle has been bent to allow clearance for the driving rod to the second axle.

Below The 'Decapod' as built is seen outside the Engine Repair Shop at Stratford.

S. D. Holden's 'Y65' Class 2-4-2T No 1304 was erected in 1909 and condemned in 1944.

was a light 2-4-2T for branch duties, and twelve were erected at Stratford in 1909 and 1910. An enlarged version (numbering twenty) was subsequently built for suburban traffic, the two types being classified 'Y65' and 'G69' respectively. The major design to appear during Holden Junior's brief tenure – he vacated the position in 1912 – was the 'S69' Class 4-6-0, which would be a mainstay of the main line for many years subsequently. Several batches were built over nine years beginning in 1911; seventy-one were built, fifty-one at Stratford and the remainder by W. Beardmore & Co in 1920/21; this was the first time a contractor had been used since the 1880s

and was the result of the strain being felt in the workshops after the First World War. The principal dimensions when built were a boiler with a diameter of 5ft 1in – reducing to 4ft 9in –with 1,633sq ft of heating surface, a Schmidt Superheater and a working pressure of 180lb per sq in, a Belpaire firebox with a 26.5sq ft grate, two 20-inch by 28-inch cylinders, 6ft 6in driving wheels, and a tractive effort of 21,970lb.

With regard to coaching stock, Holden made the biggest mark on the suburban trains when he introduced new sets of eight vehicles, 54 feet long and 8ft 10in wide seating 808, and bogies were made standard. The 1st Class was arranged with five-a-side seating, with both 2nd and 3rd Class having six-a-side; just under half of the capacity was reserved for non-smoking patrons. The set had the ability to be split in order to be accommodated in longer or shorter formations. Fourteen were built up to the outbreak of war and another three appeared towards the end of hostilities.

Before Holden left he oversaw the reconstruction of the Smithy. This process saw the roof raised and the wooden beams replaced by steel girders, a dividing wall demolished and better ventilation provided. This latter was done by installing three 48-inch-diameter Keith-Blackman fans powered by electricity, replacing the gas lighting previously in use. An additional role fulfilled by the fans was the extraction of smoke created by the many hearths used by the smiths. Two chimneys expelled the fumes into the atmosphere, considerably fewer than the thirty-two formerly performing the task. The construction work was necessarily carried out quickly as the smiths could not be

Holden 'S69' Class 4-6-0 No 1500.

A GER six-wheel Composite carriage.

disturbed from the essential tasks they carried out, and the men had to be split into two shifts to aid this.

Having begun his career on the GER in 1877, A. J. Hill rose through the Locomotive Department to become Locomotive Superintendent in 1912. However, his opportunity to make his mark on the rolling stock was stifled by the outbreak of war and only twenty-three of his engines were built

before this event. These comprised twenty 'C72' 0-6-0Ts for passenger and shunting work and three 0-4-0T shunters. Two 0-6-2Ts appeared in 1915 and were used for testing the merits of superheaters for engines limited to the suburbs. No 1000 did not possess the apparatus and proved to be inferior to sister No 1001, leading to the adoption of superheaters for future construction, which

The interior of a GER dining carriage.

Hill 'L77' Class 0-6-2T No 1000 was the first of the class to be built at Stratford in 1915.

resumed in 1921 when ten engines were sent into service from Stratford. Furthermore, No 1000 had the distinction of being the first GER locomotive to use Walschaerts valve gear; piston valves were also used.

The *GER Magazine* ran a series of articles on the works in 1913 and the following details are of interest. C. W. L. Glaze had succeeded A. J. Hill as Works Manager and his Assistant was T. O. Mein. The Carriage Works operated under H. Parker, the Wagon Works under C. Spencer, the Chief Draughtsman was E. S. Tiddeman, and the Office Manager was A. W. Polley. The office dealt with a wide variety of matters, from invoices and quotations to applications for employment and press releases. As many as sixty people were employed in the Accounts Department, which was headed by E. Winmill, and the wages for 10,000 people were calculated and adjusted. Correspondence was received from forty employees scattered around the system relating to this task, in addition to locomotive mileages, material charges and general statistics. J. H. B. Jenkins was in charge of the Chemist's Department. A Telephone Exchange was also located on site and this handled the calls from 100 telephones, amounting to approximately 1,300 a day. Stratford Power Station supplied the electricity used by the works, which was delivered to five sub-stations at 6,600 volts, then converted to 440 volts to be used by the various machines. Coal was still required for a number of functions and nearly 400 tons were used at Stratford weekly.

Stratford was obliged to cater for carriages that used wooden-centred Mansell wheels, even though steel had gained favour for new construction. The Wheel

Shop was arranged with all the machinery and benches alongside the walls with the centre left free for a set of tracks, with a third rail on the left-hand side for a crane to manoeuvre the wheel sets around. The axles arrived at Stratford roughly forged and the first task was for the axle journals to be turned on a lathe, then finished by a grinder. The wheel bosses were made from scrap iron, the piece being formed by the steam hammer into the centre. A flange was added to the centre when both were heated to a certain temperature and the mating was performed by a 500-ton hydraulic press. The hole for the axle was punched out soon after and the bolt holes drilled.

The wooden disc for the centre was made from teak imported in blocks from Burma, and these were planed and cut diagonally to form the segments, the angle being determined by the number of pieces necessary. The wood was then weighed and marked so that pieces of equal weight could be placed opposite each other to create balance. Matched segments were then bound together for the centre to be bored and the bolt holes drilled out. The axle was then introduced and forced into the centre by hydraulic pressure; a specific value was required to be attained otherwise the centre had to be used on another axle. After this was successfully achieved the tyre was shrunk on in the normal manner and cooled off in water. The outer retaining ring was then fastened on to the tyre, which was subsequently turned to profile. Balancing of the wheelset was performed to reduce hammer blow when in traffic.

A new weighbridge for locomotives was installed

in 1912, supplied by H. Pooley & Sons of Birmingham, to replace the original by Kitchin of Warrington, which had been put down in 1870. While the latter only had six weighing tables at the start, another two were subsequently added and it was kept in use, being moved to Norwich. The new bridge had twelve scales, each capable of carrying 12½ tons, or 150 tons total. Measurements from two of the tables were delivered to one quadrant box – there being six in total – and these were displayed accurately by pointers without the need for making any adjustments with counterweights. Weighing tables were kept in position but the quadrant boxes could be disconnected so that locomotives could travel over them without disturbing the apparatus.

As soon as the war commenced Stratford was busy fulfilling orders for the war effort. The first of these included 1,750 stretchers, a great many picketing posts and pegs, and ambulance trains to run both at home and on the continent; two would later be made for the US Army. The Wagon Shops supplied a number of covered vehicles, as well as several types of wagons being converted – such as vans being equipped with machine tools, etc – and sent to the front line. General service wagons were also built by the company in quantity for the armed forces. As many servicemen of different nationalities were involved in the Allied forces, the opportunity was taken by some to visit Stratford Works to learn about railway matters before shipping home. The *GER Magazine* in 1919 reported that this had been the case for fifteen servicemen from New Zealand the previous year.

The Machine Shops were fully engaged in shell production, with 37,000 6-inch shells completed, and the manufacture of a large number of components, mainly involving copper and totalling 952,650 items. Only 18-inch cartridge cases were refurbished, but the number dealt with during the conflict came to an impressive 2,360,000, which would amount to more than 1,600 a day from 1915 to the end of the war. Stratford was also delegated the task of cutting 150,000 tons of steel bars to length ready to produce shells either at the works or elsewhere. The process started with the bars (15 or 20 feet long) arriving from the steel mill by rail and taken into the works for marking off, then being cut by a 250-ton hydraulic press. The Boiler Shop diversified by producing short sections of rail that could be laid quickly. As the motor lorry was in the ascendency during this period, the workshops produced a number of parts for vehicles used near the war zone.

To honour fallen comrades the GER Hospital Fund sought subscriptions from the workshops to donate a bed for Queen Mary's Hospital, Stratford. The response was very generous and some 500 guineas was raised to ensure that a bed was provided, together with toys for unwell children and a commemorative plaque.

During 1916 Hill introduced several members of the 'T77' Class 0-6-0 goods type, being a slight development of the earlier 'E72' 0-6-0; a total of twenty-five were built up to 1920. At this time a more powerful 0-6-0 was designed to meet both present and future traffic requirements. The basis was the 'S69' Class, and the two shared the same boiler, cylinders and valve gear, but the 'D81' Class 0-6-0 was rated with a higher tractive effort of 29,044lb, giving the class the distinction of being the most powerful 0-6-0 in the country. The locomotives were built in three batches between 1920 and 1922, totalling twenty-five.

In 1920 the *GER Magazine* told the story of how the £200,000 worth of textiles the company purchased annually was dealt with by the Stores and Testing Department at Stratford. Extremely high standards were said to be necessary as any lapse would encourage some vendors to dispatch less than their best materials! A high benchmark was used to ward off this practice, save money in the long term and generally present the company in a good light to customers, etc. A machine from Goodbrand & Co of Manchester was employed by Mr Aspinall in the Laboratory to evaluate specimens sent in by the stores, which included rope, canvas and sacking. The warp and weft of canvas were tested to destruction, the former having to withstand 450lb of pressure and the latter 600lb. In addition, the number of yarns per inch had to meet a specific figure to be accepted, as did the weight, which was required to be 16oz per yard. The material – generally cotton – for the 100 different types of uniform in use by 17,000 employees of the GER was also put through its paces as outlined above, and was checked for the quality and durability of the dyes used. Sponges were also thoroughly soaked and dried several times to measure any discrepancies from the specification.

A straining machine was used to test ropes and wires, the limit being 1 ton. Hemp and manila ropes were unravelled and assessed by single strands on an instrument supplied by Wright & Co of Manchester. Generally, both ropes and strands had to withstand 200lb before they could be passed for use. The article noted that approximately 80 miles of rope was in use by the company, with a value of £20,000.

At the Grouping in 1923 there were a certain number of changes in the management and staff positions as the GER became a small part of the LNER system. A. J. Hill took retirement at this time and his position was absorbed by Gresley. C. W. L. Glaze was made District Mechanical Engineer, Stratford, and J. H. B. Jenkins was made Chief Chemist of the LNER. Other notable appointments from former GER staff included S. A. Parnell, General Manager, who became Divisional General Manager for the Southern Area, and T. Chew, Solicitor, who took a similar post with the company.

Hill's designs continued to be produced during this period, with ten 'L77' 0-6-2Ts (classified 'N7' by the LNER) being turned out from Stratford between December 1923 and March 1924. These were ordered by the LNER, but were not too different from their predecessors, the main alteration being the use of eighteen-element Robinson superheaters, which was an increase of six elements compared to the apparatus fitted to earlier locomotives.

As 'N7' No E999, this locomotive was the last to be erected at Stratford. As BR No 69621, it is seen in a rather sorry state at Stratford shed in the late 1950s or early 1960s. *Bill Reed*

The company also placed an order for ten more 'C72' 0-6-0Ts, although they remained as they had been originally designed. Stratford also produced the final development of the 'Claud Hamilton' 4-4-0 in 1923. This had a 'S69' 4-6-0-type boiler with a twenty-one-element superheater, which was first fitted to No 1805 in early 1923 before the new locomotives were erected between June and September 1923.

This experimental 20-ton brake van, made from concrete by Holst and mounted on underframes, was completed at Temple Mills in 1929.

Unfortunately for the workforce at Stratford, Sir Vincent Raven, who was commissioned to compile a report on the workshops inherited by the LNER, did not recommend the continuation of locomotive construction. This was due to a lack of modern machinery (at the end of the First World War Hill had recommended that £30,000 should be spent on replacing old machinery) and the expense of employing people living in the London area. The Board accepted this recommendation and new construction was discontinued in March 1924, when the last of the batch of ten 'N7s' was completed, this being No E999. Up to this point 1,702 engines had been built at the works. Repairs were still performed on the classes employed on GE Area lines and the Carriage Shops continued to build new carriages, albeit on a reduced scale. Temple Mills was also a casualty of the Grouping and had to accept a reduced role as a repair centre. The latter task had become pressing after the end of the war and had caused orders for wagons to be placed with the trade, even though these were not of the same standard as the GER examples.

The final carriage orders to the GER's designs were placed in 1923, and were for more bogie suburban stock. Stratford built fourteen each of the 2nd Class, 3rd Class, and Brake 3rd designs as well as ten 2nd Composites, then in 1924 a further two of each were completed, excluding the last-mentioned, which had another ten added to the ranks. Subsequently, LNER standard non-corridor stock for the GE Area would retain the 54-foot length as used by these vehicles, in addition to Westinghouse brake equipment. The company undertook to replace a large

LNER Class 'J20' (GER 'D81') Class 0-6-0 No 8280 was the first British locomotive to be fitted with poppet valves.

number of the older suburban stock during the late 1920s and much was obtained from private contractors.

Also in need of replenishment was the main-line stock, and in 1925 the Carriage Works received authorisation to erect new coaches for the 'Hook Continental' service and the boat train for Antwerp. The former comprised a Brake, three 1sts, a restaurant 1st, restaurant 2nd, three 2nds and a Brake, while the latter was similarly formed but had a 1st, 2nd and restaurant 1st missing. The carriages were slightly wider than the standard at 9ft 3in. The general service trains were dealt with the following year when Stratford contributed fifteen vehicles serving 3rd Class passengers, and Composites were built in 1927. A small number of 1st Class carriages appeared in 1928; all were 52ft 6in long and had a compartment less than the normal stock used elsewhere on the LNER.

The final items from the Carriage Works were a number of vans for the transportation of general goods as part of the passenger formation, the last being constructed in 1929. At this time the whole of Stratford Works was dedicated solely to the repair of the rolling stock in operation on the GE Section. This reduction in responsibility given to the workshops gave rise to rumours that the site would be closed by the LNER, causing the Chairman, William Whitelaw, to dismiss them, as reported by *The Engineer* in January 1929:

'Speaking recently at a prize distribution at Stratford Works Mr William Whitelaw remarked that since the amalgamation there had been speculation that the works would be closed. He added that the directors judged such matters on merit and he could wholeheartedly say that Stratford would not be closed.'

While the locomotive shops were only concerned with repairs, an interesting project was put in hand whereby 'J20' (GER 'D81') Class 0-6-0 No 8280 was fitted with Lentz poppet valves in May 1925. This was the first application of the equipment to a British locomotive, even though railways on the continent had experimented with the valves for several years previously. The poppet valves were developed to combat some of the problems experienced with piston valves, which were relatively new in themselves. These had disadvantages of wear due to movement and the carbonisation of the lubricating oil employed to reduce this aspect of their operation. Whereas piston valves moved across their ports, poppet valves lifted off seats to allow steam in and out of the cylinder, resulting in improved port openings, little need for lubrication and virtually no wear.

'B12' Class 4-6-0 No 8525 was converted to poppet valves in September 1928.

'D56' Class 4-4-0 No 1791 took part in the GER's feedwater heater trials and carried this Weir type until just after the Grouping.

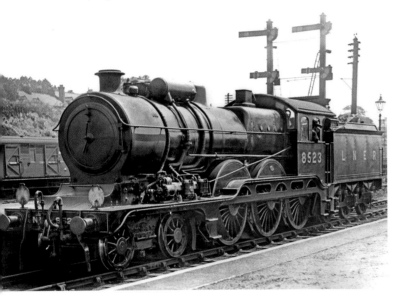

Even though feedwater heaters were successful on railways in Europe and America, British engineers never experienced the full benefits; No 8523 has the ACFI type here.

Experience with No 8280 in traffic was positive, and tests conducted against classmate No 8287 showed a slight saving in coal consumed. The main benefit was the mileage obtained between general repairs, which was 64,410, compared with the average of the class (46,642). Gresley was satisfied with this application and subsequently authorised another experiment with the 'B12' ('S69') Class 4-6-0s, and No 8516 was the first locomotive equipped in December 1926. A difference between the two arrangements was that the 'B12' had the valve chest cast with the cylinders, whereas the 'J20' had this bolted to them. Further trials again showed savings, though not as pronounced. Nevertheless, Gresley

ordered further conversions and six more 'B12s' had poppet valves by mid-1930. He had also made the bold step of having the valves fitted to ten new 'B12s' built by Beyer, Peacock & Co in 1928. The locomotives (classified 'B12/2') soon began to suffer problems with the cylinders and camshafts, necessitating expensive replacements, and this was deemed undesirable so the standard piston valves used by other members of the class were substituted, all being dealt with by February 1933. This directive spread to the conversions, and the last had its poppet valves removed in February 1934.

With the GNR, Gresley had fitted a number of freight locomotives with feedwater heaters. This device was another import from the continent and had attracted his attention because of the meaningful savings in fuel consumption, which could be expected to be in the region of 10-15%. In general terms, the device operated by using exhaust steam to heat the water through suitable heat exchange apparatus before it entered the boiler, thereby reclaiming some heat that would have otherwise been lost and reducing the energy needed to turn the water into steam. Several manufacturers produced the equipment and Gresley fitted Worthington, Weir and Dabeg examples to a small group of engines from several classes.

After the Grouping the ACFI version was put on trial, later becoming the most extensively used on the LNER. In December 1927 'B12' Class Nos 8505, 8517 and 8523 received the arrangement, which was of the 'open' type where the steam came into contact with the water, rather than being kept separate as in some systems. A suction reservoir, situated below the water level of the tender, delivered the feedwater to a tandem pump (with two cylinders for dealing with hot and cold water separately and operated by live steam) mounted on the running plate. From the pump the water was delivered to a water drum placed on top of the boiler between the chimney and the dome. Here the water mixed with exhaust steam siphoned off from the blast pipe, with exhaust steam from the water pump also being utilised, both being passed through an oil separator before going into the mixing chamber. The water entered the drum and into a perforated pipe that forced it to hit the top of the chamber and fall as a fine spray. The water was further divided by apertures in a metal plate, allowing it to be heated quickly. The product of the mixing chamber was then delivered into a second drum, located adjacent to the first, where gases produced by the process of heating were removed through a vent and liberated into the atmosphere. From the second chamber the water flowed to the hot-water cylinder of the tandem pump and was then admitted to the boiler. Two 'C7' Class 'Atlantics' and an 'A1' and 'A3' 'Pacific' received sets of the equipment at the end of the 1920s, before fifty 'B12s' were modified at Stratford between 1931 and 1933.

The association that some of these locomotive had with the ACFI heater was quite short, as a reboilering programme was started in May 1932. The new type was based on the 'B17' boiler, being 5ft 6in in diameter with

Rebuilt 'B12' No 8579 is pictured at Shepreth Branch Junction with a down slow train, possibly the 11.07am Bishops Stortford to Cambridge service.

143 small tubes and a twenty-four-element superheater, but with a shorter barrel and a larger grate area with a round-top firebox. Other changes made at this time encompassed completely rearranged motion, the provision of slightly smaller piston valves than the standard, and a new cab and running plate. The task soon spread to the whole class and continued apace during the 1930s, eventually drawing to a close in 1944.

Most of the above alterations were carried out under the supervision of Edward Thompson in the capacity of Mechanical Engineer, Stratford. He was posted there as Assistant Mechanical Engineer in 1927 and succeeded C. W. L. Glaze in 1930. Thompson's main task upon arrival was overseeing the reorganisation of the Carriage & Wagon Departments, given his experience with those at York under both the NER and LNER. In 1931 he wrote a description of the workshops in the *LNER Magazine* as the task came to an end. He states that the objective was 'to systemise the work, increase output and improve the upkeep for the rolling stock.' The majority of the changes took place in and around the main Carriage Shops on the original works site. The northern end was relaid for coaches to be assembled in a set system depending on the nature of the repair required before being taken into the Lifting Shop. This had seen the demolition of two of the roof spans so that a pair of 15-ton overhead cranes could be provided to work over a pair of bays that had previously been devoid of this luxury. Space in the shop was given over to machine tools, etc. Mechanical hauling gear was installed so that the coach bodies – set on trestles – could be moved through the various different stages of repair; the same process was applied to the bogies. Two electric traversers 55 feet long located at the end of the shop replaced the old steam-powered 26-foot example. A return to service after a light repair was said to be possible in just 14 hours.

After being split from the body, the bogies were moved to an adjoining bay where they were refurbished on the necessary machines, which included wheel turning and grinding, a journal lathe and a centring lathe. The oil in the axleboxes was drained into an oil tank and they were then cleaned by being lowered into a bosh. Afterwards any necessary attention to the bearings was completed and the springs were tested before the various parts came back together as the bogie reached the end of the shop.

The body would have the doors removed first, then be stripped of paint if necessary. Platforms were arranged at either side of the bays to facilitate access to the interior as well as for work to be completed easily on

The interior of the Carriage Repair Shop, c1960.

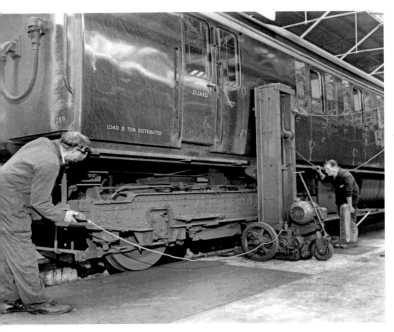

Care is taken as the delicate process of reuniting the bogie with the coach body is carried out.

The overhead crane in action in the Carriage Repair Shop.

the exterior. As movement occurred down the bay any further repairs would see the coach lifted to one of the two repair bays where replacement of panels, frame sections, etc, would take place. The next sector saw the interior fully examined and brought back to standard, including painting, and the last area dealt with the finishing touches. A full repair was estimated to take nine days, with the various movements performed at the end of each shift. The ancillary shops, such as the stores, sawmill, etc, had also been completely reorganised to support this fluency of movement. Thompson closed by recording that the number of carriages under or awaiting repair had been halved after the adoption of the new system.

Peter Grafton in *Edward Thompson of the LNER* states that Thompson encouraged the men at the Stratford Mechanics' Institute during his tenure and there was a revival of the old GER Director's Scholarship. This had been discontinued some time previously and was revived at the instigation of William Whitelaw, but with only six scholarships for the whole of the company. Three of these were for Stratford employees, whose education was furthered at East London College, later Queen Mary College.

Stratford Works was honoured by a Royal visit on 6 July 1927, and the party was received by William Whitelaw, Lord Faringdon, H. N. Gresley, C. W. L Glaze and T. O. Mein. The first event on the tour was the introduction of the King and Queen to six of Stratford's employees, each having more than fifty years' service in the workshops: Mr W. Covell (engine turner, 50 years); G. Crabb (engine turner, 50½ years); F. Gower (coachmaker, 51 years); J. Mahon (smith, 50½ years); A. Splatt (engine turner, 50¾ years); and W. J. Osborn (engine fitter, 45 years, although kept on as Secretary of the Hospital Committee). The tour then commenced, taking in the Erecting Shop, Wheel Shop and Steam Hammer Shop, where the foremen were ready to explain the machinery to Their Majesties. In the Carriage Paint Shop the stock in various stages of undress was inspected before the group moved through the 'Flying Scotsman' train.

Thompson moved back to the North Eastern Area in 1933 and was succeeded by A. H. Peppercorn. One of the

An upholsterer at work, c1960.

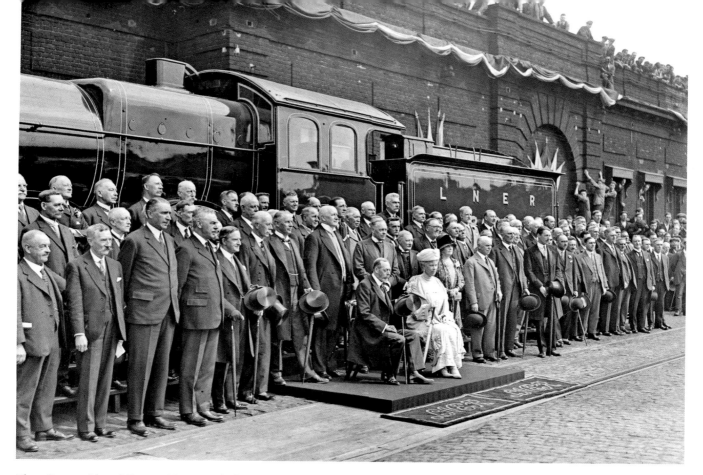

King George V and Queen Mary mark their visit to Stratford by posing for this photograph; Gresley is fourth from the left and Chairman William Whitelaw stands behind the King.

tasks carried out under the latter was the rebuilding of a number of the 'Claud Hamilton' 4-4-0s with round-top fireboxes, and some were fitted with new cylinders using piston valves, based on those fitted to the 'J39' Class 0-6-0s. Peppercorn was also present when £25,000 worth of new machine tools were installed in the mid-1930s, giving a welcome improvement to those already present. He was promoted to Mechanical Engineer, Southern Area in 1937, and F. W. Carr took his position at Stratford. K. S. Robertson, who was the Carriage & Wagon Works Manager, also moved on and was replaced by H. C. L. Edwards.

Like many of the other railway workshops, Stratford

held Open Days in order to raise money for good causes. In 1937 such an occasion was organised by a committee headed by Works Manager S. L. Baister to help Queen Mary's Hospital. A number of locations were available on Sunday 6 June, such as the Boiler Shop, Erecting Shop and Carriage Shops, and around 10,000 people inspected them. Trips were also given in a Saloon dating from the 1850s and, for an extra charge, the guests could be admitted to the Chemist's Department. At the end of the day some £300 had been raised.

During the Second World War, as Stratford was relatively close to London's docks, in addition to being a target in

'D16/3' No 8900 *Claud Hamilton* as rebuilt with a round-top firebox and piston valves.

Youngsters get involved at an Open Day at Stratford in the mid-1950s.

Men in the Smithy are served tea during a break from their exertions early in the Second World War.

itself, the works was hit several times during the Blitz. The Foundry was damaged, together with the Erecting Shop and Offices, while the Chemist's Department was completely destroyed, although much of the equipment had been transferred away; as result the staff were moved to Doncaster to establish a new laboratory. The Foundry also migrated north to Gorton Works as the men and machinery were more productively employed there for the war effort. Stratford did not receive as much work as other LNER establishments, as the shops were given

a remit to repair and maintain rolling stock, even taking some locomotives from Doncaster. Stratford did embark on the production of some gun parts and the assembly of US Army 'S160' Class locomotives, and several repairs to these were also carried out. An ongoing collection was taken at Stratford Works throughout the war years for the Russian Red Cross. A total of £2,000 was raised and presented to Stalingrad Hospital, which was said to have recognised the donors on a plaque placed in the building's entrance.

Class 'F4' No 7071 was lent to the War Department during the Second World War and was armour-plated and camouflaged for hauling coastal defence trains around the Canterbury area.

One of the few carriages built at Stratford after the Grouping was this six-wheel van to Diagram 358 in 1950.

During the late 1940s and into the BR era Stratford's role changed very little. As at the Grouping, the workshops became a small part of a much larger group, in this case being one of nine establishments not erecting new engines but carrying out heavy repairs. The facility was responsible for 1,062 locomotives, each of which could expect to be present for 20 days while the necessary attention was carried out; more than 700 repairs could be carried out annually. The Carriage Works dealt with the repairs for well in excess of 5,000 vehicles, 1,000 of which required lifting. Temple Mills saw 20,000 wagons pass through the shops during the year, the majority of these just requiring light work. The staff numbered just over 2,000 in the locomotive department, 1,500 were employed on the carriage duties, and 400 on wagons. Both the main works and Temple Mills enjoyed the provision of wash houses in the early 1950s as BR splashed out nearly £10,000.

While encouragement was given to hygiene, the artistic talents of thirty-six members of staff from across the works were supported with an exhibition of 120 pieces in the works' canteen over the week of 2-6 April 1951. These ranged from framed oils and drawings to bowls and

A view of the Repair Shop during the 1950s.

A section of the Boiler Shop at Stratford dealing with boiler tubes.

Machinists hard at work during the 1950s.

A set of iron ore wagons receive attention at Temple Mills Works.

vases carved from walnut. The *British Railways Magazine Eastern Region* explained:

'This exhibition was the result of a spontaneous suggestion made to Mr W. C. Darby, the Chairman of the Stratford Locomotive Works Canteen Committee, by Mr T. Ash, a clerk in the Locomotive shops and Mr E. Childs, a labourer in the Carriage and Wagon shops. The suggestion was acted upon promptly and, following an appeal for cooperation, a gratifying response was received from all grades, including foremen, painters, clerks, woodworkers, fitters and boilermakers and, with the assistance of the Canteen Committee and the Carriage and Wagon Engineer's department who provided the handsome stands upon which many exhibits were displayed, the Exhibition was soon an accomplished fact.'

In 1953 a similar show was arranged, and due to popular demand family members of the employees were also allowed to submit works.

An unusual task carried out during this period was the overhaul of Colchester shed's turntable, which had been built at Stratford in the early part of the century. The work was carried out swiftly as the apparatus was required before the Easter holiday trains commenced.

In 1953 the *British Railways Magazine Eastern Region* reported that an accident had been averted by a quick-thinking worker, painter L. G. Serradimigni, at Temple Mills. The traverser was set in motion while a labourer was walking across, causing him to fall in front of the apparatus and catching his foot. Mr Serradimigni witnessed this and sprang into action by catching the tumbling man, supporting his weight and walking backwards to prevent the traverser running over them. The driver of the traverser was told to stop and serious injury – with the likelihood of death occurring – was avoided.

With the formulation of the Modernisation Plan in 1955, BR also had to develop a strategy for the maintenance of the new diesel locomotives. For the Eastern Region this meant the provision of smaller repair depots, such as that built at Norwich, which supplemented the main workshops at Doncaster and Stratford. The latter was given the responsibility of keeping the diesel locomotives in the London and East Anglia areas in traffic. The Erecting Shop built earlier in the century was to be turned over to the work and as a result saw new equipment and plant installed. The plans were produced in 1956 and the conversion began during the following year. The building was said to be of sound condition and quite suitable for the change of use. Measuring 480 feet by 150 feet and 40 feet tall, the shop possessed five overhead cranes, four of 40 tons capacity and one of 10 tons. Other equipment installed included battery charging sets, injector servicing equipment and sump oil cleaning plants. A large stores was also established for the accumulation of parts to be distributed to the workshops and to servicing depots.

There were three bays: Bay 1 dealt with main-line locomotives; Bay 2 housed spare parts; and Bay 3 was used to strip diesel engines. Space in Bay 1 allowed for six locomotives to be given general repairs as well as a small number of light repairs. One of the tools provided in this area was an Atlas tyre profiler, and there was also a test bed for the locomotive to be run up to full power so that any problems could be detected before it returned to traffic. Half of Bay 2 was used as the stores, while the other half was dedicated to machine tools, lathes, and equipment for changing tyres. Bay 3 had dedicated beds to support engines once they had been removed from the locomotive, in addition to degreasing tanks and numerous

An electrician at work inside a diesel locomotive.

Maintenance is carried out on a diesel engine component.

cranes. There was an electrical section in this area where repairs to main generators, traction motors, etc, could be undertaken. A heating system using radiators with water heated from an oil-fired boiler was also provided.

The new Atlas machine allowed a considerable saving in

time over the old method of profiling. Part of the economy was due to there no longer being a need to disconnect the traction motors or disassemble the wheelsets, which brought the timeframe down from days to just several hours. The major change in the profiling method was the

Diesel locomotive No D5064 (built at Crewe in January 1960 and later a member of Class 24) is seen outside the Repair Shop on 17 August 1962. *D. J. Dippie*

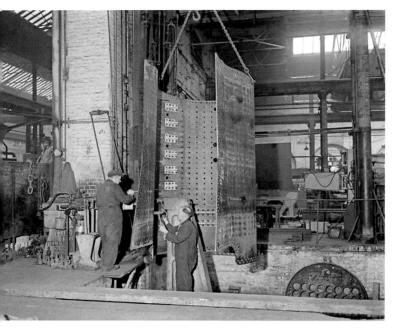

use of a milling process rather than turning, and this also prolonged the life of the tyre. The apparatus was housed in a pit and locomotives were moved on to a track above for the cutters to be raised to the wheels, which were supported by driving rollers. Track over the pit was then moved away for the cutting to begin.

Modernisation of the Erecting Shop and provision of repair facilities at a new diesel depot on the site of the old steam sheds left the original works outdated and unwanted. Consequently the site was closed in 1963 with the loss of many jobs, and the area was cleared later in the decade. Temple Mills was allowed to continue as a major repair centre for BR's modern new stock of containers, bulk wagons and car transporters until the early 1980s, when the shops were no longer required.

Repair work being carried out on a firebox.

Cylinders and axleboxes receive attention.

9

York

The York & North Midland Railway (Y&NMR) was founded in the mid-1830s to connect York with the Leeds & Selby Railway (L&SR). From that point the company would have access to several industries, such as textiles and coal mining, as well as new areas for distribution of the products of York and the surrounding area. George Stephenson was engaged to survey the line and the work was completed for opening on 30 May 1839 (the official ceremony was performed the day before). At York there was a temporary terminus outside the city walls, which was subsequently replaced by a permanent station inside the walls in the south-west corner on 4 January 1841.

Locomotives used by the company in those early years mainly consisted of 2-2-2 types that had been built by Robert Stephenson & Co, and subsequently included 2-4-0s from that firm. The L&SR was taken over by the Y&NMR in 1840 and the engines used by the company also became the responsibility of the new owner. This led to the formation of locomotive repair shops a short distance away from the temporary station of 1839, and these were overseen by the line's resident engineer, Thomas Cabry, who was also provided with a house nearby – Holgate Villa. Over the next few decades the site grew to a respectable size and catered not only for locomotives but also wagons.

The shops reached their height in the mid-1860s. At this time the works consisted of a Tender Shop, Smiths' Shop, Wagon Shop, Fitting Shop, Joiners' Shop and Stores. In 1854 the Y&NMR was taken over by the North Eastern Railway (NER), which soon decided that the wagons could no longer be accommodated on the relatively small site and they were removed to 10 acres of land to the west of the station on the north side of the line. The new shops were completed in 1867 and consisted of an Erecting Shop and Smiths' Shop. The space vacated at the Locomotive Repair Shops was turned into a new Erecting Shop and this was later extended. As wagons had been inherited from several different companies, which in turn had bought them

York Locomotive Works Erecting Shop.

from a number of outlets, there was little standardisation between the many types in use. With the arrival of T. W. Worsdell a start was made to rectify this situation; 8 tons was the capacity for many of the new designs, with grease lubrication. York Wagon Works' role was on a par with Shildon in producing and repairing the standard types, but also building many of the more specialised wagon designs including plate, bogie bolster, boiler, trolley and propeller wagons through to the Grouping.

Consideration was given to the provision of carriage workshops at the end of the 1870s and land was bought directly to the south of the wagon works; communication between the two was later affected by means of a footbridge across the running lines. The construction process was carried out in stages spanning the years 1880 to 1884, and in all the work cost around £90,000. The first shops to be laid out were the Building Shop and Paint Shop, which were the closest to the running lines; the shops built later were placed to the south of these. By the

Another view in the Erecting Shop.

Locomotives are in various stages of repair at York; note the proliferation of vices on the bench fixed to the wall on the left.

end of the project there was a Machine Shop, Repair Shop, Smiths' Shop and Stores and Offices in use, together with extensive sidings to the south-west of the works.

When the Carriage Works opened, the NER was in the midst of discontinuing the construction of four-wheel carriages and adopting six wheels as the standard, this type having been in production since the late 1860s. Ten years after the opening of the workshops a change was made to clerestory roof carriages and these were fitted with four-wheel bogies. Approximately 100 were built every year until 1906, when elliptical roofs became the mainstay of the design for passenger vehicles. The majority of the NER coaching stock featured compartments, and there was only a small number of corridor carriages built for the company's services. This was because the majority of the main-line types were for the East Coast Joint Stock (ECJS) and these were designed and – until 1895 – built

at Doncaster. From the start of the 20th century York took a greater hand in the construction duties, but was still limited in the design work. The shops were engaged in the mid-1900s in building a number of carriages for the Great Northern/North Eastern Joint Stock for the King's Cross to Newcastle trains, as the North British Railway (NBR) was unhappy that some of the ECJS vehicles were in use on these services and were even being sent to the company's shops for repair at NBR expense!

At the end of the 19th century there were major additions to the Carriage Works as the move from six-wheel to bogie coaches had reduced capacity in the existing shops. In 1896 authorisation was given by the Board for a new Lifting Shop, Frame Shop and Brake Shop, and several extensions to existing structures. This latter work affected the Paint

York Carriage Works Repair Shop in the early 20th century.

A number of carriages are seen under construction at York, c1900.

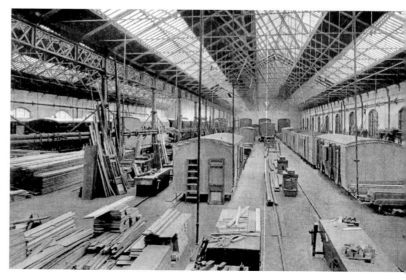

NER Composite Dining Saloon No 1855.

Shop, Building Shop, Machine Shop and Repair Shop. New electric cranes were bought for several of the shops, the total expenditure on these being more than £86,000. A shed was also provided for scrapping old carriages in the works yard. The site now covered an area of 45 acres, with some 15 acres under cover.

During 1903 York Carriage Works constructed new carriages for the electrified lines from Newcastle to Tynemouth, which were opened in 1904. These had clerestory roofs, matchboard sides, gate partitions and seating for sixty-four. A driver's compartment was provided at one end only, while controls were located in a cupboard at the other end should they be required; two driver's compartments were later standard features. Subsequent electric stock was also given steel underframes and before the First World War this became mandatory for all new carriages.

While the Carriage and Wagon Works were being developed to meet the traffic requirements of the time,

the Locomotive Shops were left behind and eclipsed by the expansions at Darlington Works. As a result the Locomotive Shops were closed in 1905, but the buildings subsequently found several other uses. The newest Erecting Shop was taken over by York Railway Institute, while the original Repair Shops were converted into a railway museum by the LNER in 1928, bringing together a large number of historical items from the collections of the 'Big Four' railway companies.

In the early days of the First World War a battalion of men was raised from NER employees in the Hull area as well as some from York. Those left behind in the Carriage and Wagon Works were soon busy making 634 general service wagons (a further 250 would be built to the end of the conflict), more than 1,000 stretchers, 3,000 picketing posts and 17,000 picketing pegs. Covered wagons were converted to transport the sick and injured and before the end of the war a seventeen-carriage ambulance train was completed, in addition to a set for the Director General of

The works had a long association with Royal Mail carriages and were still constructing examples into BR days.

The NER was early in adopting the idea of self-propelled railcars and produced a number at York in the early 20th century.

Transportation on the continent. A large number of gun parts were produced – a similar amount being turned out from the Locomotive Works, which was taken over by Armstrong Whitworth during the conflict – and many of the copper bands used by Darlington in the 6-inch shell shop were made at York. Works Manager at York at this time was R. Pick, who also supervised the recruitment of men in the shops to specific tasks in the armed forces.

Of the 21,000 carriages inherited by the LNER at the Grouping, approximately 4,000 belonged to the NER and as a result York Carriage Works was an important facility for keeping these in traffic. The capacity for new construction was not overlooked and the shops were embraced as major contributors to the requirements of the company.

On the other hand, the Wagon Works was in the midst of a transition to a repair centre thanks to the erection of new wagon shops at Faverdale. However, York would sporadically contribute some types of wagons throughout the LNER's existence, but mainly built containers following their introduction in the 1930s.

Immediately after the Grouping, York Carriage Works continued to erect NER designs. These consisted of a number of 1st and 3rd Class carriages (49 feet long by 8ft 6in wide) with seating for fifty-six and eighty respectively, and 3rd Brakes that had six compartments seating sixty people. In 1924 York was employed in building the new standard designs that were to be incorporated in the new 'Flying Scotsman' set. The 3rd Class carriages were 61ft

The interior of an NER railcar, a layout that has stood the test of time.

Inside an ambulance train built at York during the First World War.

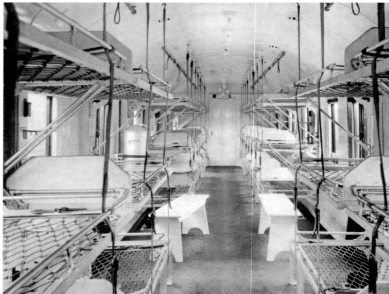

A 20-ton capacity ballast wagon built at York in 1914.

6in long by 9 feet wide, with eight compartments seating a total of forty-eight people. Exterior panels were of teak mounted on 60-foot underframes, all being carried by 8ft 6in bogies, with pressed steel frames, and positioned at 43-foot centres. Also constructed were a number of composites and locker composites, which had a small space to carry luggage. More NER designs were also turned out from the shops, and comprised Open 1sts, Open 3rds, Composite Brakes, 3rd Brakes and 1st Brakes.

Further standard carriages were built in 1925, a number of which were 3rd Class vehicles to Diagram 23. A small batch of composite sleeping cars also emerged from York, and these contained six 1st Class compartments, which were convertible from seating to beds, and two 3rd Class compartments that were fixed. In 1928 the works built the first 3rd Class sleeping car. There had been concerns that such a facility would draw passengers away from 1st Class, which was quite popular at the time, so the

fulfilment of this project had been delayed for several years. The sixteen new vehicles – to Diagram 95 – had seven convertible compartments, which seated fifty-six in the day and twenty-eight at night, and were used on services from King's Cross and St Pancras to Edinburgh, Newcastle, Inverness and Aberdeen. These proved so successful that a further nineteen were built in 1929, and a number of orders were placed in the 1930s.

In 1928 K. S. Robertson, Assistant Carriage Works Manager at York, recorded in the *LNER Magazine* that the workshops were capable of building 200 carriages a year as there had been a reorganisation and rationalisation of the processes taking place, in addition to new equipment and machinery being installed. This allowed sections of the carriages to be completed independently, then fitted together quickly. Accordingly, the typical production time had fallen from 5½ weeks to just 2½ weeks. The Frame Shop was capable of holding five sets of 60-foot

This well trolley wagon built at York in 1922 had a capacity of 70 tons.

LNER 3rd class carriage No 1007 was erected at York in 1924 for use in the 'Flying Scotsman' set and also contained the hairdressing salon and ladies' retiring room.

3rd Class sleeping carriage No 1336 was the first of ten built at York to Diagram 148 in 1931.

An interior view of the ladies' retiring room, c1938.

frames, or seven at 51 feet, and the production time for these was two days, with gangs of men responsible for certain aspects of construction, such as the riveters connecting the various pieces of metalwork. The adjacent Machine Shop prepared the solebars and the channels, among other items, and oxy-acetylene cutters were used. The wheelsets were assembled in the Smiths' Shop, with springs, brake components and drawgear being attached.

The Wood Shop had been greatly improved by the addition of new tools and the adoption of templates and jigs to speed up production. One machine that was said to be difficult to use was the heavy planing and moulding machine, on account of the time spent setting it up. However, a good deal of wood could be put through after this had been done, and many different pieces were produced. An electric recessing machine was adaptable to several tasks and a number of sanders had been installed to eliminate the need for the men to do this laborious

The Sawmill.

The 'Flying Scotsman' restaurant triplet (Nos 16481-16483) in the Repair Shop.

duty. To ensure greater security in the joints, such as those in the doors, hydraulic cramps were used instead of the old screw type.

In the Building Shop all the various sections were brought together for fitting. The underframes had the floor attached, followed by the ends and the interior partitions. The quarters, screens and roof were put in place before the doors were mounted, then the electricians were allowed access to install the fittings. The body was then lifted on to the bogies, moved outside and transported to the Cabinet Makers' Shop for more detail fixtures to be mounted. After this was completed the carriage was moved again into the Paint Shop where three weeks were spent as the various coats of varnish were applied and given time to dry. Final detailing was carried out upon completion in the Cabinet Makers' Shop, then a thorough test of all the components was

The Building Shop with Royal Mail carriages under construction.

made before a trial run was taken. Upon the successful conclusion of this the carriage was sent into service.

At the Grouping the LNER had very few Post Office sorting vans that were of recent design, and throughout the 1920s pressure was put on the company to update them. Finally, in 1929 three vehicles were built at York to Diagram 131; they had 60-foot underframes and were 9ft 1½in wide. On the inside the van was arranged for sorting at one end with tables mounted below tiers of letter boxes, which numbered some 270, 216 of which had bottoms made of glass to allow the sorter to see if any letters were left in them. There was also a space for sorting registered letters, and this had a new design of roller shutter for security. A newspaper sorting table was also provided. Staff amenities included a toilet with hot and cold running water, in addition to a hot ring for the preparation of refreshments. Apparatus was provided in

The interior of Royal Mail carriage No 2339.

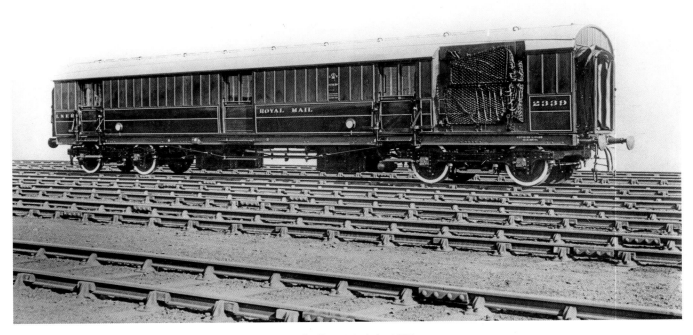

An exterior view of sorting office vehicle No 2339, built at York in 1929.

the doorway at each end for the collection and delivery of mailbags from various points along the King's Cross to Newcastle route for which the three carriages were built, although they were transferred to the GE Section around three years after entering service and replaced by a new type. A double-door was also fitted centrally on the opposite side to allow movement of mail at stations. Electric lighting was used and heating was delivered by a 2-inch-diameter pipe suspended from the ceiling.

There were around 3,000 people employed at York Carriage and Wagon Works in the early 1930s, but unfortunately 400 redundancies were made in 1930. *The Engineer* of 15 August reported that the National Union of Railwaymen, which had the largest branch in the city, was attempting to get the company to change the decision and adopt short time as an alternative, but this does not appear to have been adopted, given the mechanisation of the workshops and the financial climate of the time. A number of orders were still received for the year, although from 1931 to 1934 the amounts were quite a bit below that of previous years.

A type that gained prominence during this period was the open carriage, and several variations were built at York. Semi-open 1sts were constructed in 1930, which had four compartments supplemented by a seating area for eighteen travellers. Open 3rds erected during the year were to Diagram 27A and had two saloons accommodating forty-eight in a 2+1 arrangement. A variant on this was the Diagram 186 design produced in 1934, which had lavatories installed and the seating arranged in one saloon. These carriages were also the first production series to have welded underframes, signalling the start of the general adoption of this technique. York

had dedicated machinery installed in the Frame Shop at this time for the task, including jigs and four arc-welding machines.

Although there was much gloom throughout the years of the trade depression, York Carriage and Wagon Works kept spirits up by holding an annual Horticultural Show. The exhibits were awarded prizes, then sold to raise money for local good causes, but mainly for the hospital, which over the previous decade had received £191. The Wagon Works' Comic Band was on hand to give the event added colour.

Further improvements in the methods of construction and the tools used occurred in the early 1930s. With regard to the latter, two large lathes were acquired for turning carriage wheels, electrically powered by 35-horsepower motors. A. H. Peppercorn, then Works Manager at York, wrote an article for the *LNER Magazine* in 1931 detailing the changes made to the construction systems as a result of experience gained since 1928. Instead of a number of groups of workers being allocated a coach to assemble, they were now given a section of one coach to build, and the carriage moved through the building on a system similar to a production line. A variation from the old method saw the underframes mounted on their bogies at the first stage so that the assembly could be moved to the next stage on wheels rather than being lifted from one to the other. The required components were brought to the relevant stage, rather than one area, and platforms were erected around the sides of the carriages so access could easily be gained for the necessary work, whereas previously trestles were put up as and when required. A time saving of 30% was achieved by having work carried out continually.

Above 'Tourist Stock' buffet car No 43511.

Below A simplistic arrangement was adopted for the buffet car kitchen, as only light snacks were served.

Formerly, processes such as hanging the doors saw work concentrated on that task, then work continued on other items afterwards. In the new system, the doors were fitted as plumbers and electricians busied themselves in the interior and underneath the carriage. A total of seven stages were in use and the time spent at each was determined by how quickly the carriages were needed in service. Where possible all the carriages in the Building Shop were moved forward together. By 1936 the workshops were constructing one carriage a day and repairing as many as sixteen. At this time alterations were also carried out along the eastern and western sides of the shops as traversers were installed to improve the transfer of coaches between shops. Along the former side a certain amount of remodelling to the frontages was necessary to squeeze the apparatus into the space between the main shops and the Smiths' Shop and Stores.

Although introduced earlier, 1935 saw York turning out buffet cars to be used as part of the 'Tourist Stock', which had been formulated at the height of the depression years as a means to offer a cheap alternative to coach travel for weekend and holiday traffic. To save money plywood was employed liberally and only 3rd Class accommodation was offered. Two buffet cars were placed in the 'Tourist' formation and these had a kitchen at one end, a serving counter and an open saloon to seat twenty-four people. The kitchen had gas equipment, a boiler and refrigerator to offer light refreshments in keeping with the 'no frills' service. The success of these carriages led to the introduction of buffet cars for general use, and these orders were fulfilled at York in 1936 and 1937. These were generally similar to the earlier vehicles but had electric cooking equipment and were used on several medium-distance passenger trains.

With the introduction of the high-speed trains in 1937, a certain standard came to be expected for all main-line services. One to receive an upgrade was the 'East Anglian', running between Liverpool Street station and Norwich, stopping at Ipswich. York was engaged on the project and built six carriages, the set comprising a Brake 3rd, restaurant 3rd, 3rd, 1st, restaurant 1st, and Brake 3rd. Armchair-style seats were provided and Rexine and aluminium trim and fixtures were used throughout. For

The interior of a 1st Class carriage used as part of the 'East Anglian' train.

Inside a 1st Class compartment of a 'Hook Continental' carriage.

1938 ten carriages were ordered from York to form the 'Hook Continental' set, comprising two bogie Brakes, a Semi-open 1st, Open 1st, restaurant 1st, Open 1st, Open 2nd, restaurant 2nd, Open 2nd, Open 2nd, 2nd, and Brake 2nd. The widespread use of open carriages followed on from the streamline sets, which employed this arrangement allowing meals to be served at seats to improve the capacity. Interior decoration and fittings were also similar to those used elsewhere at the time.

In 1939 the outbreak of the Second World War made these glamorous trains fade into a different era. By the end of the year York was building ambulance trains – for use at both home and abroad – and these

sets were formed of nine carriages for the former and sixteen for the latter, all being 57 feet long. Other items built included aeroplane parts, tank components and motor launches. The workshops were steadily employed through to 1943, when new construction was halted; during this period production consisted mostly of 3rd Class types. Production in the latter days of the war was not helped by the destruction of the Building Shop by an accidental fire. When rebuilt it was quite similar to the original, but was slightly taller and had improved lighting. A similar calamity had struck the Wagon Works Sawmill in the early 1930s and a new Lifting Shop was later built to replace this.

The 'Hook Continental' formation.

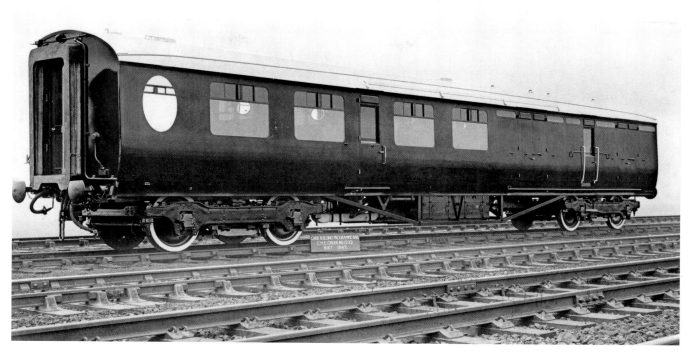

Above New construction at York increased after the end of the Second World War, and one of those built was Brake 3rd No E1905 for the 'Junior Scotsman' in 1947.

Below The layout of the brake portion of No E1905.

The interior of BR's standard 1st Class carriage.

Welding components to form the gangway end of a carriage.

Construction of new carriages at York began again in 1946, and these were of the new design featuring steel panels for the sides, 61ft 6in underframes and a 63-foot-long body, but they remained 9ft 3in wide. Many of the carriages for the 'Flying Scotsman' and 'Junior Scotsman' were produced during 1947 and into 1948. These consisted of the new standard designs, in addition to two new vehicles specially built. A ladies' retiring room and buffet lounge were constructed – only the former at York, the other at Doncaster. The ladies' room was included in both a 1st and 3rd Class carriage, and boasted a sink and other comforts. The LNER's carriage designs continued to be built through to 1950.

As at the Grouping, both York's Carriage and Wagon Works were indispensible for their respective functions

1st Class seats are being refurbished in the Upholstery section.

for the newly formed British Railways. Once the standard designs for carriages were formulated, the first orders were placed in the workshops and amounted to 826 vehicles; some 363 were also obtained from private carriage builders. There were no surprises with the new types, and all were of steel construction with 8ft 6in-wheelbase bogies, 63ft 5in-long welded underframes, automatic couplers, Pullman-type gangways and automatic vacuum brakes.

York was engaged to build 115 coaches of several types. The first to be completed were three Open 1sts to Diagram 71 – Nos 3000-3002 – which seated forty-two passengers in a 2+1 arrangement separated by a table. Following were six Open 2nds for Southern Region boat trains, which differed slightly from the aforementioned. Accommodation was for forty-eight, doors were placed centrally and the two toilets were placed at one end – instead of at both ends as in the 1sts. York also turned out eleven 1st Class and fourteen 3rd Class restaurant carriages, these being laid out in a similar manner to their standard counterparts. Finally, there were eighty-one corridor 3rd Class carriages to Diagram 146, which seated forty-eight in eight compartments.

The first three orders had been completed by mid-1951, but the later ones did not appear until the same period in the following year. Nevertheless, BR wanted more Diagram 146 coaches, and in March 1951 York and Derby were asked to build twelve and forty respectively. Also requested from York at this time were sixty-seven compartment Brake 3rds and seventy-five gangway Brake carriages to Diagram 711. The former consisted of six compartments to seat a total of seventy-two people, with more than 18 feet of the carriage given over to the brake/guard's compartment. Completion of these two types did not occur until March 1955 and September 1954 respectively.

With all this work in hand BR did not trouble York again until May 1952 when the Diagram 146 corridor 3rd and a variation of this – to Diagram 147 – was ordered. These had increased seating for sixty-four passengers as the armrests were omitted and the seats were intended to be occupied by four people rather than three. This kind of arrangement soon spread to the open stock and for several programmes subsequently York erected Diagram 93 carriages, with seating for sixty-four and two toilets at one end. A total of 378 were constructed through to October 1957.

As three of the 'Big Four' companies had built sleeping carriages around the time of nationalisation, BR did not contribute a design until ten Diagram 1 vehicles, for 1st Class travel, were included in a small number of orders placed in October 1955. York produced the vehicles, which had entered service by the end of 1958; they had eleven compartments, two toilets and an attendant's compartment. A further thirty-four would follow before the end of the decade in addition to a 2nd Class version (2nd having replaced 3rd by this time) to Diagram 10, which was quite similar to the 1st Class.

One of the final new types built by York as part of the Mark 1 series of BR coaching stock was the miniature

Above A BR 1st Class sleeper.

Below BR continued the practice of providing buffet facilities on short-distance trains.

Carriages for the Southern Region in the Erecting Shop.

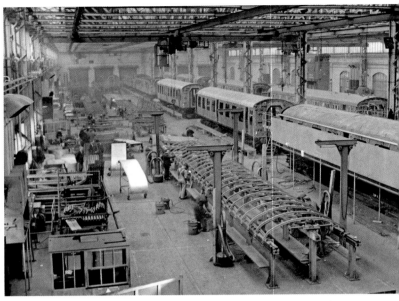

Roof members on a welding jig at York.

buffet. As with the LNER version some years earlier, this was an attempt to offer a cheap alternative to the restaurant cars; at first trialled on the main services, they were soon adopted on many other trains. The design was to Diagram 97 and there were two seating areas – for forty-four people – split by a drink and snack bar, with two toilets provided at one end. Experience with these initial twelve showed that not enough space was given to the buffet, and consequently a cupboard was built at the side, causing the seating to be reduced to forty-four.

From 1959 York Carriage Works concentrated on building electric multiple units (EMUs) for BR's growing number of electrified lines. The first of these was the stock

for the former London, Tilbury & Southend Railway line, and comprised Motor Brake 2nd, Driving 2nd, Trailer Composite and Driving Trailer 2nd vehicles. The total number of these, which were built to 1960, was 286 and, when joined with those built at Doncaster, formed Class AM2, later Class 302. At this time the Enfield to Chingford route was being converted and the three-carriage stock was formed in 1960, numbering 156 individual vehicles or fifty-two sets. The three types used were Battery Driving Trailer 2nd Open, Motor Brake 2nd Open and Driving Trailer 2nd Open; their designation was Class AM5, later Class 305. Rounding off this group was the stock for the Liverpool Street to Clacton electric services. Built in 1962 this comprised Motor Brake

BR 3rd Class Brake carriage No E43130, designed for suburban services, is seen on the traverser at York on 12 January 1955.

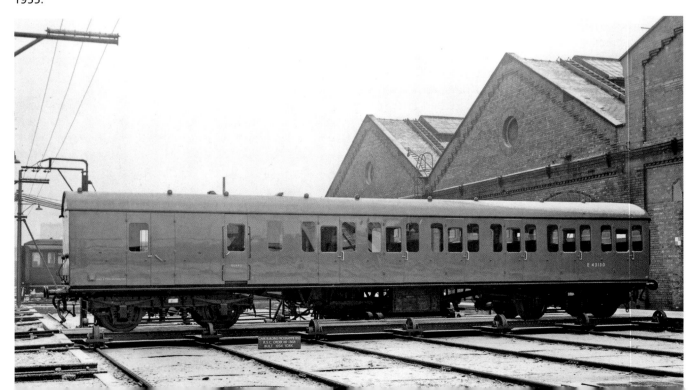

2nd, Driving Motor Brake 2nd, Trailer Restaurant Buffet, Battery Driving Trailer Composite, Battery Driving Trailer 2nd, Trailer 2nd Open, and Driving Trailer Composite. Twenty-three sets were created from these vehicles (including some from Wolverton Works), in twos, threes and fours, which were also often coupled together.

The late 1950s saw the Southern Region's main lines electrified and a large portion of the new stock for this was received from York at a rate of four carriages a week. Construction began in 1964 and the four-coach sets were made up of Driving Trailer Composite, Motor Brake 2nd, Trailer 2nd and Driving Trailer Composite. Power was from the third rail at 750V DC, delivered to four traction motors each of 250 horsepower. A total of 166 of these sets were built in 1964 and 1965, in addition to twenty-eight trains that included a buffet instead of the Trailer 2nd; the two types would later be classified 421 and 422 respectively. As with the Eastern Region stock, these sets had the ability to be coupled together to form longer trains when necessary. Similar units were also built in 1966/67 for the Bournemouth route. However, these were much more powerful as there were to be three or four carriages running without traction in the formation, being taken between Bournemouth and Weymouth by an electric locomotive. This group consisted of a Driving Trailer 2nd, Trailer 1st, Trailer Brake 2nd and Driving Trailer 2nd, being later classified 438 and numbering thirty-four. The power units used eight English Electric traction motors of 400 horsepower and the carriages were a Driving Motor 2nd, Trailer Buffet, Trailer 1st Brake and another Driving Motor 2nd. Only eleven of these Class 432 EMUs were built initially before another four were added in 1974.

York Carriage Works was fully modernised for the continuation of EMU work, beginning in 1965 and completed in 1967, at a cost of nearly £1,000,000, with repair work also remaining part of the remit. Unfortunately, the Wagon Works was obsolete by this time and closed in the early 1960s as the work was transferred to Shildon, while some container repairs were carried out on the Carriage Works site. The Paint Shop and New Building Shop remained in use for those tasks, but were fitted out for modern requirements, such as spray booths in the former and welding jigs in the latter. This shop was still arranged to the 'progressive' system with the various components coming together at specific stages. The next building to the south-west became a Store – previously having been the Wood Machine Shop – while the Machine Shop for metalwork retained this function and had an area dedicated to tool manufacture/refurbishment and jig construction. The old Frame Shop was transformed into two sections, one being the Traction & Electric Motor Shop, where the traction motors and wiring were fitted to the underframes and repairs and maintenance to the components took place. The other half was the Plumbers' Shop, where the fixtures and fittings were installed and looked after, in addition to the cooking equipment for the restaurant and buffet carriages.

A hive of activity in the Building Shop.

The Repair Shop handled fifty carriages weekly, and if they were split from their bogies a spare set would be used so that the carriages could to be moved easily between the various stages. The Frame Shop had moved into part of the Lifting Shop and new frames and bogies were built there using many jigs and welding. The last-mentioned area contained equipment for maintaining the wheelsets,

Apprentices hard at work learning their craft in York's Apprentice School.

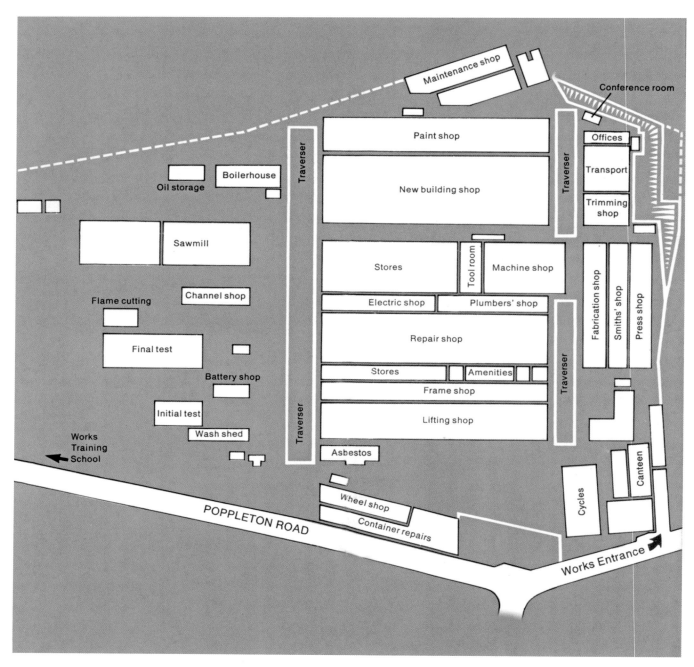

A map of the works, c1965.

such as lathes, balancing apparatus and flaw detectors. Along the south-western perimeter with Poppleton Road was the Wheel Shop, where the axles and wheels were brought together and the tyres fixed and profiled. Further along on this side was the Apprentice Training School, which was founded in 1962 and admitted sixty pupils for a year's course in the basic skills required for a career in BR's workshops and motive power department. In the southern corner of the site was the works' canteen, which could hold 500 staff, and the offices. A short distance away along the perimeter was a large block consisting of Fabrication, Smiths' and Press shops. The former was equipped with electric arc-welding apparatus for several items, including gangway faceplates, for the whole of

the company. In the Smiths' Shop the laminated and coil springs were tested and overhauled together with several components being heat-treated. Body panels and details were created in the last-mentioned as several types of press were present, the largest being of 500-ton capacity. All the panels were treated in the building to guard against corrosion before being sent out for use. Next door was the Trimming Shop, which dealt with all the seating and interior details such as curtains, etc, and the flooring.

Just under 3,000 people were employed at York Carriage Works at this time and, with the improvements made at the site, the shops were well placed for the future. In the late 1960s York was still constructing 'traditional' carriages, including Post Office vehicles. These used the

Above A door receives a coat of paint in a small spray booth; note the large number on the right still to be similarly treated.

standard coach dimensions and bogies, while the internal fittings and layout were little altered from the LNER examples built some thirty years earlier.

During the late 1970s and throughout the 1980s York was engaged in constructing nearly all of British Rail's second-generation EMUs. However, BREL was privatised in 1987 and bought by ASEA Brown Boveri. Class 465 and Class 365 EMUs were completed under the new management in the early 1990s. Then, ASEA Brown Boveri was forced to end just over 110 years of high-quality carriage construction and maintenance at York due to challenging conditions in the market place.

However, this was not quite the end, as US firm Thrall acquired the workshops and began construction of wagons for English, Welsh & Scottish Railways in 1997, which continued until 2002, when the site was finally shut down. Since then some of the buildings have been demolished, such as the Smiths' Shop, while the others remain standing and are in the possession of Network Rail. Parts of the former sidings are used for small business offices and sections have been reused for housing.

Right Checking the electrical systems.

Bibliography

Allen, C. J. *The Great Eastern Railway* (1961)
    The London & North Eastern Railway (1966)
Backtrack Magazine – various issues
Barclay-Harvey, Sir Malcolm *A History of the Great North of Scotland Railway* (1998)
Bonavia, Michael R. *A History of the LNER: 2 The Age of the Streamliners, 1934-39* (1985)
    A History of the LNER: 3 The Last Years, 1939-48 (1984)
British Railways Magazine: Eastern Region – various issues
Brown, F. A. S. *Nigel Gresley: Locomotive Engineer* (1975)
Clough, David N. *British Rail Standard Diesels of the 1960s* (2009)
    The Modernisation Plan: British Railways' Blueprint for the Future (2014)
Cox, E. S. *British Railways Standard Steam Locomotives* (1966)
Dow, George *Great Central – Volumes 1-3*
Emett, Charlie *The Stockton & Darlington Railway: 175 Years* (2000)
Everett, Andrew *Sir Vincent Raven: North Eastern Railway Locomotive Engineer* (2006)
Fawcett, Bill *A History of North Eastern Railway Architecture – Volumes 1-3*
Gordon, Hugh *Great North of Scotland Railway Locomotives* (2008)
Gourvish, T. R. *British Railways 1948-73: A Business History* (1986)
Grafton, Peter *Edward Thompson of the LNER* (2007)
Great Eastern Magazine – various issues
Gresley, H. N. 'The Three-Cylinder High-Pressure Locomotive' (*Proceedings of the Institution of Mechanical Engineers*, Volume 109, July 1925, pp927-67)
Groves, N. *Great Northern Locomotive History – Volumes 1-3B*
Hale, Don *Mallard: How the 'Blue Streak' Broke the World Speed Record* (2005)
Harris, Michael *Gresley's Coaches* (1973)
Hoole, K. *Rail Centres: York* (2004)
    Rail Centres: Newcastle (2008)
Jackson, David *J. G. Robinson: A Lifetime's Work* (1996)
Jenkinson, David *British Railway Carriages of the 20th Century Volume 1: The End of an Era, 1901-1922* (1988)
Johnson, John and Long, Robert A. *British Railways Engineering 1948-1980* (1982)

Journal of the Institute of Mechanical Engineers
    Visit to Cowlairs Works (1895, p482)
    Visit to Cowlairs Works (1923, p773)
    Visit to Darlington Works (1925, p1061)
    Visit to Doncaster Works (1885. p453)
    Visit to Doncaster Works (1903, p617)
    Visit to Doncaster Works (1936)
    Visit to Doncaster Works (1953)
    Visit to Dukinfield Works (1929, p752)
    Visit to Faverdale Works (1925, p1064)
    Visit to Gorton Works (1894, p430)
    Visit to Gorton Works (1929, p714)
    Visit to York Works (1936)
Larkin, Edgar *British Railways' Workshops* (2006)
LNER Magazine – various issues
Newsome, N. *The Development of LNER Carriage and Wagon Design, 1923-1941* (*Journal of the Institution of Locomotive Engineers*)
Nock, O. S. *Locomotives of the North Eastern Railway* (1954)
North Eastern Record – Volumes 1-3
Parkin, Keith *British Railways Mark 1 Coaches* (2006)
Railway World – various issues
RCTS *British Railways Standard Steam Locomotives – Volumes 1-4*
    Locomotives of the LNER – Parts 1 to 10A
Rowland, Don *British Railways Wagons* (1985)
Spencer, B. 'The Development of LNER Locomotive Design, 1923-1941' (*Journal of the Institution of Locomotive Engineers*, Volume 37, Journal No 197, Paper No 465, 1947, pp164-226)
Steam Railway – various issues
Steam World – various issues
Teasdale, John G. (ed) *A History of British Railways' North Eastern Region* (2009)
The Engineer – various issues
The Railway Magazine – various issues
Thomas, John *The Springburn Story* (1974)
    The North British Railway – Volumes 1 and 2
Townend, P. N. *Top Shed* (1989)
Tatlow, Peter *LNER Wagons – Volumes 1-4B*
Tuffrey, Peter *Cock o' the North* (2015)
Wrottesley, John *The Great Northern Railway – Volumes 1-3*

Index

York

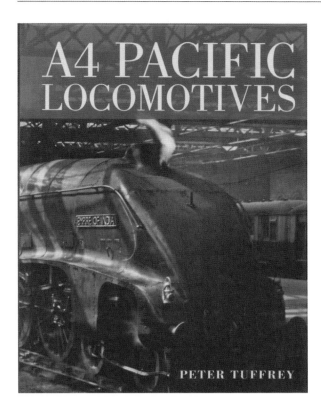

A4 Pacific Locomotives

Peter Tuffrey

The 'A4' class of Pacific locomotives was arguably the most distinctive type of steam locomotive built in Britain. Designed by Sir Nigel Gresley for the London & North Eastern Railway in the 1930s, their streamlined design not only reflected the art deco and modernist style of the era, but was also functional, enabling them to travel efficiently at high speeds. On 3 July 1938 the most famous locomotive in the class, Mallard, broke the world speed record for a steam locomotive, travelling at 126mph. This record has never been broken.

A total of 35 of these beautiful locomotives were built from 1935-38. The efficiency and speed of Gresley's design ensured they continued in top link service into the BR era, particularly London-Edinburgh but also in later years on the hilly Glasgow-Aberdeen route. In 2013, to mark the 75th anniversary of Mallard's record breaking run, all six surviving A4s were gathered together in the UK for the first time since the 1960s and fittingly Bittern set a new world speed record of 93mph for a preserved steam locomotive.

This is a glorious history of the construction, design and service of the 'A4s' for over 30 years with the LNER and British Railways by author Peter Tuffrey. It is an uplifting account of the career of the six remaining A4s in preservation and a must have for all railway enthusiasts.

Hardback, 144 pages
ISBN: 9780711038479
£22.50

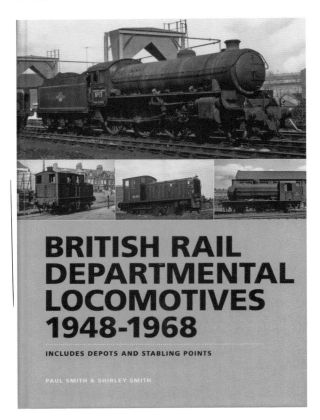

BR Departmental Locomotives 1948-68

Paul Smith and Shirley Smith

BR Departmental Locomotives 1948-68 provides a single reference work to all the departmental locomotives - steam, diesel, electric and battery - both standard and narrow gauge operated by BR from 1948 to the end of steam in 1968.

Although the railways employed the vast bulk of their locomotive stock on commercial passenger and freight traffic, many also employed a number for departmental duties. These may have been narrow gauge, for use in the major workshops such as Crewe and Horwich or withdrawn ex-main-line locomotives that eked out their final days or months in a secondary duty at a locomotive shed. At Nationalisation in 1948, BR inherited a number of these departmental locomotives from the 'Big Four' companies and, over the next 20 years, a number of further steam and other locomotives were transferred to departmental duties, including a significant number used as stationary boilers.

The transfer of locomotives from capital to departmental stock did not cease with the end of steam and examples of diesel and electric locomotives being renumbered into the departmental series continued effectively until the end of BR in the early 1990s.

BR Departmental Locomotives 1948-68 includes information about the locations at which the locomotives worked and provides full details of each individual locomotive's record in departmental service. The book is richly illustrated throughout with Ordnance Survey maps and photographs of the locomotives and locations.

Hardback, 96 pages
ISBN: 9780711038004
£20.00

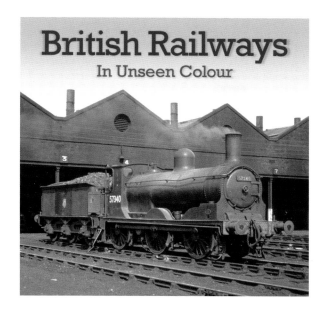

British Railways in Unseen Colour 1948 - 1961

The Classic Railway Colour Photos of Roy Vincent
Edited and Compiled by Kevin Robertson

British Railways in Unseen Colour 1948 - 1961 celebrates the contributions of Roy Vincent, a railway photographer whose work has received little coverage until now, but deserves to be seen in the first rank of those working in colour.

Roy was a railwayman based in both London and the north-east, however his work covers much of the country in geographical terms including the Southern and Western regions. Using quality film, he concentrated on taking pictures in good light and weather conditions resulting in a portfolio full of superb photographs published here for the first time.

Memorable images, with work-stained and weary machines intersperse with gleaming locomotives fresh out of works and present a fitting and long overdue tribute to a fine and original photographer whose work has hitherto not received the credit it deserves.

Hardback, 160 pages
ISBN: 9781909328839
£20.00

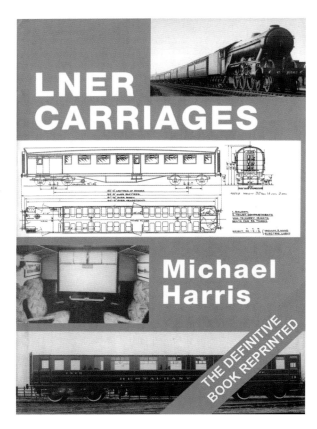

LNER Carriages

Michael Harris

The name Michael Harris will be synonymous with that as the acknowledged expert on LNER - and indeed a number of other types of railway coach.

Greatly adding to the author's previous title Gresley's Coaches, *LNER Carriages* includes additional archive material and fully covers the reasons why particular designs and types were specified and how these carriages were used in service.

All carriages built for the LNER between 1923 and 1947 plus post-war carriages built to LNER design are included together with detailed and comprehensive appendices including re-numberings. Official photographs, service shots and line drawings provide a full record of all types and serve as an authoritative guide for modellers and railway enthusiasts alike.

Paperback, 160 pages
ISBN: 9781906419523
£19.95

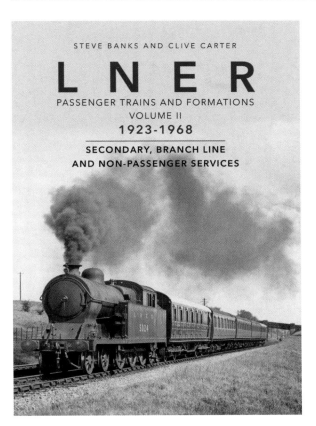

LNER Passenger Trains and Formations Volume II 1923-1968
Secondary, Branch Lines and Non-passenger Services

Steve Banks & Clive Carter

LNER Passenger Trains and Formations Volume II follows on from the authors' previous successful volume which focused on the principal services operated by the LNER and its successor, the Eastern Region of British Railways.

Many secondary services declined over time and the sometimes eclectic range of rolling stock in the steam era is often overlooked today. The variety of traffic they had to convey such as mail, parcels and newspapers along with types of perishable traffic such as fruit, fish and milk and passengers' luggage in advance added to the wide range of vehicles that could be seen on these services.

In addition to scheduled services, special trains were a regular feature of the Working Timetables. Trains were provided to cater for itinerant theatrical companies and excursions of all types to many destinations were frequently promoted by the railway operators to enhance revenue.

This detailed analysis of the formations used on these services will be of great interest to those absorbed in LNER and BR(E) history and railway modellers intent on recreating new layouts.

Hardback, 256 pages
ISBN: 9781909328792
Price: £35.00

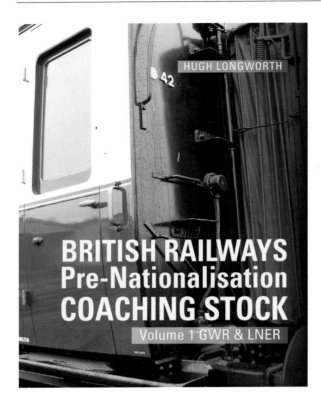

British Railways Pre-Nationalisation Coaching Stock Volume 1 GWR & LNER

Hugh Longworth

At nationalisation in 1948, the newly formed British Railways inherited the coaching stock of the 'Big Four' and continued to build new vehicles based on their designs until 1951. This is the first of two planned volumes dealing with that inheritance.

British Railways Pre-Nationalisation Coaching Stock Volume 1 GWR & LNER provides a complete listing of all the coaching stock absorbed by BR from the GWR and the LNER including any pre-grouping stock which came into BR ownership in 1948.

Entries for each individual vehicle include details of when it was built and subsequently withdrawn from service. Passenger carriages, sleepers, buffet, griddle, kitchen and other catering vehicles plus non-passenger stock permissible for use in passenger train formations such as horseboxes, fitted vans and milk tanks are also included. Vehicles converted for use as Departmental stock complete this wealth of comprehensive information for the railway historian and modeller alike.

Hardback, 338 pages
ISBN: 9780860936756
Price: £40.00